DATE DUE

Demco, Inc. 38-293

YOUR EVIL TWIN

BEHIND THE IDENTITY THEFT EPIDEMIC

BOB SULLIVAN

WILEY

JOHN WILEY & SONS, INC.

Published by John Wiley & Sons, Inc., Hoboken, New Jersey
Published simultaneously in Canada

For general information on our other products and services, or technical support, please
contact our Customer Care Department within the United States at 800-762-2974, outside
the United States at 317-572-3993 or fax 317-572-4002.

Wiley also publishes its books in a variety of electronic formats. Some content that appears in
print may not be available in electronic books.

For more information about Wiley products, visit our web site at www.wiley.com.

Library of Congress Cataloging-in-Publication Data:

Sullivan, Bob.
    Your Evil Twin: behind the identity theft epidemic / Bob Sullivan.
        p.   cm.
    Includes index.
        ISBN 0–471–64810–8 (cloth)
    1. False personation—United States. 2. Credit cards—Forgeries—United
States. 3. Identification cards—Forgeries—United States. 4. Privacy, Right
of—United States. I. Title.
    HV6684.U6S85 2004
    364.16′3—dc22   2004002214

Printed in the United States of America

10 9 8 7 6 5 4 3 2 1

To Angelo Giuseppe Roncalli, and to all who live in
the spirit of *aggiornamento*.

CONTENTS

FOREWORD

Millions of Americans have been victims of identity theft. They have been subjected to a kind of out-of-body crime spree, one where a second self has charged thousands of dollars in purchases, opened wireless phone accounts, and even committed crimes using their identity. When the harms from these experiences materialize, victims find themselves in a Kafkaesque nightmare, where the confluence of interests among credit bureaus, collection agencies, retailers, banks, and the police are oriented in different directions. Credit bureaus collect and continue to report information about impostors' activities to victims' employers and banks. Collection agencies harass victims, demanding that they pay debts incurred by impostors. Creditors report debts in the victims' names even after they have been notified that the charges are fraudulent. Banks continue to issue credit in victims' names to anyone with a bit of personal information. And finally, the police sometimes won't take a report from a victim, or worse, they can become convinced that a victim is guilty of a crime actually committed by the impostor.

Bob Sullivan's *Your Evil Twin* is an important step in awakening Americans from this nightmare. Sullivan's understanding of technology and clear writing puts a face on the forces of identity theft. No longer is identity theft simply a manner of shadowy fraudsters and computer hackers. Sullivan fully develops the nuances of identity theft, showing how clever individuals can easily take advantage of credit practices that are premised on a "grant first, ask questions later" business model. His survey of the crime covers credit card fraud, the problem of new accounts being opened in victims' names, and the worst-case scenario, criminal identity theft, where the impostor uses the victim's identity in altercations with the police.

Sullivan highlights new, more daring forms of identity theft, including criminals who buy new automobiles on others' credit, criminals who hijack hundreds of online auction accounts, and even those who send authentic-looking solicitations to individuals in order to get them to divulge personal information. He also shows how this crime is more serious than previously thought— identity theft is now recognized as a principal source of funding for individuals wishing to commit crimes of terrorism against the country.

Now that Sullivan has elucidated the nuances of this crime, as a society we need to take steps to eradicate it. That path, too, is difficult. In 1999, Congress passed the Financial Services Modernization Act, which paved the way for mega-financial companies spanning the insurance, brokerage, and banking industries. This has led to the creation of an industry that is overwhelmingly powerful in Washington. In the 2000 election cycle, financial services companies were the biggest donors to Republicans and Democrats in Congress and then-candidate George Bush. In that session of Congress, a banker-friendly bankruptcy bill quickly moved through the legislature that tightens the screws on individuals in financial trouble. Later in 2003, the financial services companies won again, this time by preventing states from passing stronger identity theft and credit reporting laws. The Department of the Treasury is furthering this trend by attempting to sweep away state laws that protect consumers from predatory lending and usury. And, as I write this during the

2004 election cycle, again financial services companies are the strongest backers of President Bush's reelection campaign. Combating the influence of powerful lobby is a principal challenge in curbing identity theft.

New identity theft risks are being raised by advances in data processing efficiency as well. In 2003, it was discovered that financial institutions, tax preparation companies, and even hospitals were shipping our personal data to telemarketers and data processors in India and other countries. Serious questions remain unanswered regarding the privacy, security, and accountability of these business practices. Already, this "off-shoring" of personal information processing has led to extortion and identity theft cases. As pressure mounts in Congress for accountability in off-shoring, the financial services industry has activated its special interest groups to stymie reform.

Scholarship in the area of identity theft has properly framed the crime as a result of information policy in the United States.

Professor Daniel Solove of The George Washington University Law School has argued that Americans collectively are in a state of vulnerability created by information brokers, by businesses that are loose with personal information, and by credit card companies who recklessly issue accounts to impostors. The current architecture places us in the information-age equivalent of a home without locks, or a neighborhood without police protection. We should expect identity theft to occur because the current system is easy to exploit, and because companies still make more money by placing profit over process, privacy, and precaution.

I have argued elsewhere that we need to change the architecture of information policy in order to curb identity theft. Specifically, we need to put individuals in control of their credit reports, so that they can freeze their financial DNA from release to both creditors and criminals alike. Sullivan's book continues this vein of conceptualizing identity theft as a crime that results from the architecture of information policy. It explains why this crime is so easy to commit and so difficult to prosecute. If you are interested in identity theft, whether you are a victim, a public policy maker, or just someone who wishes to avoid the crime, Sullivan's book is a must read.

—CHRIS JAY HOOFNAGLE
Director of Electronic Privacy Information Center
Washington, D.C.
March 2004

PREFACE

Well, as many people have told me, my destiny lies in hell, where, of course I will just take over some poor sap's identity and then go to heaven.

—Video Vindicator, in "I.D. Hopping"

One hundred years ago, Sigmund Freud taught us what poets have known forever—there is more to you than meets the eye. Deep inside is the subconscious you, intangible yet very real, governing most of your actions, your choices, your impulses. Ignore the subconscious at your peril, and the peril of all you love.

This book is about yet another you who must be considered— not the inside you, but the outside you, another person poets have always known. Your honor. Your good name. Your reputation. Your influence. Your financial power. Your heritage. Each step we take in the world, a mighty wind is generated. Consequences cascade off your decisions. And now, nearly all those decisions are recorded in some book, on some piece of paper, and increasingly on a computer. The sum of these decisions form a history book now, a history book that is often sold to the highest bidder. The car you bought last year. That one drunken mistake you made in college. The e-mail you sent to your lover. For a few dollars, anyone can see this book.

Like the subconscious, in many ways, this outside you is just as real—if not more real—than your flesh and blood, more you than the you who is holding these pages right now.

If you doubt that, consider this: more than half of all major corporations now conduct computerized background checks on job applicants. If the report says the applicant is a convicted felon, he or she will be quickly turned away, perhaps without ever knowing why. Even if the company is good enough to offer an explanation, the applicant often has little chance to protest. Imagine a man who really didn't commit the crime that turns up on the background check. Imagine him telling the human resources manager, "It was just a case of mistaken identity."

Who will she believe? Him, or the computer?

This book is about this other you, this outside you, your digital twin. And it is about the perfect crime—identity theft—when a criminal manages to become this outside you, now your evil twin.

Acting as an imposter is hardly new. In old movies, criminals who wanted to move freely around a secret location would bop a security guard over the head and don his uniform. The imposter had free rein, until someone got close enough to see his face.

But identity thieves are one step better than these imposters. Look closely at a stolen credit card number. It looks just like the real thing. So does a state-issued driver's license obtained by an ID thief armed with the right papers. There is no recognizing the imposter. In fact, an ID thief is not an imposter—he is you. Or rather, he is a perfect copy of you, your digital, evil twin. A computer can't tell the difference between a number and a copy of a number. Once ID thieves have your numbers, they can do anything you can do.

An amateur ID thief can buy your credit card number in a chat room, then pretend to be you for a few hours. A professional can get a driver's license and birth certificate in your name, buy a new BMW, take out a loan against your home and even—as this book will show—commit murder in your name. Perhaps, as the ID thief at the beginning of this section boasts, he can steal your place in Heaven.

Today, people enter this dark world of the digital imposter in many ways—they receive a harassing phone call from a collection agency, they are denied a home loan, they endure a false arrest, or they are just a victim of excessive interest charges from credit card firms recovering their fraud losses. But once a victim crosses into that threshold, once a Social Security number has been used by another, there is no turning back. You're out there now. There is, forever, a certain loss of control, a helplessness. Even if you eventually recover all the money taken from you, several studies suggest you will lose between $500 and $1,000 chasing down the paperwork associated with identity theft and in lost wages. Victims can spend 100 hours or more filling out forms, doing damage control. And they learn quickly that their reputation and honor are not theirs alone to keep, and in fact, they can be as slippery and changeable as the 1s and 0s of a computer file.

Identity theft provides an intriguing window into many of the ills facing America today, from hyperconsumerism to terrorism, from excessive personal debt to digital alienation. It is the fastest-growing white-collar crime in America. It victimizes more people than any other crime in the country. It's profitable, nearly unpreventable, and hardly ever prosecuted. Some estimates say 10 million Americans are victims each year now, and the crime shows no sign of letting up.

Many who describe identity theft make a variety of distinctions about the crime, from merely having your credit card used to make an unauthorized purchase to so-called full-blown identity theft, which can see someone steal hundreds of thousands of dollars in your name. In some versions of the crime, already existing bank accounts are raided; other flavors see the creation of brand-new accounts, or even brand-new identities. I do not make these distinctions, which often create confusion and can be used to minimize the size of the crime—as in, only a third of the 10 million ID theft victims suffered from full-blown identity theft. In fact, ID theft is all of these things, and I refer to all of them whenever I use the term, unless otherwise noted.

This book examines the perfect storm that created the petri dish for identity theft, the crime of the twenty-first century. The storm is driven by massive corporate negligence. Given years of advanced warnings, the American credit industry did almost nothing to quell the epidemic and still enables digital imposters by choosing profits over privacy at nearly every turn. The book also chronicles the government ineffectiveness, law enforcement indifference, and consumer impatience that have stoked the flames of ID theft for years. It highlights individual heroic efforts being made, privately, to soothe consumers reeling from their Kafkaesque trials as they attempt to recover their good names after a bad bout with an imposter. And lastly, it examines some of the forward-looking projects designed to stem the epidemic.

When I began this project, a colleague shared with me a piece of artwork her child had done recently while in daycare. The project had been completed on donated scrap paper, a thoughtful gesture intended to help the center and to help the environment. But on the back of the artwork was a medical form. It revealed the patient's Social Security number, name, address, birthday, and details about his medical conditions. Her 4-year-old had come scurrying home with this treasure trove of personal information. Thanks to decades of marketing and consumer education, we are, as a nation, far more attuned to recycling issues than privacy issues. It will take initiatives as large and as consistent as environmental awareness programs to get a grip, and place the proper priority, on the privacy issues facing our country, and our world.

Ignore the world of this digital, evil twin at your peril, and the peril of all you love.

ACKNOWLEDGMENTS

While this book is about identity theft, it is a book inspired by the victims. Without their stories of endless toils, their heartbreaking discoveries, their disappointing credit rejections, their false arrests, there would be no crisis. Any gesture of gratitude towards them would be insensitive. But here, I would like to honor them. Thousands have sent me e-mails during the past several years at MSNBC.com, screaming for help, having found none in the usual channels. Their banks had ignored them, their police departments had turned them away, their credit card issuers left them in voice mail limbo. Their voices were haunted by helplessness. As a reporter, I couldn't help, either. But out of their cries this project was born. What I can offer is an amplifier for those quiet, anxious, oft-ignored voices, and I hope I have done so. First and foremost, I acknowledge all the victims of this crime, and I acknowledge their pain and frustration, the depth of which can only be understood by those who have suffered the crime. I wish them peace and a renewed sense of empowerment, or, barring that, acceptance of the helplessness brought on by this crime and our digital age. I do especially thank those who have taken the time to share their pain with me directly along the way.

Many thanks also to my editor at John Wiley & Sons, Debra Englander, who quite literally was the only one willing to take a chance on this first-time author. Before the Federal Trade Commission revealed 27 million people had been hit by this crime in recent years, validating the term *epidemic*, she saw the importance of a book exploring the topic, and took the risk. Thanks also to an army of fine people at Wiley, for their dilligent work on my text, particularly Greg Friedman and Todd Tedesco.

Thanks also to my agents at Venture Literary, Frank Scatoni and Greg Dinkin, who many times went the extra mile for me, and did so much more than negotiate on my behalf. They plucked me off the heap of Internet writers, encouraged me to ponder a full-length book project, never seemed to doubt that I could do it—even when I did—and kept positive energy flowing my way during my grueling six-month odyssey.

But at the top of my list of thanks are my colleagues at MSNBC.com, who were flexible with my work and recognized the urgency required by this project, allowing this book to happen on an accelerated schedule. Identity theft really is an Internet story, and I was lucky to begin attacking the problem from the top Internet news site. Thanks to the miracle of e-mail, which we now all take for granted, MSNBC.com gave me access to countless thousands of victims who formed the core of this project. In particular, thanks to editors Gary Seidman, Lori Smith, and Colin Hurlock, who continually allowed me to juggle news reporting with book work, and to editor-in-chief Dean Wright, who created an environment where writers can pursue deeper, more in-depth projects. Thanks also to Mark Stevenson, my first editor at MSNBC.com, who showed excessive and, perhaps at times, reckless confidence in me when few others would. And to MSNBC.com founder Merrill Brown, who from the outset saw our news site as more than a place to get the latest wire stories and stock quotes, but as a place where journalists could distinguish themselves by taking risks and creating original, made-for-the-medium journalism.

In addition to the many victims who indulged my endless questions, a wide array of professionals with very valuable time spent plenty of it with me during this project, explaining this complicated world of white-collar crime. They are too numerous to thank individually, but some merit special recognition for also agreeing to review my work and steer me clear of errors. I am certain many of them have far greater knowledge than I and could indeed craft a better book than I have done here. These include Linda and Jay Foley of the Identity Theft Resource Center, Chris Hoofnagle of the Electronic Privacy Information Center, consumer attorney David Szwak, U.S. attorney Sean Hoar, privacy consultant Rob Douglas, *Credit Card Nation* author Robert Manning, Dan Clements of CardCops.com, fraud consultant Tom Trusty, Beth Givens of the Privacy Rights Clearinghouse, and Gartner analyst Avivah Litan.

Cheers also to the crowd at Murphy's, which each Sunday night gathered after mass and over pints of Guinness and Irish coffees, tolerated endless prattling by me as I bounced my minidramas off of them, one by one, turning them, perhaps unwillingly, into my first and perhaps most important editorial review board. I hope I did not tax our friendships too much. Thanks also to the members of Corduroy, and of the St. Benedict choir, who reminded me that singing always makes you feel better.

To Beau and Lucky, who provided the never-ending love and optimism that only dogs can and who suffered many walks cut short so I could get back to work.

And thanks to Rosa Duarte, who from the first moment I brought up the idea of writing a book simply smiled and said, "Of course, you can," even though neither of us had any idea what that really meant at the time.

Any solid reasoning you, dear reader, find in these pages is probably to the credit of my fine Jesuit education at Fairfield University, and to professors Rev. Tom Regan and Bill Abbott, who taught me to think, and to question, and to always go right to the source. Thanks also to Pat, who has taught me through the years that nothing is more important than hearing the little voice inside, and letting it grow.

And finally, thanks to my family, Don, Rose, Jim, Donnie, Margaret, and Shannon. From the first, they instilled in me a dedication to fairness and honesty and to finding the truth, and the ability to persist when people don't listen right away. Above all, they taught me to notice when people are hurting, or are in trouble, and to do what I could for them.

1

CEOs IN MY CLOSET

"It's so very simple to be anyone you please, on any given morning you awake."

—James Rinaldo Jackson

As the CEO of a Hollywood studio, Terry Semel certainly didn't want to be bothered at home by budding writers peddling two-bit scripts. His home phone number was unlisted. His assistants at Warner Bros. knew better than to give out his address. In 1993, well before the popularization of the Internet, before fan stalker web sites existed, before nationwide telephone lookups were just a few mouse clicks away, maintaining an unlisted number offered reasonable protection against crackpots and fanatics.[1]

So Semel, today the CEO of Yahoo! Inc., must have been surprised that day in 1993 when a Federal Express package arrived at his home. Inside was, of course, a movie pitch from a would-be screen writer. Film producers are used to seeing all manner of desperate attempts to get their attention, but this pitch was very different. As Semel shuffled through the papers, perhaps he realized that he was staring at a shocking mirror of himself, or rather, of his financial self. Somehow, the screenwriter had sent Semel a copy of his Social Security number, bank account number, credit card number, and part of his credit report.

And that was just the beginning.

Semel turned the pages and found dozens of other digital dossiers, all manner of personal data not meant for his eyes, belonging to a Who's Who in Hollywood: Steven Segal, Mel Gibson, Michael Ovitz, Danny DeVito, Sydney Pollack, Leonard Nimoy, and the screenwriter's favorite, Steven Spielberg. Next to each name were private financial account numbers, mother's maiden names, itemized purchases from credit card billing statements, and more.

"There are leaks in the system," the letter said. The author was an inmate at the Millington, Tennessee, federal prison camp.

The prisoner wanted a movie deal. But with the offer came what sounded like a warning: Someone is planning to commit a massive fraud against all these famous people, it said. Lawrence Tisch, Arsenio Hall, Tom Cruise, Lew Wasserman, Alan Ladd, and many others. They were all on a hit list. Someone should do something. Perhaps a movie would help.

The prisoner understood better than most what was about to happen to our digital world. His tone in this letter was at once childlike and prophetic. In one breath, he pitches his wife "Princess" and his friends for roles in the movie. In the next, he describes the coming billion-dollar crisis. Perhaps that's why no one took the June 1, 1993, correspondence very seriously.

"Millions of citizens across America have been or will become victims of fraudulent activities caused by other criminal-minded individuals," he wrote. "In other aspects, illegal purchases of real estate, expensive automobiles, and fine jewelry and easy access to other people's bank accounts, credit cards. . . . It's time for these matters to be dealt with on a more realistic basis and put to a screeching halt."[2]

***

James Rinaldo Jackson is, among other things, a Steven Spielberg fanatic. Such a fanatic, in fact, that for an entire year in the mid-1990s, he knew everything Spielberg purchased on his American Express card. "He has awesome taste, class, and style you won't believe," Jackson says now about Spielberg.

Everything Jackson learned about Spielberg, he learned while in prison, much of it using a cell phone supplied by a family member. Jackson says he never tried to steal anything from the famous Hollywood director. He just wanted to snoop.

"When you like and admire someone of his phenomenal talent, you don't even attempt to step on his shoes," he said. But you might drop his name, and some personal data, to get the attention of a big movie producer.

Just a few calls while in the care of the federal prison system, and Jackson scored all sorts of data on Spielberg and about 100 other Hollywood types. All in a single day's work. He started by calling the Screen Actors Guild and tricking an operator into sharing the name of the guild's health care insurance provider. Then he called the provider's toll-free number and pretended to be an administrator at a medical provider looking to verify coverage for billing purposes. Helpful operators spat back Social Security numbers, dates of birth, addresses, and other private information.

"All I needed was a name," he said. Then, he would start his "prowl."

"I called up American Express. The rep asked me for my account number when I gave him my name as Steven Spielberg. He was a young-sounding guy who appeared to be overwhelmed and excited to a degree until he asked me, 'Is this *the* Steven Spielberg?'

"Calmly, my reply was no. Then I said, 'I'm mistaken for him every single day of my life.'

"So he relaxed somewhat and proceeded to ask me for my account number when I told him I didn't have my card with me at the time. Then I remember saying something to the effect of, 'Unfortunately I left home without mine, I'm certain the real Steven Spielberg would never do such.'

"After I told him that, he said, 'Well, that's okay, how about your Social Security number?' Thanks to the Screen Actors Guild, I had that. So I called out all nine digits. Then the rep asked me for my date of birth and I gave him that. The rep then went on to say 'How can I help you?' I asked for my balance, which was nearly $100,000. Then the representative started to give me a detailed billing of the charges, where he had dined, establishments where the card had been used, amount of last payment, current payment due. This guy had real good taste. He spent wads of money on brand-name clothes and expensive jewelry, wined and dined at the top-of-the-line hotels. . . ."

It took a year before guards discovered Jackson was committing identity fraud while behind bars. On daily outdoor work duty at a nearby military base, Jackson had only his memory of toll-free phone numbers and payphones to work with. Still, he managed to score stolen credit card accounts and other funds from a host of wealthy people. Other inmates helped; accomplices who stood guard while he made the phone calls were paid off with pizza, beer, Nike sneakers, jogging suits, jewelry, watches, even money, all funded by credit card accounts pilfered over the telephone. They even watched his back so he could find time alone with a blue-eyed, blonde-haired female Naval officer stationed on the base. When their love affair was ratted out, he was sent to solitary confinement. Later, he was only allowed work detail near the prison, doing simple landscaping and garbage collecting under the constant watchful eye of prison guards. But even that didn't stop him.

Jackson's brother-in-law drove up one day, discarded a crumpled-up fast-food bag, and missed the trash. Jackson picked it up, as was the plan, and later took out the cell phone and car charger that had been left inside. He could chat on the phone while sitting in the prison's landscaping truck, which he was still allowed to drive around the compound. He hid the phone inside the truck's air vents when he left.

The scheme worked for a few months, until Jackson got too greedy yet again—when he tried to steal thousands of dollars from Dean Witter executives, including CEO Charles Fiumeffredo, he set off red flags. It meant another two years in a federal prison, and finally, he said, "I was put inside a place with barbed wire." Only then did he temporarily stop posing as America's elite for his own financial gain; but it was just a temporary hiatus. A few months after his release in 1998, he would be back at it again. His best work was still ahead of him.

While he did get the thrill of being Steven Spielberg for a while, Jackson never got his movie deal. He did have several telephone conversations with an assistant to Terry Semel at Warner Brothers during several weeks in 1993, who encouraged Jackson. But shortly after that, Jackson was moved to another prison where he had no phone privileges, and he lost contact with the movie studio.

"I didn't get the movie deal because identity theft wasn't a major concern . . . back then," Jackson said. "I felt then it would eventually become a fast-growing crime in America. And it did!"

As if to fulfill his own prophesy, Jackson ended up scamming some of the famous people on the list he sent to Semel. Many never knew Jackson was the culprit, even though he should have been an obvious suspect, given the typewritten preconfession. Victims from the Semel letter include Robert and Patricia Stemple, then CEO of General Motors; and CBS's Lawrence Tisch. "I'm extremely remorseful," he says now, addressing the victims. "Please forgive me."

***

James Rinaldo Jackson had an unusual childhood for Memphis, Tennessee in the 1960s. His mother was black and his father white; at school, he was quickly given the nickname, "Zebra," and it stuck. The teasing was painful, but young James turned the tables by embracing the label. At times, he remembers refusing to answer when his parents called him James–he insisted that his name was "Zebra." Then, when he was given a guitar for Christmas, he began imagining he was a member of the Beatles. Call me John, Paul, or Ringo, he demanded. Like many kids, he would break out in song, blaring, "She loves you, yeah, yeah, yeah!" and not always at the most appropriate of times. His parents laughed it off; his babysitter spanked him when she got irritated, but no one really took notice how much energy James put into being other people. Or how good he was getting at it.

His musical affections quickly turned local, and Elvis became the target of his obsession. By the time he was 12, he insisted on eating jelly donuts, peanut butter sandwiches topped with banana slices, and wearing blue suede shoes for special occasions.

One day, his father told him, gently, that "God made you and there's only one you in the whole wide world," attempting to urge the boy to start to find his own personality. But it was devastating for James, who realized then that there must be only one Elvis, too. He says he burst into tears at the kindly remark. "That man doesn't know what he's talking about," James remembers thinking. "He's got life all wrong."

By a stroke of luck, Jackson attended Humes Jr. High, where Elvis had attended high school. The obsession became complete. He even imagined he was shitting in the same place Elvis did.

"I wanted to say that I sat bare butt on the same toilet (Elvis had), to describe the wonderful feeling of sensation from the rim of a commode where Elvis sat," Jackson wrote in a private memoir he hopes to publish some day. He would end up in detention for creating disruptions as he broke out into Elvis songs during school.

Just as James was about to reach high school, his father died suddenly. Now he felt he had something else in common with The King, who had lost his mother when he was still young. James remembers staring at Elvis' retired football jersey in the school's trophy case, crying, and singing *That's Allright Mama* to himself. He prayed for his dad and his mom, and soon vowed to transfer schools so he could get away from his overwhelming desire to be someone else.

But his attempt at self-rehabilitation didn't last, because right about then he learned that he could make good money pretending to be other people. And with his father now gone, his mother sure could use the help.

It began innocently enough. The golden age of rock-and-roll radio brought with it intense competition and stations quickly learned the best way to steal listeners from each other was to pay them. Cash giveaways and other prize games were everywhere. Just by knowing what songs the stations were playing, and calling at the right time, James could win $300 at a clip. Sometimes he won five prizes a day, calling shows in the morning before school. His most prized winnings at the time was a ladies' Wittnauer watch worth $150, which he was able to give his mom as a present when he was only 15 years old. Of course, 15-year-olds weren't supposed to win; and no one was eligible to win contests repeatedly each day.

James says he beat the system by setting up a bank of telephones at home and quick-dialing them repeatedly, by hand, so he could be caller number 10. Then, when he won, he would disguise his voice—sometimes as a 90-year-old grandmother, sometimes a young, excitable woman. And he would use various names and addresses all over town. Next, he'd simply wait for the valuable mail to arrive, sneak into the mailbox, and collect his winnings. He also won free blenders, toasters, grills, kitchen ware and other appliances for his family. At the time, he felt "the ability to talk my way out of anything I wanted or for that matter, talk my way into retrieving anything I wanted, too."

Jackson didn't last long in college; instead, his true college was the University Club of Memphis, where he waited tables on the rich and famous from his teen years to his early 20s. Charming, exceedingly polite, and patient, he learned how to talk the way powerful people talk, with confidence and back-slapping humor always at ready disposal. He also learned to dislike the smug elite, and he acquired a taste for outsmarting people who were supposed to be smarter than him.

From the Federal Correctional Institution in Forrest City, Arkansas, where he is serving an 8-year term for his most recent frauds, Jackson, for the first time, offered elaborate details of his 15-year identity fraud crime spree. Fueled by a burning desire to demonstrate that he is sorry for his crimes, which could reduce his prison term, Jackson agreed to a lenghthy set of correspondence interviews, offering an intimate look at criminal imposters and the broken systems that enable them.

"It's 7:06 A.M., I've had my M&Ms, it's time to exert some positive energy," he wrote. The perfectly typed, single-spaced letters of about four thousand words each could have as few as two paragraphs and contained even fewer typing mistakes. "As the ole saying goes, the early bird gets the worm. . . ."

***

To say that Jackson is starstruck would be quite an understatement. In the early 1990s, just as Oprah Winfrey's stock was headed from star to superstar, Jackson learned that Oprah's father owned a barbershop in Nashville, a couple of hundred miles away from Memphis. No matter; Jackson decided he just had to have his hair cut by Vernon Winfrey. More than a decade later, he still remembers their first encounter in vivid detail. One of the other barbers had an open chair and offered it to him; he refused, of course. When Winfrey's chair came open, he turned on the charm.

"I've never had my hair cut by the father of a famous daughter," Jackson said, getting just a little laugh. Then, the two bantered back and forth about Jackson's hometown of Memphis and Winfrey's whimsical idea that the city should really be part of Mississippi. After all, Oprah was born in Mississippi.

Jackson remembers driving to the barbershop in his stolen pearl-white Mercedes Benz 420 SEL. Winfrey, who noticed the car, said his daughter had recently bought him a similar Mercedes, a 560 SEL with heated seats and a bigger engine. He didn't like driving it, though, because it didn't fit in well with the neighborhood, a poor section of Music City. Eventually, Jackson learned Winfrey still lived in the tough area, which Jackson called "the hood," despite Oprah's recent gift of an expansive, half-million-dollar mansion in the suburbs.

"He told me that Oprah nearly begged him and begged him to move into the home; he kept putting it off . . . he point blank said to me, 'James, that's my daughter's money and fame. I am so happy right here where I am, where I've been living among average, everyday kind of people nearly all my life. I don't need all of that.'"

He went on to say that Oprah had offered to buy him a brand-new barbershop, or to rebuild the one he had, but he refused.

On the Winfrey barbershop is a wall with thousands of pictures from well-wishers who have stopped by to meet the famous father. Before he left, Jackson thanked Winfrey for being gracious, shook his hand, gave Winfrey his picture, then waited to make sure it ended up on that wall.

The elder Winfrey's kindly ways probably saved his daughter a financial headache in the future. Jackson, a sort of digital-age Robin Hood, declared Oprah off-limits after the visit.

"He was an amazingly warm and sensible gentleman that I grew to love, admire, and respect all because he treated me like a customer who was there spending a million bucks on fine, fine jewels," Jackson says now. "It made me not ever want to commit an identity theft crime against anyone that had close ties to Mr. Winfrey." Others among the world's famous and elite weren't so lucky.

***

He started small, rigging car accident claims involving rented cars in the late 1980s. With a band of disciples in tow, he honed that craft and ultimately staged some 50 accidents, netting the crime gang $642,000. But car accidents were hard work, and another, more lucrative money-making scheme was emerging.

While working as a delivery driver for Federal Express, Jackson met a Nigerian "professor" who explained the ins and outs of the insurance industry and the methods for tricking customer service telephone operators into divulging critical data on anyone. Watching CNN one night in the late 1980s, he saw Time Warner's Gerald Levine being interviewed and decided to give it a whirl. Moments later, he had a full digital dossier on Levine. It was as easy as lying to the man's health insurance company.

Within two years, Jackson had worked his way through much of corporate America, impersonating such luminaries as Edward Brennan, CEO of Sears, Charles Lebreque, former head of Chase, and about 25 other CEOs, which he still won't discuss. But he had his biggest early score by hitting a victim in his own backyard.

The Belz family is one of the most influential real estate developers in the south—certainly in Memphis, Tennessee, where the family owns a series of malls and office complexes. But no one noticed in 1990 when Jackson stole a letter addressed to Jack Belz, then CEO of Belz Associates, and applied for a credit card in Belz's name. He managed some $116,000 in purchases and cash withdrawals on credit cards in Belz's name before he was finally stopped.[3]

In the meantime, he was living in style, chilling in a $150,000 home he had purchased in Georgia using a false ID. He had amassed an impressive fleet of luxury cars via identity theft. In addition to the Mercedes, he had a Lincoln Continental, a BMW, and a Nissan Pathfinder. A Corvette he once owned had been exchanged for a Lotus Esprit SE.

The women came easily, too, especially when he wasn't paying. Jackson says he regularly carried FBI and U.S. Marshal Service credentials that often earned him free sex. When he checked into hotels, he got into the habit of flipping through the yellow pages and calling a local escort service, ordering one or two girls at a time. When he was finished with them, he'd let them dress and then flash a badge "smack dab in the middle of their face," read them their rights, and announce a sting. He'd offer to let the girls go if they returned his money. He'd even make a crank call and carry the gag further, until they returned the cash. "It worked like a charm 99.5 percent of the times I pulled this scheme," he wrote. "The other 0.5 percent nearly cost me my life."

While pimps never caught up with Jackson, the cops eventually did. Law enforcement agencies began to circle Jackson in late 1990, and his world would begin to unravel the next year. Insurance investigators from Geico and a local furniture store he had bilked had him arrested. But perhaps as a bit of poetic license, his first conviction involved theft of airline travel, using a technique not unlike that of famed impersonator Frank Abignale. Jackson had assumed the identity of a Federal Express employee with the same name and had been flying around the country for under $50, round trip, using the other Jackson's employee discounts.

When he was arrested, federal authorities also found a $55,000 Cadillac Allante and a $40,000 Lexus in his driveway, both purchased using fake Social Security numbers. Court documents indicate he was arrested with a series of credit cards under assumed names, including "those of top executives of major U.S. corporations."

While awaiting trial, Jackson continued to show his ability to acquire hard-to-find information. The master imposter sought revenge against the FBI agent who helped catch him, reporting a domestic disturbance at the agent's home. Jackson called from jail, telling dispatchers someone had been stabbed inside the agent's home during a family fight. The address was supposed to be a federal secret. But soon a sheriff, an ambulance, and several fire trucks were outside the agent's home. He messed with my family, I'll mess with his, Jackson said at the time, according to court documents.[4]

Later, to convince Judge Julia Smith Gibbons that conditions inside the jail where he was being held were unlivable, Jackson sent a box full of bugs, which were gathered in his cell, to the judge's home. Thanks in part to such jail-cell shenanigans, he found himself in federal custody for the next seven years.

***

When Jackson found his way back out on the street in 1999, much had changed. The Internet made his research easier than ever. Jackson was surfing the Net one day in late December when he decided to browse the *New York Times* obituaries. Only the kind of people Jackson served at the Memphis University Club have their obits published in the *Times,* Jackson noted, so the section proved to be fertile ground for potential victims.

There he learned about the death of Gordon Teter, CEO of Wendy's. The obit listed Teter's age, hometown, and the name of the funeral home taking care of the arrangements. The obituary in Teter's Dublin, Ohio, hometown paper provided more details. Then, back to his old tricks, Jackson called the funeral home, posing as an insurance company representative who needed to verify Teter's personal information. Without it, he threatened, the funeral home might not be paid. At this point, Jackson didn't even know what company held Teter's policy, but he didn't need to. The only verification the funeral home employee insisted on was a "yes" answer to the question, "Do you work for Mr. Teter's insurance company?" The operator then gave him Teter's Social Security number, date of birth, and home address.

"I knew it would only be a matter of time before I would actually be impersonating Mr. Teter," Jackson said. "And that there would be one good advantage of stealing the identity of a dead person. They wouldn't feel it; it's not like they could come back to life and call in their accounts as a fraud. I knew this was the perfect caper to pull off."

Now, Jackson simply had to find Teter's money. Years of experience had taught him that executives often have personal bank accounts in the same bank as their company's corporate accounts. So he called Wendy's corporate offices, pretending to be an entrepreneur who was in the process of opening a new franchise. Jackson said he was concerned that he might have bounced a check sent to Wendy's. The operator shared the name of the bank, Fifth Third Bank, in Dublin.

The next day he called the bank and talked to a female operator, asking to check the available balance on Teter's account. The operator asked for his account number; he didn't have one. But he had Teter's birthday, home address, ZIP code, and Social Security number. And that was enough.

"Which account are you referring to?" he recalls her asking.

"Which ones do you show?" he replied.

In a moment, she was voluntarily revealing Teter's checking account numbers and credit card account numbers. In fact, she told Jackson so fast he didn't even have pen and paper ready the first time. She repeated the numbers more slowly on request.

The checking account had a balance of more than $300,000.

***

Stealing someone's private information is often as easy as asking for it. Customer service telephone employees have always been the best source for professional identity thieves. Early on, Jackson learned how to read customer service representatives by ear. Not every one is naïve. The more experienced and middle-aged the operator, the more likely the scam will fail, he says. At that point, a con artist who spots trouble must delicately hang up.

"An account can easily go from gold to dirt" if any suspicion is raised, he says. But if the voice on the other end is "eager to help and youthful sounding, bingo." And the more money in the account, the less likely the ID thief will be hassled. After all, no one wants to be fired for giving the bank's best customer a hard time.

"Let's make Mr. Teter happy. Customers first. Actually, it's Mr. Imposter first."

Like a kid in a candy store, Jackson set out to cash in on Teter's $300,000 account. A week earlier, he had seen magazine advertisements for Mondera.com and Ashford.com, two online diamond stores. He'd ripped the ads out of the magazine and shoved them into his wallet. Now, he took out the crumpled papers and looked jealously at the Rolex watch in the ad. After settling on an initial purchase, he called Mondera.com and got the right account information to wire money to the web site.

He called back First Third Bank, posing as Teter, and said he wanted to make a wire transfer. The operator who answered said he'd have to come into the bank branch personally to sign the papers.

"Fine, I'll be in shortly," he answered, not to raise suspicion. Of course, he couldn't—he was hundreds of miles away from Dublin, Ohio, in Memphis, Tennessee. But distances have no impact on identity thieves. He just hung up, called back, and got a young woman named Mary with a pleasant-sounding Irish voice on the line. He honed his story a little bit, this time saying he was in an important business meeting in Beverly Hills and needed cash quickly to buy stocks, so he couldn't come into the bank. Mary complied. She said she could wire up to $100,000 for him, as long as he provided a call-back number that could be used to verify his identity. So he asked her to wire $96,000 to Mondera.com's accounts. Then he gave her a voice mailbox he had used before, which was based in Milwaukee, Wisconsin, set up with a stolen credit card. He hung up and quickly changed the voice message to say, "You've reached the offices of Gordon Teter. I'm sorry, I'm unavailable."

Within a day, just in time for Christmas, the bank wired the money.

The only obstacle left was receiving the diamonds, and for this, Jackson also had a plan. He made a reservation at a local hotel in Teter's name and had the diamonds shipped there. The hotel clerk would accept the delivery because Teter was supposed to be a guest. Then Jackson or an accomplice would pick up the diamonds. When asked to provide positive identification, that was no hurdle. Jackson had been dealing in fake driver's licenses for years. When he was arrested back in 1991, he was found with 2,000 fake Tennessee licenses and another 2,000 fake New Mexico licenses.[5] In fact, well before Internet sites and laser printers made creation of imitation licenses easy, Jackson had done it the hard way, once buying a Polaroid license printer for $3,000 right from the manufacturer.

His diamond scam worked like a charm. He picked up the rocks from the hotel without a hitch, and now, he thought he had finally hit on the perfect crime. In quick succession, he ordered another $200,000 in diamonds during the next two weeks, draining Teter's account, which was "paying off like a slot machine in Vegas." He was rich again.

But not rich enough, so he had to keep going. Before he was done, $750,000 in diamonds and expensive watches made their way to Memphis through a complicated network of hotel rooms, delivery services, and identity frauds.

During those heady eight weeks, Jackson started stealing money from two other recently deceased *New York Times* notables, James Klinenberg, former administrator of Cedars-Sinai Medical Hospital in Los Angeles, and Nackey Loeb, a newspaper publisher. Loeb, he picked on because she had been critical of then-President Bill Clinton on the editorial pages of her newspapers. Clinton had enamored himself to Jackson when he played Elvis tunes on his saxophone as a guest on the *Arsenio Hall* show.

"Those insulting comments really made me pissed," Jackson writes in his personal memoir. "So my reasons for Nackey Loeb becoming a victim of mine, very easily and well explained.

He also ordered diamonds in the name of John Alm, CEO of Coca Cola, Richard Fuld, head of Lehman Brothers, and John

Bollenback, CEO of Hilton Hotels. In some cases, he simply ordered their personal data from information brokers on the Internet, a kind of digital-age private investigator service that sells Social Security numbers and other private information to the highest bidder.

With each order, there were mild variations, as the scheme became more intricate. He faced few hurdles in cracking security systems and impersonating the rich and famous. Some dealers received counterfeit checks drawn on stolen accounts. Others agreed to simple credit card transactions. When he bought $40,000 in diamonds from Blue Nile, he charged them on Alm's and Fuld's American Express cards.[6] Knowing that most merchants perform address verification to stop fraud on high-ticket items— they only ship purchases when the billing address on the credit card and shipping address match—Jackson planned ahead. He called American Express and had Alm's billing address changed to the address of a hotel in Orlando, Florida. He had the diamonds shipped there and then forwarded to Holiday Inn Express in Southaven, Mississippi, just over the border from Tennessee.

He had no trouble impersonating his victims, even Loeb, who was a woman. Merchants often don't even check to see if the name being used to make an order matches the name on the credit card, Jackson said. As long as the account was valid, and the billing address was right, the orders would go through. So on some cases, to expedite matters, he said he was a doctor, to win added respect. Here's my phone number, but don't call me back, I'm busy with patients, he told one merchant.

"He called himself Dr. Teter," Shane Coley, owner of Time & Time Again in Boston, told *USA Today* after the crime. Time & Time Again shipped Jackson a Rolex watch after receiving money wired from Teter's bank. "He was charming. He even haggled a little bit. After we shipped him the first one, he called to say the watch was excellent. 'I love it,' he told me. 'I just finished up with a patient, and the receptionist told me your package arrived. When I'm in Boston in the spring, I'll come up to see you.'"[7]

***

But already, the end of Jackson's two-month shopping spree was near. So was his brief taste of freedom.

Manhattan's diamond district is a tight-knit community, and people talk about hundreds of thousands of dollars in disappearing jewels. While the diamond packages were delivered to hotels around the country, they all ended up in Memphis or nearby Mississippi towns. Several merchants plotted the delivery points on the Internet and realized the shipments were all headed to the same area, and probably the same person. And while the orders were placed in different names, many merchants had been given the same voice mail number.

FBI Agent Maureen Dougherty in New York began to connect the dots. The takedown was easy. In fact, Dougherty thinks Jackson probably wanted to be caught, because he kept going even after he sensed authorities closing in, frittering away his chance to get away with the diamonds and his freedom.

At the FBI, such sting operations are called *controlled deliveries,* and Dougherty had New York diamond dealers lining up to volunteer for the job. She got Diamond Cutters of Western New York to accept a wire transfer for diamonds and send an empty box to a "Dr. Redding" at Red Roof Inn in West Memphis in early February 2000. When no one picked it up, the box was returned to the local FedEx drop-off point, where Jackson and his accomplice planned to pick it up. But when the FedEx employee left the front desk to alert the FBI that the suspect had arrived, Jackson fled, sensing something was wrong.[8]

Still, he couldn't stop himself; he was convinced his plot could still work. On February 14, he placed a modest $9,000 order at American Diamond Wholesalers in Nackey Loeb's name, asking that the package be sent to Teaneck, New Jersey, just a few miles from Manhattan. A messenger arrived to pick up the package with instructions to forward it via FedEx to a Holiday Inn Express in Cordova, Tennessee. On February 25, Jackson walked into that hotel to pick up the package. FBI agents were there to arrest him when he walked out.[9]

***

After spending 15 years pretending to be America's corporate elite, once the owner of a fleet of luxury cars and a small hoard of diamonds, Jackson found himself declared an "indigent defendant." He had no money. His own bank accounts were virtually empty. Tall, soft-spoken Robert Dunn was appointed his defense attorney. The evidence against Jackson was overwhelming, and so was the recidivism. A long jail term was a certainty. All Dunn could hope for was to minimize the damage, and he wanted to.

"James is a very nice man, very personable. This is a problem he has," Dunn said. The only strategy left was for Jackson to throw himself on the mercy of the court, and hope his contrition blunted the judge's outrage. Stealing from a recently deceased man's family is hardly the best way to invite mercy.[10] He would plead guilty to all 29 felonies he was facing.

Dunn hardly knew what to expect at Jackson's plea hearing—he was well aware of his client's penchant for doing the unexpected. A few weeks earlier, while struggling to find some way to mitigate Jackson's guilt and reduce his potential jail time, Dunn sent his client to one of the top psychologists in New York. There's obvious compulsion here, Dunn thought, and maybe even multiple personality disorder. A standard battery of tests should determine that.

But before Jackson arrived in the doctor's office, the con man had already written a lengthy psychological evaluation of himself. Gambling was the problem, Jackson's missive revealed. And after a brief consultation, the psychologist agreed. He sent word to Dunn that a report was on its way that might help his client's case. The psychologist submitted a report to the court suggesting that compulsive gambling was in part to blame for Jackson's behavior.

Jackson had conned one of New York's best psychologists.

Never in his 15-year history in and out of the court system had Jackson mentioned gambling; it was an entirely unbelievable story, and in fact, Jackson now admits, was a fraud. At any rate, even if it were true, that wouldn't have been a mitigating factor, wouldn't have landed him a shorter jail term. But Jackson had convinced himself that compulsive gambling would earn him sympathy from the judge, so he played that last card. And lost.

"He out conned his God-damn self," Dunn said.

***

"Mr. Dunn, leave him alone," Judge Deborah Batts barked during the plea hearing. "I am actually trying to understand what is happening here."[11]

Like any defense attorney, Dunn wanted his client to say as little as possible while offering his guilty plea. But it was too late. James Rinaldo Jackson was in the zone, in his element, bragging about his journey through the financial system, his time pretending to be some of America's most famous and wealthiest people. A tug on Jackson's arm went unnoticed.

"I am sorry for the interruption by your counsel, Mr. Jackson. Just proceed," the judge said. There was an elaborate chart in the courtroom, explaining the 29 felonies and the complex net of financial crimes listed in Jackson's indictment.[12]

But the judge wanted more; she wanted a true confession, not just a guilty plea. "Just forget the chart," she said. "Just talk to me. Tell me what you did, how it got started, what you agreed to do." Only later would Jackson, the great seducer, learn he was being seduced.

By the time he was finished, his pride was so obvious it out-shone any contrition. The U.S. attorney's office would take the unusual step of asking the court to keep Jackson behind bars as long as possible—in this case, eight years, at the very top of the sentencing range for the crimes he committed—because it was clear he couldn't resist the temptation and thrill of it all. A letter from U.S. Attorney Jason Weinstein to Judge Batts, urging a stiff sentence, drove home the point that Jackson was proud of his work. While in prison the last time, the letter said, Jackson began writing "a self-help book for budding credit card fraud-sters and identity thieves . . . his opus, entitled *Personal Info of a CEO, or Anyone Else by James R. Jackson,* includes a 21-chapter table of contents featuring chapter titles such as 'The CEO Syn-drome,' 'Gathering the Personal Info,' 'Getting Positive ID Any-time,' 'The Credit Report of a CEO and What to Do and How I Did,' 'Buying the Car of Your Choice Without a Job,' . . . and 'Mad Judge and Intimidated FBI Agent.'"[13]

But Batts wouldn't need the U.S. Attorney's Office's arguments to convince her that Jackson should go away for a long time. He did that for her.

"Yes, your honor. What happened, I was going through some magazines, and after going through the magazines I saw dia-mond merchants listing their web sites. . . . I decided, gosh, I can log onto a web site and actually, you know, look at these dia-monds, and after looking at the diamonds then of course I came to myself and I said boy, this is impressive. I said I would sure like to get some of these diamonds to just have."[14]

What followed was a blow-by-blow account of the diamond heist, including a boast that the master imposter had simply glanced at Who's Who in America to pick his victims. Jackson thought he was getting on the judge's good side by explaining every last detail, explaining how he stole money from the dead. The judge didn't have to know about the incident at the funeral parlor, Dunn said. But she pushed him, and "he lights up like a Christmas tree." She found that incident particularly reprehensible.

"Amazing. Simply amazing," the judge said, goading him on. She set him up. To give Jackson the stiff eight-year term she wanted to, she needed to "enhance" the sentence by establishing that he had used "sophisticated means" to commit his financial crimes. And that determination would have to stand up before an appeals court. Jackson made her case for her. The diatribe he offered, perhaps the best public testimony yet on the methods of identity thieves, made successful appeal of the extraordinary means enhancement unlikely.

Dunn liberally agreed that his client was a con man who needed to do hard jail time. But extraordinary means?

"What he really did couldn't have been any simpler," Dunn argued. "There was nothing sophisticated about it. He just exploited gaps in the system." What should really be on trial, Dunn says today, is the system that made Jackson's scams so easy.

***

A month after being nabbed in the sting, while awaiting trial at Metropolitan Detention Center in Brooklyn, Jackson met scruffy, overweight Abraham Abdallah. Abdallah was also a career identity thief, in and out of jails since his teenage years. And, like Jackson, Abdallah had slowly escalated from simple frauds to far more serious identity thefts involving America's rich and famous. The two spoke only a few times; Abdallah was also awaiting his day in court. Their conversations were shallow and chatty. Abdallah, like most Americans, had never heard of Jackson, and had no idea who he was. He knew nothing about the diamonds, nothing about Steven Spielberg, nothing about all those CEOs in Jackson's closet. The two didn't talk shop. But Jackson certainly knew of Abdallah. Much of the world did, at least for a few days in March 2001.

Overnight, Abdallah had become a global celebrity by boldly impersonating global celebrities. His was a billion-dollar crime—in fact, tens of billions of dollars were at stake. When his takedown finally happened, it came with all the trappings of a Mafioso roundup, complete with a New York City cop dangling out the sunroof of the getaway car. When two investigators managed to subdue Abraham Abdallah and stop the car he was in, they put an end to potentially one of the biggest-ticket crimes in New York City history.

But this was no mob takedown. Detective James Doyle remembers it more like a Keystone Cop routine. When a detective spotted Abdallah at the sting scene at the Brooklyn waterfront, Abdallah ran back to his 2000 Volvo jumped inside and simply locked the doors. There was no place to drive, all the exits had been cut off. [15]

Detective Michael Fabozzi noticed the sunroof was open and leapt into the car. While Fabozzi, upside down, tried to handcuff Abdallah, the identity thief tried to squirm under the dashboard. Doyle, who joined Fabozzi in the sunroof, tried to help subdue Abdallah by pounding on him with an empty plastic Pepsi bottle—the only thing he could find nearby. In moments, Abdallah went from being the world's richest man, 200 times over, to being a suspect in handcuffs clinging to a dashboard with all his might, as if he could cling to being Microsoft cofounder Paul Allen for just a few more moments.

Abdallah was a high school dropout, a New York City busboy, a pudgy, disheveled, career petty criminal. Almost 20 years earlier, he had been arrested for simple credit card fraud. He even made a video at the time, called "Crime of the 20th Century," with the U.S. Postal Inspector's Office, in exchange for a reduced sentence. The video is still used as a training tool in some financial companies.[16] But now, Abdallah was on the front page of the *New York Post*. He had committed the crime of the twenty-first century.

The only evidence prosecutors needed was the dog-eared copy of *Forbes* magazine that was sitting on the passenger seat of Abdallah's Volvo. It was the special "Forbes 400" issue, splattered with pictures of the usual suspects—Warren Buffet, Steven Spielberg, Oprah Winfrey, and Bill Gates. But the pages were jammed with scribbled notes: checking account numbers, cell phone numbers, brokerage accounts, balances, and everywhere, names and phone numbers of key financial advisers Abdallah had tracked down.

That year, 2001, Bill Gates was at the top of the *Forbes* list. Gates escaped unscathed, but only because Abdallah had chosen not to go after him—too well known, according to the *New York Post*'s Murray Weiss. But after passing on No.1, the rest of the list was up for grabs. Abdallah scored with more than 200 other celebrities on the list, working his way from Buffet and Oprah to Martha Stewart and Larry Ellison. Using a cell phone, some voice mailboxes, and free e-mail accounts, he had fast-talked his way through receptionists and security questions for six months. Eventually, he had access to billions of dollars.[17]

***

It all unraveled when Abdallah got very greedy very quickly. He asked Merrill Lynch to move $10 million from software magnate Thomas Siebel's account to a new account in Australia, and that set off alarm bells. "Operation CEO" began in earnest. Digging behind that transaction, Detective Fabozzi eventually found an elaborate net of e-mail addresses, voice mails, and P.O. boxes purchased in the name of the world's richest people.

Fabozzi arranged a sting, not much different from the FBI's controlled delivery to Jackson. As is often the case, this white-collar criminal playing in the make-believe world of bits and bytes was caught when he was forced to step out into the world of reality, just for an instant. Authorities almost always catch cyber criminals at the end of a package.

On February 23, 2001—only 48 hours before James Rinaldo Jackson stepped into a Holiday Inn in Cordova, Tennessee, and walked out into the waiting arms of FBI agents—Abdallah was in

Brooklyn awaiting delivery of $25,000 worth of equipment used to magnetize and manufacture bogus credit cards. As usual, the delivery was to be made in stages, in an effort to obscure his trail. The package was to be shipped via UPS to a bogus Bronx location, then picked up by a courier service and delivered to an auto shop near Brooklyn's waterfront. There, Abdallah figured he could pick up the package in safety. But police intercepted the initial UPS delivery. Detective Jamal Daise then took the wheel of the courier service van and headed for Brooklyn. Detective Doyle didn't want Daise driving alone, so he climbed into the back of the truck.

Delivery vans almost never come with two employees. As luck would have it, the minivan was full of windows, so Doyle had to hide. He jumped into a garbage bag and ducked down in the back. He sweated all the way from the Bronx to Brooklyn.

The plan was simple. When Daise said "Have a nice day" to whomever accepted the package, Doyle would pop out of the bag and help cuff the suspect. A few minutes later, the van arrived at the auto shop, and Daise was met by a mechanic.

He was quickly cuffed—and even as the mechanic tried to explain he was only there to accept a package, Abdallah's Volvo pulled up. Still sweating from his time in the garbage bag, Doyle raced toward the Volvo at the end of the waterfront. But Fabozzi, who had trailed the van, got there first and leapt inside.[18] Moments later, Abdallah was in custody.

Abdallah never strayed far from his childhood neighborhood in Brooklyn. But as far as the world's financial companies knew, for that glorious six months, he was everyone and he was everywhere.

Martin Biegelman, the Postal Inspector's officer who first busted Abdallah in the 1980s, was sitting in the subway the next day when a fellow passenger held up a copy of the *Post* to read it. That's Abdallah, he thought, eyeing the scruffy face splashed on the cover. That's the kid I busted for getting credit cards using fake letterhead 20 years ago. Within hours, Biegelman was on

CNN and dozens of other television stations with the "I knew him when" part of the story.

"He was a petty criminal, not exceptionally good. But he did stay with it. He advanced with the technology," said Biegelman, who 20 years earlier had talked Abdallah into appearing in the fraud video mentioned earlier. "He was very cooperative. A good kid, really."[19]

Abdallah's main technique then, requesting account information on faked or stolen letterhead, still did the trick in 2001. When police caught up with him, he had rubber stamps bearing the names of Goldman Sachs and Bear Stearns, two prestigious New York investment companies.

The stamps turned out to be a key element in Abdallah's scheme. It all started with letters sent to credit reporting companies, sent on official-looking letterhead, requesting credit reports on the world's richest people. The credit reporting companies complied, and that gave Abdallah the head start he needed. He knew victims' Social Security numbers. And he knew where their accounts were. He could call Paul Allen's broker and request a transfer, leaving what appeared to be a West Coast callback number. But it was just a voice mailbox. He used virtual fax machines and even anonymous e-mail accounts to do his dirty work. And when it came time to receive stolen goods, he used drop locations and hired runners to cloak his trail. For six months, he lived it up as the world's rich and famous.[20]

When Abdallah's story hit the front page of the *New York Post*, the Brooklyn kid was hailed as a genius who had used "sophisticated cell phones." He had so many accounts and so many deliveries headed to so many places in New York, it was amazing he could keep them all straight, police said. He had evaded authorities and for months was only an "electronic blip" on the web. In hundreds of publications worldwide, Detective Fabozzi, who had worked electronic and financial crimes in New York for a dozen years, was quoted as saying Abdallah was "the best I ever faced."

***

That, both Doyle and Fabozzi now say, was an exaggeration, a bit of over exuberance by the publicity department at New York's Finest. Abdallah made dozens of sloppy, amateur mistakes. He was caught trying to move $10 million at once, an amount sure to trip alarm bells. The requests came from two free Yahoo! e-mail addresses. When Merrill Lynch checked its customer database, it discovered Abdallah had used those same e-mail accounts in connection with five other wealthy Merrill Lynch clients. In fact, he had used the e-mail addresses all over Wall Street. Had Abdallah been even a little cautious, he would have created hundreds of disposable e-mail addresses to not raise suspicion. And he certainly wouldn't have tried to move that much money all at once.

Meanwhile, by 2001, cell phones with Internet access were hardly "sophisticated," and neither were remote voice mailboxes.

Abdallah was not a genius—he just outsmarted a very dumb system.

There were open cases all over New York involving Abdallah's fraud, Fabozzi said, but not because Abdallah had eluded police—more because "no one cared." When a bank or a credit card company loses money, the lending institutions generally just write it off. They have a high-dollar threshold for pursuing an investigation; and so does law enforcement. It's the same everywhere, Fabozzi says, with all white-collar crime investigations. A huge paper trail is a lot of work. Criminals know that. They can stay under the radar forever committing small paper crimes of $10,000 or less.[21]

Abdallah knew that, too. But he went after Siebel's $10 million, anyway. He wasn't a genius. He wasn't even the best Fabozzi had ever faced. He was just compulsive. As he pled guilty to 12 counts of mail and wire fraud in October 2002, Abdallah admitted as much, telling Judge Loretta Preska in a Manhattan court that he was on medication for depression and obsessive-compulsive disorder.

"I wish I could say that this was all about money—then I'd have a reason to explain why I've ruined my life," he said.[22] The only technique that might be considered resourceful was his method for obtaining the critical credit reports on the world's richest people from the credit bureaus—his use of corporate seals from Wall Street firms to forge the paperwork for the requests. After all, even to the irreligious, a credit report is a sacred personal document.

The nation's three main credit bureaus—Experian, Equifax, and TransUnion—are the financial historians of America, the Santa Claus of money. They know if you have been naughty, and if you have been nice. They have pages and pages of data on every American who has participated in the credit economy. They are entrusted with this information, which is central to every American citizen and his or her basic rights to buy a house or a car. The firms and their data are also central to the smooth operation of the economy as a whole. For Abdallah to crack that system wide open, to get copies of credit reports on the world's richest and most famous people, credit reports that obviously receive extra care, he must have employed true criminal genius. Could it be that easy to crack the country's most personal archive? Philip Cummings, an underpaid help-desk worker at a Long Island software company, had already discovered the shocking answer, authorities allege.

***

Something was very wrong at the Ford Motor Credit office in Grand Rapids, Michigan, during the early part of 2002. Thousands of credit reports had been slowly stolen from Experian through the automaker's branch office. Most of the reports weren't even run on Ford customers. Complaints started coming in from consumers who noticed unusual activity on their credit files. A trace showed the downloads had been going on for 10 months, since April 2001. The leaking data wasn't discovered until February 2002.[23]

Ford did the right thing, a few months later, once it determined a little more about what was going on. In May, it sent 13,000 letters to victims around the country explaining that their credit reports had been downloaded by a criminal, someone posing as a part of Ford Motor Company. Check your credit report, the letter said; you will likely become a victim of identity theft, if you aren't already. Contact authorities if you are.[24]

Reports began to flood in from victims, including one elderly woman who only had $1,000 in her bank account but discovered criminals had withdrawn $35,000 from it. The scope of the crime slowly became obvious.[25] Someone had managed to crack the entire credit reporting system. Whoever it was, they could now download the financial history of anyone in the country and arm themselves with all the data they needed to commit massive frauds. It was a highly organized effort. Whoever ordered the reports had carefully plucked out addresses in affluent neighborhoods all around the country.[26]

Upon discovering the leak, Ford changed the codes it used to order credit reports and shut down the criminals' doorway into the credit reporting world from Grand Rapids. But that hardly put a dent in the crime. Whoever it was, they were still out there ordering credit reports. Another 6,000 credit reports were ordered from the Experian credit bureau by someone using the initials "M. M." in the name of Washington Mutual Bank from March to May of that year.[27]

But the criminals weren't just picking on Experian. About 1,100 credit reports had been ordered for Washington Mutual through Equifax, a second credit bureau. They, too, were ordered by "M. M." In May, "M. M." moved on again, downloading thousands of credit reports while posing as several smaller companies: MGA Vintage Apartments in Houston, Texas; Dollar

Bank in Cleveland, Ohio; the Sarah Bush Lincoln Health Center in Illinois. The FBI became actively involved in the case.

Months would pass before an investigator from Equifax called FBI Special Agent Kevin Barrows with an obvious break. During that delay the equal opportunity criminals continued to scoop up America's financial secrets. In September, about 4,500 credit reports were ordered from the third of the major credit bureaus, TransUnion. This time, Central Texas Energy Supply's account had been used to order the reports.

Then on October 17, Barrows was told that telephone records had linked "M. M." to a residence in New Rochelle, New York. Whoever ordered those credit reports was simply calling up Equifax's 1-800 number for clients and ordering them from home.

Six days later, FBI agents searched the New York home of Linus Baptiste, where they found five computers, a pile of credit reports, and a batch of documents bearing the names Equifax, TransUnion, and Experian.

Baptiste immediately ratted out his alleged supplier.[28]

***

Just like Abraham Abdallah, Philip Cummings was 32, overweight, with an odd mixture of smarts and sloppiness. An English immigrant, Cummings was black, over 300 pounds, and never amounted to much more than the telephone help-desk job he landed at tiny Teledata Communications, Inc. in Bayshore, New York, on Long Island in 1999. But the annoying hourly wage job turned out to be a goldmine, seemingly a license to print money, once Cummings made the right friends, authorities allege.

Teledata makes "credit prompter boxes," easy-to-use credit check terminals found at more than 25,000 companies around the country. The terminals make it simple for a car dealership, cell phone shop, or apartment rental office to perform routine credit checks. As one of hundreds of third-party service providers hooked into the nation's credit reporting system, Teledata had access to all the credit report data at Experian, Equifax, and TransUnion. And, Baptiste realized, so did Cummings. Simply by using the right codes, Cummings could impersonate almost any company authorized to obtain credit reports from the credit bureaus. He approached Cummings with an idea: I have friends, he said, a few dozen Nigerian friends, who would pay good money for credit reports. And you have codes that can enable us to commit identity theft on virtually anyone.[29]

They settled on a price: $60 apiece, split evenly. That set the market price for ruining someone's financial history. Eighteen months later, while the credit bureaus took their sweet time checking telephone records, Cummings and Baptiste had allegedly pulled off what authorities called the largest identity theft in history.

Cummings wasn't at Teledata long. He left in March 2000, after spending just a few months at the firm. But court documents say he left with what might as well have been a printing press from the U.S. mint: He had a spreadsheet of user names and passwords to access credit reports at all three credit bureaus.[30]

It's a dialog box nearly everyone has seen. When a typical home user sits down to their PC at night, their computer offers this simple challenge: supply a user name and a password to log in. That same line of defense was all that stood between Cummings and his 33,000 victims. Simply by applying the right user name and password, Cummings was allegedly able to impersonate firms like Ford, giving him the keys to almost any citizen's personal financial kingdom. Such golden keys, one might think, would be carefully guarded. They weren't.

"Any help-desk representative has access to confidential passwords and subscriber codes of (Teledata) client companies that would have enabled that employee to download credit reports from all three credit bureaus," Barrows said in his deposition. Teledata was a disaster waiting to happen.[31]

But it wasn't only Teledata's fault; Teledata was merely the first symptom of a very sick system. Even more than two years after Cummings left the firm, the passwords he had allegedly stolen still worked. When a firm finally caught on and changed the codes, the FBI says Cummings just went down the list to the next sucker. None of the companies exercised even the most basic stewardship of such vital information. And the three credit bureaus, who know best the explosive nature of such credit terminals, failed to enforce even the most basic security measures, for examples, by insisting passwords be changed regularly. Meanwhile, those three companies, which were in the best position to notice all the data flying out of their computers, spent months before realizing their system was infiltrated by someone calling from a home in New Rochelle through an 800 number. And that someone was robbing America blind.

Over 33,000 victims were caught up in the scheme the FBI says Cummings masterminded scheme. Hundreds called in to describe the devastating consequences: homes, boats, loans obtained in their names. Uncounted millions of dollars in losses for consumers and businesses; perhaps incalculable losses of time and energy cleaning up the mess.

Cummings was indicted by a federal grand jury of 22 counts of conspiracy, wire fraud, computer fraud and forfeiture. He pled not guilty and is awaiting trial. In January 2003, Baptiste pled guilty to four counts of conspiracy, wire fraud, identity fraud, and access device fraud in connection with the scheme.

James Jackson and Abraham Abdallah were merely playing with the system, going on a high-tech financial joyride, always more than willing to leave the stolen cars on the side of the road and walk home. They see themselves a bit like Robin Hoods of the digital age. Perhaps they don't readily give to the poor, but they can take the rich down a peg or two, and all in a harmless way behind a keyboard and a telephone. Steven Spielberg and Paul Allen were none the worse for wear after their identities were stolen.

But America's real identity thieves, the ones who cause real heartache, they steal from real people. They are rarely caught. And the system makes their work exceedingly easy.

***

"This is the first time it's ever happened. . . . it's a pretty unique situation," Donald Girard, director of Public Relations for Experian, said after the Cummings incident.[32] Security measures were added in the wake of Cummings's arrest, he said, but wouldn't elaborate. But the problem of internal employees abusing the powerful credit terminals had been well known in the industry for at least a decade. In 1994, consumer attorney David Szwak wrote several articles highlighting the issue. He described the 1991 theft of $100,000 by a car salesman in Orlando, Florida, who used his dealership's terminal to steal credit from a series of consumers around the country with the same name.[33]

The flaws in the system were obvious, and Cummings's alleged scheme was completely predictable. So were the flaws exploited by Jackson and Abdallah. And in fact, so, too, was the entire identity theft epidemic predictable—and preventable.

It is an epidemic. Until the middle of 2003, the best estimates suggested a few hundred thousand victims had been hit every year, but quiet rumblings among fraud investigators, along with a never-ending stream of noisy consumer victims, suggested the number was far higher. Experts would tell stories that at any given family gathering, when the question was asked, someone would raise their hand and say they had been hit. Finally, three major studies, including one commissioned by the Federal Trade Commission, shed light on the size of the problem in 2003. Studies since then agree that there are millions of victims each year now, and perhaps as many as 1 in 10 adults have been hit by one form of identity theft. More Americans now are victims of identity theft every year than any other crime.

And why not? It's easy, lucrative, and almost entirely risk free. A Gartner study in 2001 suggested that as few as 1 in 700 identity thefts are eventually prosecuted. Meanwhile, the payoffs, in time and invisibility, are enormous.[34] In stirring congressional testimony during 2002 support of identity theft legislation, Sen. Diane Feinstein offered powerful examples of now far identity theft can take a criminal.

An administrator of Kmart Corporation's stock option plan was accused of stealing the identity of a retired Kmart executive and exercising 176,000 options in his name. In another case, a Chicago man allegedly killed a homeless man to assume the victim's identity and avoid pending criminal charges for counterfeiting.[35]

Identity criminals can get away with murder, literally; government officials now outwardly express concern that such digital crimes will be an essential component enabling terrorism. And, in fact, identity theft had an important role to play in the tragedy of September 11. Authorities believe at least 2 of the 19 hijackers initially may have entered the country using stolen passports. An Algerian national was convicted of stealing the identities of 21 members of a health club in Cambridge, Massachusetts, and giving the identities to an individual convicted in the failed plot to bomb Los Angeles International Airport in 1999. There is ample evidence that terrorist groups regularly fund their activities with simple credit card frauds, and there have even been reports that al-Qaeda training manuals encourage it.[36]

Certainly, criminals are to blame for the identity theft crisis. But so are the stewards of our electronic lives, those entrusted with our electronic identities, our digital twin. The institutions designed to protect our identities have let us down and enabled this epidemic. Corporate America had shirked much of its responsibility for the problem, looking the other way while signs of the coming crisis have been in plain view for years. Credit card companies, in their rush to push the "miracle of instant credit" at consumers, in an effort to simply push profit margins a little higher, have created the systematic flaw that allows identity theft to be profitable in the first place. The real headache for most victims, however, is the paperwork nightmare faced once the crime has been committed. Put simply, many victims find their credit is ruined and can spend years fixing the pockmarks left by their imposter. The nation's credit reporting agencies and their incestuous relationship with the credit card companies, are solely responsible for this most painful revictimization of consumers.

Law enforcement, meanwhile, has often been slow to react to the crime, refusing to even take criminal reports from victims in many cases. In others, detectives refused to get involved, citing the complex investigations and rarity of meaningful jail time for convicts. Many government agencies have been even slower to react; our nation's identification systems, driver's licenses and Social Security cards, are meaningless relics from the past. Congress has refused to pass meaningful regulation on the companies largely responsible for the mess, with many elected officials choosing instead to side with a lucrative lobbying force. And the Internet has made life easy for criminals, as they can steal the data they need from the comfort of their own homes and, in many cases, can simply trick consumers into handing over personal financial information willingly.

Ten years ago, James Rinaldo Jackson's pleas for attention to the fundamental systems that enable the crime fell on deaf ears. As a result of that neglect, some 27 million people have endured the emotional and fiscal trauma of dealing with a crime some refer to as financial rape during the past five years. Identity theft is much more than a paperwork headache for victims. The crime has been blamed for everything from divorce to suicide to murder. It threatens happy retirements as well as college student loans. In its very worst form, it can even land innocent people in jail. The trials victims endure can be more surreal and maddening than anything Franz Kafka ever imagined—and their stories must be seen to be believed.

2

THE PAIN

"Police from Florida contacted my parents trying to find my brother. Apparently, the man who stole his ID had murdered two women. One was found in a trunk in Florida. My brother was now wanted for murder."

—Sister of ID theft victim Michael Berry

Tales of famous people being hit by identity theft could fill *People* magazine for a year. Take Tiger Woods, for example. Starting in August 1998, Anthony Lemar Taylor spent a year successfully pretending to be the golf superstar. Taylor's $50,000 spending spree included a big-screen television, stereo speakers, a living room set, even a U-Haul to move all the stolen goods. Taylor, who looks nothing like the golf legend, simply obtained a driver's license using Tiger's real name, Eldrick Woods; then, he used Woods's Social Security number to get credit in his name.[1]

Defense Attorney James Greiner was astonished that the scheme worked at all, let alone for a full year. It's ridiculous that retail clerks believed Taylor was one of the world's most recognizable athletes, he said in court.

"Does he just walk into Circuit City? What they're saying is Anthony Taylor, my client, walks in and says, 'Hey, I'm Eldrick Tiger Woods,'" Greiner said, tongue firmly in cheek, during Taylor's trial.[2]

When Tiger himself testified during the case in 2001, Taylor, a 30-year-old career criminal, didn't stand a chance. Woods's star power helped the state throw the book at Taylor. He was sentenced to 200 years to life under California's strict three-strikes rule. The firm, swift justice might have made other potential identity thieves think twice, but for this: Precious few identity thefts are even investigated, let alone prosecuted to the full extent of the law. The average victim has enough trouble getting the police to bother filling out an incident report.

While sensational crimes against the rich and famous steal the headlines, identity theft isn't really about them. Victims like Tiger Woods will never face difficulties securing new credit cards or home loans because of a few pockmarks on their credit report—obviously, they have plenty of credit. A few VIP phone calls easily cleans up the mess. With identity theft, who you know, and who you are, really does matter. And now, the credit bureaus have a "protected list" of important people whose data receives special treatment—politicians, influential judges, and the like. It's locked away in special files, accessible only under special circumstances, says consumer attorney David Szwak. That prevents the wrong people from getting hurt, which would draw a little too much attention to the problem and the financial institutions that allow it to happen.[3]

The real world of identity theft, the world where some 10 million people found themselves in 2002, is a much more perilous place. It is a haunting, paperwork nightmare, one often compared to financial rape, littered with small and large tragedies. People commit murder in the name of identity theft. Couples can't buy homes because their credit is damaged. Identity theft victims are often denied access to the lowest interest rates and can pay as much as 50 percent more to borrow money. Teenagers can't get student loans because their parents ruined their credit before they were even able to drive. And thousands of people face hundreds of hours of electronic trials against their erroneous credit reports and eventually end with fraudulent debts and endless nightly threatening calls from collection agencies. James Pittman, for example, says he received such calls for five years after Capital One sold his defaulted credit card account—an account really opened up by an identity thief—to a collection firm. Eventually, he was told that if he wanted the whole matter cleared up, he "should be willing to pay what the person who had stolen my identity had charged, plus interest and collection fees."[4]

After the fallout of a tough bout with identity theft, many face emotional consequences—such as paranoia or guilt—similar to victims of physical abuse. Relationships and marriages even dissolve because of the drama.[5]

Because the methods are so easy and the prosecutions so rare, the identity theft explosion has spawned a variety of subcategories for the crime. Each one puts in motion a different kind of nightmare and leaves a very different kind of emotional wake. Stories from this underworld border on the unbelievable–such as the tale of one woman who was forced to undergo a physical examination to prove she was not the mother of a crack baby, recently abandoned by her imposter.[6] To really understand identity theft, and the human cost of this epidemic, it's essential to get to know some of the real victims and their stories.

***

Malcolm Byrd was at home with his two children on a Saturday night in January 2003 when a pounding knock came at the door. Three Rock County, Wisconsin, sheriff's officers were there with a warrant for Byrd's arrest. Cocaine possession, with intent to distribute, the warrant read.[7]

This time, Byrd thought, I just can't take it anymore. Why bother to explain? During all the other arrests, all the other times he'd been fired from his job, the times his driver's license had been taken away, no one listened. It's because I'm black, he thought. No one believes a black man when he says he's innocent. No one believes him when he says, "You've got the wrong man."

On this night, Byrd's wife was at work. The sheriffs intended to cart Byrd away, no matter what he said, and they couldn't leave the children alone. So they threatened to call child protective services to take his two- and four-year-old daughters. Their grandmother arrived just in time to watch Malcolm led away in handcuffs.

As he sat in jail later that night, Byrd's mind raced through every episode of the past five years—every time he tasted asphalt after a routine traffic stop; every humiliating conversation with his human resources department. The injustice was so intense he could almost chew it, the hate pounding so hard in his chest he couldn't even think of sleeping. At least until the second night, on Sunday, which he also spent in the county jail.

Byrd's nightmare had begun five years earlier. It was the simplest of identity thefts. A man arrested on drug charges in a nearby town gave the name Malcolm Byrd when he was booked. Byrd still doesn't know why. But that single misidentification, now forever planted in national law enforcement crime databases, became a seemingly immortal virus in Byrd's life.

Thanks to an article in the local *Janesville Gazette,* the real Malcolm Byrd found out about that initial identity theft and headed to the police to correct the error. The newspaper ran a correction, too. It was over, Byrd thought.

Nothing happened for four months. Then, he was pulled over for speeding. That was the first time he tasted pavement and felt handcuffs around his wrists. The correction hadn't been made. Police records still showed that he was wanted for drug dealing. He was tossed in the back of a squad car and carted to police headquarters. The matter was cleared up when officers compared a booking photograph of the suspect to Byrd—they looked nothing alike. The incident cost Byrd half a day's wages, but not much else.

Then, things went downhill quickly. Soon after, Byrd was fired from his part-time job as a nursing assistant because he was accused of lying about his criminal record on his job application. It wasn't me, Byrd said. No one listened.

Months later, when he was laid off from his full-time job, he was denied unemployment benefits because of his criminal record—just as his wife Carla was about to give birth to their first child. The benefits were reinstated, but at about the same time, he received notice from the Department of Motor Vehicles that his license had been suspended for failure to pay traffic fines.

Byrd's imposter just kept committing crimes, and kept getting away with pinning the transgressions on the wrong man.

A year later, while surfing the Internet, Byrd discovered his impostor had been arrested again, this time in a neighboring county. Byrd had a new idea. To clear his name, he visited the county district attorney's office and submitted his fingerprints. In exchange, Byrd received court documents proving his innocence. He carried them everywhere.

The papers were insurance against another wrongful arrest. Byrd wasn't crazy about the idea, which reminded him a bit of World War II–era Germany, when citizens were forced to "present their papers." But it was better than the alternative, ending up in handcuffs again. The papers didn't help, however, when he lost his driver's license again in 2000, thanks to an automated process that noticed a set of unpaid fines tied to his license number.

And those papers didn't stop two more arrests. In April 2002, Byrd was pulled over again. Once more, he found himself in handcuffs in the back of a squad car. Officers quickly discovered their mistake, thanks in part to Byrd's paperwork, but not before he lost another day's pay. His sense of personal humiliation was mounting, but at least he had managed to clear his name before he was forced to spend a night in jail. That ultimate humiliation had never happened to Byrd—until the Martin Luther King Day weekend in 2003, a full five years after the initial identity theft.

Byrd had lent his car to his niece for a Saturday night drive, while he stayed home. She was pulled over by a police patrol.

"Do you know where Malcolm is?" they asked her. He's at home, she said. Minutes later, three deputies were at Byrd's house, armed with arrest warrants from three counties. They carted him away, grandmother and two children left behind.

Byrd's wife, Carla, got word of what had happened and raced to the sheriff's department around midnight with court papers clearing her husband's name. But that didn't help—the warrants were dated after Byrd's "declaration of innocence." He could have committed the crimes after the judge issued the papers, the cops said.

"They said there was nothing they could do," Carla said. She went home without her husband, who spent his first night in jail that evening. In fact, Byrd didn't even know his wife had come to visit him until the following morning.

Byrd was cleared on the local Rock County, Wisconsin, warrants soon after, but the sheriff's office wouldn't release him until the other two counties gave their permission. The bad luck of being arrested on a holiday weekend made things much worse. There was no way to clear up the other two warrants until that Tuesday, when government employees showed up for work again. So Byrd ended up spending three nights in the jail. In fact, the final clearance arrived just moments before Byrd was to be hauled into court for an arraignment.

Exasperated, Byrd and his wife finally made the heart-wrenching decision to change their name in an attempt to avoid further harassment , both for him, and their son, who shares Malcolm's name. Soon after their episode received national attention, the family finally received some welcome news. Byrd's imposter was arrested after a routine traffic stop near St. Louis. Police found four kilograms of cocaine in the imposter's car, and on further searching, evidence that he had been using several fake identities to duck prosecutions. The suspected imposter, Dearnear Gary, was eventually convicted on drug trafficking charges, and is awaiting sentencing. Five years earlier, Gary had begun Byrd's nightmare when he gave Byrd's name after an arrest for drug possession with the intent to distribute. But at Gary's trial in a

Milwaukee federal court, prosecutors didn't bother pressing the identity theft charges against him because the drug charges carried much more severe penalties.

***

Criminal identity theft is the worst-case scenario for ID theft victims. Losing your clean credit history is one thing; losing your freedom is another. And victims of America's fastest-growing crime are discovering they often have much more to worry about than the hundreds of hours of paperwork necessary to clean up the financial mess associated with ID theft. Sometimes, they have to worry about ending up in jail—again and again.

There's nothing new about criminals using aliases to evade the law—suspects often try to give their buddy's name, address, and date of birth to dupe police. But the explosion of identity theft, and the ready availability of stolen digital dossiers on innocent victims, makes it just as easy for a criminal to give a stranger's personal data during an arrest.

Match that problem with the increased use of state and national computer crime databases, and you have a recipe for disaster. Once police book a suspect under a fake name, that mistake can plague a victim for life.

There are no accurate studies of how many Malcolm Byrds there are every year, but interviews with dozens of ID theft–trained cops suggest the problem is far more widespread than many realize.

The problem is so common that California now has an ID theft victim's registry, called the California's Identity Theft Data Base, that's available to cops on the beat. Victims in the midst of a wrongful arrest can ask officers to call an 800 number that connects to the database and essentially lets the arresting officer know the suspect is really an identity theft victim. Consumers need to submit their fingerprints, and must obtain a court order verifying "victim status," to be listed in the registry.[9] Virginia, meanwhile, started issuing identity theft victim ID cards—called Identity Theft Pass-ports—during 2003 in response to a string of wrongful arrests.[10]

A false criminal record is virtually impossible to completely erase. Once a name is used as an alias by a criminal, it generally stays in police data files forever.

"Officials of criminal records (databases) are—for good rea-son—reluctant to remove information once it's been placed in the database," said Beth Givens, executive director of the Privacy Rights Clearinghouse. "It's very difficult to clear your record if you are a victim of criminal ID theft."[11]

And that alias becomes a disease for the victim; it may not be terminal, but it can be incurable. There are endless nightmare stories to be found that combine identity theft and false arrests. California resident Clay Henderson simply lost his wallet while vacationing in Daytona Beach in 1987, but the momentary care-lessness ended up costing him 14 years of headaches, including a week in jail during the mid-1990s. For more than a decade, police say, Douglas Staas lived his life under the name Clay Hen-derson, becoming his evil twin: Staas bought and sold homes, opened bank accounts, obtained credit, married twice, and was arrested at least three times. Meanwhile, the real Henderson was rejected when applying for apartment leases and credit card accounts and had civil judgments levied against him. The inci-dent even hurt his career: As a computer worker on a U.S. Air Force base, Henderson was denied some security clearances because of his poor credit rating and criminal record.

But perhaps the worst part of the ordeal happened when he was denied his freedom. In 1995, Henderson was picked up on an outstanding arrest warrant issued in Seminole County, Florida, a place he had never been. The charges were dropped after he provided his fingerprints to authorities in Florida, but the process took more than a week.[12]

Staas eventually pleaded guilty to nearly 50 counts of fraud, and was sentenced to eight and a half years in state prison.

Things were almost much worse for Michael Berry. He never spent a night in jail. But he did make the *America's Most Wanted* television show's web site—as a murderer.

A soft-spoken Washington, D.C., lobbyist and chief operating officer of the conservative Independent Women's Forum, Berry's financial life had suddenly unraveled in January 2002 when he was rejected for a new credit card. An investigation into his credit report revealed that a cornucopia of credit cards had been opened in his name and maxed out just as quickly, riddled with lush expenses like $400 flower deliveries.[13]

Weeks later, as Berry scrambled to fix his credit, things went from bad to worse. Orlando, Florida, police called to tell him a nationwide warrant had just been issued for his arrest. A man using Berry's identity, an already convicted murderer, was wanted for two more gruesome killings. The local police knew identity theft was part of the crime—they knew their suspect was really a short black man named Demorris Hunter. Berry is tall, thin, and Caucasian. It was Hunter who had gone on the spending spree using Berry's information, police said. But Berry's name was listed in Hunter's electronic criminal file. Be careful, the officer told Berry. Any officer around the country could pull him over at any time. And it would likely be at gunpoint.

Within days, John Walsh and *America's Most Wanted* picked up the story of the "lady killer." The show correctly identified the suspect as Hunter and steered would-be tipsters to its web site for more information. But the site's profile of Hunter listed Berry's Social Security number. Calls to the show's web site couldn't convince its producers to remove Berry's information; the information only came down after a call from Sen. Diane Feinstein's office.

Berry's paranoia became so powerful that at one point, he flew all the way to South Central Los Angeles and visited the address listed on all those fraudulent credit card applications, just to see if he could spot his imposter.

A month later, police arrested Hunter near Houston, Texas, relieving some of the paranoia, and Michael Berry's crimal record was cleared. Hunter was charged with murder and is awaiting trial in Alamada County, California. But ever since Berry's ID theft saga was chronicled in a *Washington Post* article, he has been forced to relive again and again the trauma of being accused of murder, retelling his story repeatedly to television stations and newspaper reporters. He became the poster child of the worst kind of identity theft.

Murder and identity theft have gone together before. In 2000, Marcus Toney, a 37-year-old custodian at City College of Chicago, in quick succession lost his wife to a new man, lost his identity and financial standing to his wife's new lover, and then lost his life.

Divorcing couples with vindictive tendencies often dream of "winning" most of their joint assets in divorce court. Identity theft means not having to wait until the divorce is final to clean out your partner.

It only makes sense that much identity theft is committed by people who know the victims well and, particularly, by family members. They have easy access to all the essentials: Social Security numbers, mother's maiden name, and recent addresses. ID theft can be easy income for desperate family members with drug or alcohol problems, for example. But divorcing couples are at special risk. There's nothing new about running up charges on your spouses' credit cards out of spite as the relationship sours. Identity theft takes that vindictiveness to new heights.

Toney was a solid citizen by all accounts, attending classes at night to learn heating, ventilation, and air conditioning, trying to get ahead. But his wife, Lisa, then 46, began a torrid affair with the younger, 29-year-old, smooth-talking Sienky Lallemand. Not long after the affair began, Lisa mused openly about killing her ex-husband and skulking away with his $50,000 in life insurance. But Lallemand had a better, more profitable idea; steal Toney's identity and run him into financial ruin. All the while, the couple could be having the time of their lives at Toney's expense.[14]

And so it went. There were high-priced vacations, expensive jewelry, a cache of credit cards, even a brand-new Lexus sport utility vehicle. It all added up to a $200,000 bill for Toney. According to court papers, Lallemand had simply obtained an Indiana driver's license with his picture and Toney's personal information. Then, he filled out an application with Toyota Motor Credit Corporation to buy the new Lexus. On the application, Lallemand indicated the lessee was "Victorio Consulting." He signed the lease "Marcus V. Toney, president/CEO Owner, Victorio Consulting, Detroit, Michigan."[15] The janitor was unaware of that lofty promotion to CEO on that day, August 27, 1999. He only had six more months to live.

Toney got wise soon after the Lexus lease was signed. He started getting mail he didn't understand, indicating he owned a Lexus and a Mercedes. The U.S. Postal Inspector's Office, which prosecuted the case, said one day Toney drove to his former wife's home, saw the Lexus, and unraveled their scheme.

Toney went to the police. His ex-wife got scared. The murder plot was back on. Lallemand constructed two pipe bombs, packed them in a VCR box, gift-wrapped them, and sent them via Federal Express to Toney's home. The package sat, partially opened, in Toney's house for three or four days, friends and relatives told postal inspectors. The wait made Lallemand even more anxious, and he tried to prod Toney. A voice mail message left on Toney's cell phone February 15 taunted him.

"Why don't you just open up your little gift, and, uh, you know, take a look at what I've sent you," it said. And then, a cryptic message, "Bleed out."[16]

Later that morning, Toney opened the package and was killed instantly. A neighbor was also injured by the blast.

Lallemand tried one more time to change identities and escape the consequences of the murder. Only days after the killing, he seduced 54-year-old Sandra Lavel, an accountant for the television show *Cops*. She paid for Lallemand's $8,100 worth of plastic surgery, an attempt at disguise. But authorities eventually collared both of them. Lallemand escaped the death penalty only by pleading guilty. A jury found Toney's wife guilty of conspiracy to commit murder. Both are now serving life prison terms.

"They were just having a great time at this guy's expense, and then they blow him up," the jury's foreman said after the trial.[17]

Lavel was sentenced to 33 months in prison after she was convicted of harboring a fugitive.

***

Domestic disputes often spill over and affect the lives of children. In perhaps the most insidious form of identify theft, authorities are discovering more and more cases of parents who steal their children's identities. It almost seems too irresponsible to be true, these parents who—far from trying to provide a secure financial future for the children—are literally robbing from their children's future.

In the most tragic examples, both parents are derelict. One nine-year-old girl in Texas had both of her parents use her information to get credit. Her father is in federal prison for armed robbery. Her mother, now in jail for identity theft, was scheduled for release in April 2004. Since parental ID theft was not legally considered child abuse in Texas, the girl was scheduled to be returned to her mom then.[18]

But often one former spouse is the culprit. Somehow, seven-year-olds end up with credit files jam-packed full of loans and credit cards. And often, they don't discover the problem until they apply for a driver's license and find they already have one, or apply for a student loan and are denied because their credit has been ruined by one of their parents.

Rachel Soper met her husband in 1995 in a small Nevada town of Fallon about 50 miles from Reno. Jeremy Potter had legal troubles—he was on probation for passing bad checks—but she didn't think much of that. He had a tongue of gold and wanted to get married quickly. She didn't break off the engagement, even when signs of trouble crept into the relationship.[19]

"I was an army brat," she said. "All I wanted to do was make him a better person."

The young couple had three children from 1995 to 1998, but all the while, something wasn't right. Potter became more and more aggressive Soper says, and seemed to be less and less honest about all kinds of family matters. Finally, while pregnant with their third child, Soper left Potter. Even before their divorce was final, he already had found another woman. During their ugly divorce, Soper fought hard to limit Potter's access to the three kids. Two years later, Potter and his new wife left for Texas, and Soper thought her troubles were mostly behind her.

When Potter pulled back into town two years later, driving a brand-new four-door Ford truck and pulling behind a trailer full of elegant house furnishings, Soper knew something was wrong. His credit is terrible, she thought, and so is his wife's credit. There's no way he was able to afford all that, and certainly no one would give this convicted felon such loans.

She remembered a disturbing incident two years earlier, when Potter had called her home. Caller ID displayed the caller's name as "Nigel Weight." (The name has been changed to protect the child.) She asked around the tiny town of Fallon, Nevada, and learned that Nigel was her ex-husband's new stepchild—son of her ex's new wife. Soper's ex-husband and his new wife had put their home telephone in the child's name, a common tactic for those with bad credit to avoid running into troubles getting a phone hooked up. Nigel was nine years old at the time. They put the electricity in his name, too.

Soper looked at the truck again. She had heard her ex-husband was trying to buy a pricey condominium in town. She remembered the telephone incident. She became very scared for her seven-year-old son, who was also Potter's namesake. She raced to her computer and ordered a credit report for him online. And she couldn't believe what she saw. The credit report was pages and pages long. Her seven-year-old had been granted a series of credit cards in Texas and Colorado. There were expensive jewelry purchases made on credit. That new Ford truck Potter had rolled into town in? It also belonged to the seven-year-old. There were even loan applications filled out with his name. In all, the report included over 60 attempts to obtain credit. Potter, who wasn't even allowed to see his son by court order, had completely taken over the child's life. And he and his new wife were now living it up, on the back of his son's financial future.

It's hard to imagine how a seven-year-old can buy a car or a home, but it's easy to explain. Most credit grantors simply don't verify age when they process applications. So identity thieves with a valid Social Security number can often supply their own age on credit applications. There is a way to verify the date of birth of the applicant, which would provide a reality check on credit applications. But credit bureaus don't provide the service unless asked, and most grantors don't bother asking. In fact, during the late 1990s, the credit industry opposed a California law designed to mandate such basic fact checking.

Former credit card fraud investigators say the credit industry believes such laborious fact checking would slow down the application process too much, creating far too many "false positives." Any typographic error would kick back an application, risking the sale. Tests of such procedures often found as many as 9 in 10 fraud detections for suspicious items such as mismatched birthdays or nonmatching home addresses were really false positives, said a former credit bureau fraud investigator. Manually processing that many legitimate applications would cost the industry too much. So rather than making nine innocent people wait for credit, the industry lets one guilty applicant get away with fraud.

Potter was a deadbeat who had beaten the system for two years, but now he was caught red-handed. His mistake had been the return to Fallon. Soper called the police, and a detective was assigned to her case. While she waited for her turn in the legal system, she began her own investigation. One by one, she called every creditor on the report. She got copies of the credit applications, showing again and again the seven-year-old's Social Security number and her ex-husband's handwriting. By the time the detective called, the case was virtually complete. Her husband was arrested soon after.

She dumped a huge file of paperwork on her divorce lawyer, begging for help cleaning up the mess. There were 60-odd pockmarks on the credit report which had to be removed. There would have been more, except after the initial 14 accounts were granted, and Potter neglected to pay, the child's credit score began to plummet—all the way down to 511, below the territory reserved for those who file bankruptcy. The file was now thick with nothing but defaulted accounts; it would be a long time before anyone would obtain credit in his name.

If not for his mother's quick thinking and industry, Soper's son might not have discovered the problem, and had a chance to unravel the tangled web, until he was an adult. After a nearly a year of haggling with creditors—with most of the heavy paperwork performed by her attorney—all the black marks next to the child's credit report were cleared. But the episode isn't really over for Soper, who has $19,000 in unpaid legal expenses. Some of that was accrued during her initial child custody battle, but much of it during the identity theft episode, she said.

For all the trouble he caused his son and ex-wife, Potter didn't see any jail time. Only days before his scheduled trial, Soper received a call from her lawyer and the police detective. The local district attorney wanted to give Potter a break, and agreed to a plea bargain. Potter pleaded guilty to one count of a gross misdemeanor, to possession of stolen property, in connection with the pickup truck he had purchased using his son's identity. He received a one-year suspended sentence and two years on parole.

But his freedom was short-lived. Soon after, Potter's probation was revoked after he was arrested again during a routine traffic stop. A fresh warrant had been issued for his arrest, after another allegation that Potter tried to obtain a loan with stolen identity information. He is now in police custody awaiting trial on those charges. His wife, who was also arrested during the same traffic stop, was convicted of two counts of passing fraudulent checks, and is now a resident of the Southern Nevada Womens Correctional Facility, due to be released in August 2005.

***

Linda Foley had just gotten married and moved from Los Angeles to San Diego, starting her life all over, and was looking for work as a freelance writer. While having dinner in a local restaurant, she picked up a copy of *Essentially You*, a local women's magazine. Obviously a niche publication, it was slick, upbeat, and smart looking. But there were no restaurant reviews, Foley's specialty. Perhaps the magazine could use some, she thought to herself. She contacted the magazine's editor, Bari Nessel, soon after. Nessel ate up the idea, realizing she could easily pick up some new restaurant advertisers to support the column, and Foley started penning weekly dispatches.[20]

Four months later, things were going so well that Nessel asked Foley to join the staff full time, to help with advertising sales. The magazine seemed hearty enough; even doctors and lawyers were advertising in it now, and the second income would help Linda and her husband, Jay, save for a down payment on a house.

So she filled out the requisite tax forms. She didn't think twice when Nessel asked for a copy of her driver's license, since she would be driving on assignments from the firm. A few weeks later, she got a phone call from Citibank Visa, asking about her new address.

"I haven't moved," she told the operator, who insisted that several other credit card firms had reported the change of address. She hung up and called MBNA, which had also reported the change. Someone had applied for a new MBNA credit card in Foley's name. But the address listed was a P.O. box—the box used by *Essentially You*. On the card, Barry Nestle was listed as a cosigner and second cardholder. It was a corporate card, MBNA said, authorized by Foley so Nessel could spend money on business expenses.

"Aren't you the president of the company?" Foley remembers being asked.

"No! She is!" Foley answered.

Could this be a mistake, she wondered? Nessel had mentioned getting her a corporate card; perhaps this was a mix-up. So she called one of the credit bureaus and found out three credit cards had been issued in her name—one that included Nessel's son as a joint cardholder. She got a copy of one of the applications from FirstUSA. Foley's Social Security number had been scribbled in Nessel's handwriting.

"I wasn't in denial anymore," Foley said.

Fortunately, Foley was working out of her home at the time. When she went to the police, they urged her not to quit right away, so Nessel wouldn't get a whiff that the gig was up and destroy evidence. But she was told not to talk with Nessel—only to send an occasional e-mail to show that she was still working. She sent a few notes reminding Nessel that she was owed commission checks. Three weeks later, police executed a search warrant and left Nessel's house with seven boxes of evidence.

Records show Nessel was having a ball on Foley's credit. She hired a gourmet chef to deliver prepared meals to her house. She paid for nutrition counseling and expensive vitamins. She was sure to buy from magazine advertisers, the best way for any publisher to grease an ad account.

"We were living on a limited income at the time," Foley said. "She was living it up."

Eleven months later, facing 31 counts of various economic crimes, including a long history of bounced checks, Nessel told the judge that she was a terrible money manager, that she was just borrowing from Foley's name out of desperation. She planned to pay it all back, she said. The district attorney on the case agreed to plead the case down to four felony charges, including one charge of false impersonation of another.

Meanwhile, Foley was trying to work through her sense of paranoia. It took six months before she would even look for a job, and when she did, she would refuse to complete applications with personal questions such as former addresses or Social Security Number. She rarely got past the receptionist, who would report her as "uncooperative." When a store clerk asked her to write down her driver's license on a check, she refused. And sometimes, she made a scene. Husband Jay would often bail her out by jumping in and paying with cash.

Finally, she found work freelance writing for a small firm that publishes city guides. A few days before Nessel's sentencing, the local detective allowed Linda to see her case file. In it was a bad check that her digital evil twin had written to Heritage Media—Foley's new employer. Only weeks before Foley got the job there, Nessel had talked her way into a management job at the same company. They were coworkers again.

"This can't be happening," she thought, as her husband made her drink a cup of water. Nessel was later let go for undisclosed reasons. But it was clear she wasn't out of Foley's life. Later, Foley would learn that Nessel had a routine of finding midlevel management jobs at firms, then engaging in a variety of creative financial transactions, like creating false expense reports, milking the firm until it caught on.

At the sentencing in March 1999, Foley didn't know what to expect. Until this point, she had kept the affair largely private, limiting the story to an inner circle of friends. But news reporters had gotten wind of the court date, and she decided it was time to go public with her story, forcing reporters to agree to wait until the sentencing hearing.

Nessel never showed. A warrant was issued for her arrest, and local newspapers and TV stations aired the story. A booking photo of Nessel ran on the nightly news.

And Foley was terrified.

"I had just publicly humiliated her. I didn't know how she would react. I didn't know how vengeful she would be. I went into hiding in my house."

Twelve days later, Nessel turned herself in. She was sentenced to 240 days of jail time, but the judge suspended the incarceration, electing to give her five years' probation with a long list of economic conditions. These included avoiding credit shenanigans altogether.

Six months later, when a regular probation review came up, police alleged Nessel was at it again. She had gotten another job where she was able to collect personal information, violating her parole terms. This time, she was forced to serve her 240 days in jail. A hundred days later she was released for good behavior. But even as her five-year parole was set to expire, the San Diego district attorney's office was bringing her up on fresh charges that she violated her parole by attempt to pass fraudulent checks, again as part of a working relationship with a company.

***

It's hard to fathom that someone can walk into a bank with a fake driver's license or some other data and walk out with a home equity loan or drive off in a new car. But it's true. In 2002, about 10,000 people reported to the Federal Trade Commission that some kind of home loan had been taken out in their name, according to a study done by TowerGroup. The reported total losses were $300 million. And these are just the victims who thought to report the incident to the federal government.[21]

Big-ticket items, where sales competition is fierce, can be among the easiest items to pilfer via identity theft, as long as the thief is bold enough. James Rinaldo Jackson purchased seven cars this way and, generally, just used auto salesmen's eagerness against them. He recalls one saying, "Buddy, I don't care who you are or whether you've even got a Social Security number or not, make my day." And as he was buying a $100,000 Lotus Esprit SE-Turbo, the dealer said to him, "I just need a sale."[22]

Jim Thomas of Coventry, Ohio, found out the hard way how easy it can be. He had perfect credit until the year 2000, when an identity thief got a hold of his Social Security number and purchased a half-million-dollar home in California with his information. The place was a palace, a 3,100-square-foot, two-story ranch in Riverside. The criminal even spent $25,000 improving the house.

The thief was ready to close on another house—this one worth $800,000—when Thomas's own investigation halted the deal. In the usual irony, Thomas and his digital evil twin, Terral Donta Toole, had little in common. Thomas, 52, was a 6-foot-tall white man and a private airplane pilot. Toole, 32, was a 5-foot-4-inch black man, just recently out on parole after serving time for check fraud.

While the loan application included some accurate information about Thomas, the rest of it was obviously faked, he told Knight Ridder Tribune Business News.

"A 10-year-old could have done a better job" on the application, said Thomas. "To my knowledge, not one call was made to verify anything in my application—or his application, I should say."[23]

In the end, Thomas wasn't out the money, but he did spend $2,000 flying to California to straighten out the mess.

Miguel Hernandez and his extended family knew very well how to play this loan application game, and their story reveals just how easy it is. It also shows that even blatant identity thieves, who purchase big-ticket, fixed items, can get away with it. A full three years after Toole was arrested for stealing a home with identity theft, Hernandez's family moved into a dream, half-million-dollar hideaway home along the banks of the Columbia River in Vancouver, Washington, on April 1, 2003—truly an April fool's joke. The small palace was just one of 23 residences the family is said to have purchased during a two-year home-buying spree in the area near Portland, Oregon. For good measure, many of the buildings were income-generating adult care homes. The family could get rent—and sometimes double rent—from elderly residents, funding their lavish lifestyle.[24]

The Hernandez clan's tactics were not much different than the complicated leveraged property deals one might see hawked on a late-night infomercial. But underneath the entire scheme was a house of cards made of other people's Social Security numbers.

While six family members were involved, police said the group has at least 20 known aliases. They entered the country via Florida several years earlier and spent time in Texas before allegedly beginning their string of cons in Vancouver in 2001. But Vancouver Police Detective Ed Hewitt believed they had practiced their craft in other parts of the country.

"I think they came here with experience," he said. "Now the issue is figuring out who exactly they are and backtracking and seeing how much damage they have done."

The list of victims is long, but their final victim might be the most tragic, Hewitt said. Facing $60,000 bail, the fugitives' grandmother convinced a friend from church to put up his house as collateral for a bond.

"He did it without telling his wife," Hewitt said. "They're probably going to lose the house now."

The Hernandez clan was ingenious at making money on all sides of their business dealings. With each house closing, they apparently convinced the seller to pay them an extra $10,000 or $20,000 in cash for improvements—money that was supposed to be rolled into the loan. Family members even posed as tax preparation experts, filling out bogus returns for clients, exaggerating tax overpayments—and then intercepting and cashing the big refunds checks.

The complicated string of alleged crimes include allegations of vehicle loan fraud, real estate fraud, IRS tax fraud, Department of Social Services violations, and immigration issues, Hewitt said.

The scam began to unravel in 2003 when Miguel Hernandez visited Columbia Credit Union, where the family had already financed four high-ticket cars. According to Paul Hodge, chief operating officer at Columbia, Miguel Hernandez tried to finance a new Ford truck through the firm. But the financial institution's antifraud software revealed Hernandez had used a different Social Security number on a previous car loan.

"That set off some red flags," Hodge said. "So we looked at the account and determined that there were issues."

That one slip-up cost the Hernandez family its alleged identity theft home empire.

"Maybe he got a little greedy," Hodge said. "Eventually, (all criminals) get overconfident. And that's finally what it took."

The credit union called Vancouver police, which then went looking for the four cars. As agents visited the various addresses provided by the credit union, the residences followed a pattern: They were all adult foster homes.

But it was the last home that raised the most suspicion, Hewitt said. It was there police finally caught up with the Hernandez clan on September 26.

"It's a beautiful place, high above the Columbia River. There's a quarter-mile driveway to the house," Hewitt said. "And while we're sitting there, a guy pulls up in a brand new $30,000 truck with paper plates, one of the cars we were looking for."

Detectives went inside the home and arrested Miguel Hernandez, 22, and his sister Melania Hernandez, 21. Hours later, authorities were back to the home with a search warrant. And this time, they found a small identity theft factory inside.

"We hit a cornucopia of evidence. Three computer workstations and a laptop. Phony birth certificates from Cuba, with a seal," Hewitt said. "There were IRS W-2 forms, phony pay stubs. All used to manipulate their way into car loans."

Two days later, brother and sister were released on bail. Then on September 29, they failed to appear for their initial court hearing. When police visited the various Hernandez homes hunting for the fugitives, it became clear they had disappeared.

"They have totally split. All the electronics, televisions, stereos—everything is gone from their homes," Hewitt said. Even on their way out of town, they stopped by several of the foster homes and demanded early rent from some of the tenants, claiming they needed funds for immediate repairs, he said.

What they really needed was "traveling money," Hewitt said.

"It truly is a nightmare case," he said.

The Hernandez clan is still at large.

***

"How can they do that and take our house? We never had it for sale or rent or anything," said Arlene Cling, a widow in her mid-80s, in front of her San Diego home. But it was true. Someone had stolen Cling's personal information, gone to the bank, sold her home, and pocketed the cash.

"All I know is we got this letter that the house had been taken—sold—and we . . . we didn't sell it," she told NBC's Kevin Tibbles.[25]

As identity thieves grow bolder, there have been an increasing number of woeful tales involving senior citizens who suddenly discover their home has been sold right out from under them. In 2002, federal prosecutors unearthed Detroit-area crime rings that had stolen about a dozen homes this way.[26] Other elderly residents have discovered a slightly less bold form of heist; weighty home equity loans taken out in their name, draining the value right out of their life long investment.

Mari J. Frank, author and identity theft consultant, has helped elderly victims recover from the crime for years. During congressional testimony in 2002, she offered other searing images of the troubles the elderly can face when their private financial data is stolen.

"Allan and Marcia are retired and living in a gate-guarded community, in a mortgage-free home. They felt sure that their mail and finances would be safe inside the gate, yet they learned that convenience checks were stolen from their mailbox, and thousands of dollars were spent in their name. Also their own checks were stolen, credit cards were opened in their name, purchases were made across the country using their credit card numbers on the Internet. After several months, they learned that their 'mortgage-free' home now had a large mortgage and a lender was threatening foreclosure."[27]

She also told the story of Lorraine, who all at once had to deal with mourning the death of her husband and the theft of his fortune and good name.

"Lorraine, a 65-year-old widow of a deceased decorated United States Air Force General, found out several months after her husband's death that his identity was stolen to commit security crimes and credit card fraud. She is left to deal with her grieving, but also the tremendous burden of repairing her husband's tarnished reputation and addressing her own financial disaster of trying to convince the collection agencies that the debts didn't belong to her late husband."

The elderly have always been at risk from scammers who show up offering cooked-up home construction services like emergency roof repairs or aluminum siding work. But identity theft presents special risks for the elderly, since they are most likely to have good credit and least likely to use technology—such as Web-based account monitoring—to notice the problem. Nursing homes and other facilities can also offer easy access to personal information, particularly to employees who may have lessthan-caretaking intentions.

In 2003, officials in New Jersey's Hudson County unraveled a complicated ID theft ring that could only be described as depraved and macabre. A 29-year-old nurse named Sara Henry, of Philadelphia, was busted for assuming the identity of terminally ill patients and taking out bank loans in their names. Other suspects engaged in equally offensive financial attacks on the helpless, such as emptying bank accounts of psychiatric patients. Account withdrawals were made from virtually every corner of the state, authorities say. All the criminals needed were driver's licenses with the victim's data and the criminal's picture. The group wasn't shy. Members bought Jaguars, BMWs, Mercedes-Benzes, even a Land Rover.[28]

It's not just the elderly who are at risk from this kind of ID theft. Frank tells the disturbing story of George, a 55-year-old disabled veteran living in Colorado, who was suddenly denied his disability payments and hit with a large tax bill for the income that his impostor had earned working under his name in Tennessee.[29]

Senior citizen advocacy organizations have expressed concern about the ease with which identity theft can be committed against the elderly. According to a March 2003 study by the American Association of Retired Persons (AARP), 22 percent of all identity theft victims are over age 50. Additionally, a disproportionate number of seniors (51 percent versus 44 percent of the general population) report having their stolen information used to commit credit card fraud. Seniors are therefore disproportionately exposed to risks of damaged credit reports, rejection for credit, and collection calls.[30]

U.S. Secret Service Agent Douglas Coombs expressed this concern during congressional testimony in July 2002. He predicted older Americans will become an increasingly attractive target by criminals, given the fact that 70 percent of the nation's wealth is controlled by those 50 years of age and older. They are an easy mark, he added. Often, as people get older, their level of diligence in monitoring personal finances decreases. And some are embarrassed to come forward after they discover fraud or are unsure of the steps necessary to report the compromise.[31]

***

Not all ID theft is so dramatic. In fact, in some ways, victims who find $500,000 in home loans or BMW purchases on their credit reports are lucky. They meet law enforcement thresholds; their cases are taken up by prosecutors. Car dealerships are willing to act to recover their stolen merchandise.

But most of the 10 million victims every year aren't so lucky. They must go through the Jobian trial alone, winding through affidavits, police reports, bank voice mail systems, and endless record keeping with little sense of when it all might end. Even if no money is lost, the average identity theft victim spends about $500–1,000 cleaning up the mess. There is lost work time—half-day "vacations" taken to make required bank appearances and the like. And there's often a drop in work performance, due to the nagging distractions of all those personal calls required to clean up credit errors. The length of time it takes an individual to recover their identity is often between a year and a half and two years, according to Senator Diane Feinstein's office.[32]

Even while their cases might sound trivial to investigators, victims face painful, random, and sometimes shocking consequences.

Victims like Matthew Forsythe, who didn't learn he was hit by ID theft until he tried to refinance his home in 2003, during the boom of low loan rates. When his bank ran his credit report, it was riddled with bad accounts. His loan was rejected out of hand, with no chance for redemption until he cleaned off all the incorrect data. Six months of letters and phone calls later, he was still fighting with the credit bureaus. And the cheap loan rates were long gone. He still got his loan, but at a fractionally higher interest rate. Like most ID theft victims, he wasn't responsible for paying the credit card bills and loans connected to his name. But losing out on low loan rates cost him at least $15,000 over the life of his home loan, and probably more, he figures. That means the criminal didn't steal from him; the system did.[33]

The mathematics are simple: In one typical example for a home mortgage, those with a high credit score of 720 or better—the top bracket—qualified for a 5.664 percent interest rate. ID theft victims with miserable ratings, such as Rachel Soper's child, whose score was in the 500s, would pay 9.289 percent for a mortgage. But even a typical penalty of 75 points for a couple of defaulted accounts, which knocked a victim's score down to a 619, would result in a stiff identity theft penalty. Interest rates on that loan would be 7.476 percent.

Perhaps the 2 percent difference doesn't sound like much, but its impact on a loan is staggering. Monthly payments on a $200,000 mortgage would rise $240. The victim would pay a full $86,000 more during the life of the loan. Consider it an identity theft victim's tax—a penalty on the victim and a profit point for lenders.

***

We hear again and again that identity theft is a victimless crime. Anyone who spots credit card fraud on their bills is quickly soothed by the financial institutions, which brag about their zero liability policies, the panacea for all credit card fraud. And thus is the most obvious and immediate form of identity theft blunted by marketing messages—all in the name of credit flow. All the companies with a vested interest in the flow of credit have to keep a lid on the misery caused by fraud and identity theft, lest it get in the way of their free-flowing funds.

No matter what the consequence, America's financial firms and retail outlets insist on keeping the credit faucet turned on as high and as wide as possible. In virtually every victim's story mentioned earlier, a small dose of common sense, combined with a little less haste, would have stopped the pain before it started. But that's virtually impossible now. Consumer spending, which accounts for two-thirds of the economic activity in the country, is largely predicated on a mammoth marketing effort designed to convince people that instant gratification is the true path to happiness—even if it makes a few million people miserable along the way. That's the fallout from the miracle of instant credit. This miracle, created by corporations to edge profits a bit higher by shrinking the distance between a consumer's heart and his or her wallet, is really the cause of the identity theft epidemic. The credit industry, the one entity that could have stopped or at least significantly slowed the progress of the crime, instead stood by and watched.

3

THE "MIRACLE" OF INSTANT CREDIT

I pulled out the card I had in my desk and verified that it still had the "Call 800 . . ." sticker on it to activate it. . . . I asked how a card that was not activated could be used, since they use caller ID to verify the person is at least calling from the card name's phone number. Here is the important part; they said that there are other ways to activate the card. That is the problem with identity theft, there are other ways to activate the card! The reason we have the big issues we have now is people do not always do what they are supposed to do to verify the cardholder. Whether it is a credit card, a vehicle, or a cell phone, if they don't stick to their rules then there will always be another way for the thief to get what want.

—Anonymous
ID theft victim

Right now, millions of Americans can walk into an electronics store and walk out 15 minutes later with a $3,000 plasma television—regardless of how much money they might have in their wallets or in their checking accounts. The buyer might not even have to make payments on the television for a full year. A slightly smaller percentage of Americans can walk into a car dealership and drive out within in a few hours with a new car. "Zero Down!" scream the advertisements and posters cramming dealership windows across the nation.

This is the "miracle" of instant credit, so termed by Howard Beales, director of the Federal Trade Commission's (FTC) Bureau of Consumer Protection.[1]

Corporate America has seized on instant credit as its key conversion tool; that is, converting window-shoppers into buyers. You want it? You can have it—right now. The impulse buy is the engine that drives today's American economy.

Television commercials push the virtue of our have-it-all, have-it-now ways. In one recent Circuit City advertisement, a young, hip, married couple sits outside a Circuit City store vowing that they are going into the place "just looking" and won't buy anything, no matter what pitch they hear from a salesman. Of course, moments later the man gives in to temptation nearly instantly while standing in front of a mammoth television.

Instant credit means instant gratification. It is the apple in the Garden of Eden, a temptation that many consumers find impossible to resist. Shopping has become less and less a matter of "Can I afford it?" and more and more a matter of simply "I can have it." While instant credit now has enamored itself to nearly every industry, from auto dealers to cell phone retailers, the concept is really borne of the credit card industry, which is the incubator in which the identity theft epidemic first developed.

Robert Manning's groundbreaking study of the credit card industry, *Credit Card Nation*, describes the incredible cultural shift financial institutions have managed to forge through a combination of fiscal temptation and marketing muscle. Credit cards, and to a larger extent, the credit culture, have created a near-complete cognitive disconnect between how much money people earn and what they can afford to buy. The thinking goes something like this: Plastic means not having to pay until tomorrow or maybe the next day. And somehow, perhaps that day will never come, particularly if I keep shifting balances to new credit cards.

Of course, that day comes. The fallout from the credit card culture is the incredible $2.0 trillion in total consumer debt that burdens Americans—$735 billion of it owed on credit cards debt.[2] Americans carry an average of 10 credit cards each today. The 44.5 million Americans who don't pay their bill every month, so-called revolver households, carried an average of $13,000 in credit card debt during the year 2002—and they paid an average of $1,700 in interest and fees.[3] Those fees are an incredible profit engine for lenders and investors of "asset-backed securities," similar to stock options on consumer debt. Credit card lenders now get about one-third of their profits from various late fees and other penalties.[4] In some cases retailers make more money lending money in the form of credit cards than they do selling their products.[5]

Consumers are compliant in this paper economy. Nearly half of all Americans using credit cards carry a balance from month to month. That explains why a record 1.7 million people filed for personal bankruptcy in fiscal 2003[6]—an embarrassingly high rate of personal bankruptcies, higher than any industrialized nation in the world.[7]

But we Americans tend to blame the bankrupt for their plight. The puritanical thread of thinking to be found in Americans' view of capitalism dictates that those who overspend their means, even if tempted by instant credit, really deserve the blame for their economic fate. That may be true; but it doesn't mean the industry that pushed credit at the vulnerable bears no responsibility. For years, tobacco companies argued they were simply giving consumers a choice by selling cigarettes—and spending millions to market them. Eventually, as a nation, we decided it's possible to blame both the consumer and the company.

However, in the world of credit, the Puritan ethic still reigns, and this attitude gives the instant credit industry its brazen attitude, a sense of immunity from any wrongdoing. In fact, it encourages the industry to keep pushing its free money at consumers, despite the inevitable consequences for millions of

Americans, as a way to continually speed up the nation's increasingly consumer-driven economy. After all, consumer spending is king now, the biggest engine of American capitalism. It represents two-thirds of all U.S. economic activity, and it was the only leg of the economy that remained strong during the 2001–2002 recession. The age of "generous financing terms" and other forms of instant credit arguably saved the nation from a prolonged recession or even a depression during that time, as credit kept up the pace of consumer spending even as unemployment rose and wages fell.

A million or more personal bankruptcies each year is seen as an acceptable consequence of this make-believe Eden.

But now, the miracle of instant credit has another cost. If nearly any consumer can walk into an electronics store and walk out a few minutes later with a $3,000 television, so can any identity thief. Instant credit is the only tool an identity thief really needs, and the only reason identity theft is the problem that it is. Companies that grant such credit enable identity thieves to do their dirty work. By all accounts, instant credit is the prime in the pump of identity theft, the radioactive byproduct of Americans' newfound ability to have it all right now. In an age where mortgages are approved in 15 minutes, there is no time to see who is applying.

And consumers play right along with the system. After all, we want our televisions right now. We want that new car today, this afternoon, before we go to dinner. This willingness to pay for today with tomorrow's money is the fundamental reason our identities are now so fragile. Our evil digital twin, now fully separated from economic reality, can wreak almost limitless havoc.

The fundamental flaw of the credit card culture is no longer limited to those among us too weak to avoid its temptation. The fallout is greater than rising personal bankruptcy rates. Now, overindulgent consumer credit impacts all of us—27 million identity theft victims in the last 5 years, according to the Federal

Trade Commission.[8] All exposed by a system designed to enable people to buy a $3,000 television on a whim.

Still, all this bad news hasn't been enough to make the industry wonder about the wisdom of its ways. In fact, during an interview about the importance of liberal data sharing among creditors, an industry lobbyist bragged about the fact that a consumer who accidentally leaves his credit card at home is able to present his driver's license to a retail store cashier, and that cashier can look up the account and enable the credit purchase. The cashier can even raise the buyer's credit limit to make a big-ticket purchase.[9] As we see later in this book, examination of a driver's license proves nothing. But workarounds like these do keep the faucet of credit flowing at full speed.

As Americans begin to question the wisdom of the credit system, major card issuers such as Citibank have begun to take their case right to the consumers, with marketing campaigns aimed at making the creditors seem to be part of the solution rather than the source of the problem. The more bad publicity that ID theft draws to the credit system, the more marketing Americans can expect. There are incredible software projects being designed to catch identity thieves by the digital bread crumbs they leave there are "zero liability" promises to protect cardholders; there are even agreements among lenders now to share data about victims. All these steps are productive, but all of them apply only after the crime has already happened, after the consumer has already been impersonated. The one thing that would truly slow ID theft—slowing down the speed at which credit is granted in the first place—will never be discussed. Commonsense solutions such as forcing department stores to wait before issuing credit cards so they can call the new customer at home to verify who they are or verifying age and address information on every credit application—these are highly unlikely. Because the one thing the credit culture can't allow is a slowdown;

that would mean fewer transactions, and fewer transactions translates into less profit.

***

You might think credit card fraud would be a serious concern for credit card issuers. After all, the FTC says *someone* lost $50 billion dealing with the 27 million identities that were stolen from 1998 to 2002—and two-thirds of the stolen identities represented stolen credit cards.[10] But credit card companies have less economic incentive than one might think to stop some forms of identity theft. In fact, a lawsuit has been filed alleging the firms actually profit from it.

It's a bit confusing trying to determine just who loses money when a stolen credit card is used for fraud. Most people know consumers aren't out the money, as long as they dispute the charges quickly enough. But what most people don't know is credit card associations like Visa and MasterCard often don't lose money on credit card fraud, and neither do card issuing banks like Citibank. In fact, sometimes they *do* make money on fraud— and one lawsuit estimated the card associations made nearly $400 million during 2001 in profits off of such fraud.[11] Here's how.

Millions of Americans know well their part of the process when credit card fraud occurs, because as many as 1 in 5 has been hit with such fraud. A victim simply calls his or her card issuing bank and disputes the charge. To the consumer, that's pretty much the end of it.

But behind the scenes, a complex cost-shifting process has been initiated, a shell game that makes banks the winners and merchants the losers. The ingenious cost shifting also spreads the burden of fraud so thin and wide that the pain is blunted enough to prevent any real kind of public outcry.

When a stolen credit card is used to pay for an item on a web site, such as a $1,000 laptop computer, the seller learns of the fraud about a month or two later. The bad news comes in the form of a credit card chargeback. When the victim consumer calls the bank to dispute the charge, $1,000 is removed from the consumer's bill. The cardholder's bank (known in the industry as the issuing bank) then takes the $1,000 it's missing from the seller's bank (the "acquirer" bank), which then issues a chargeback to the seller, or merchant, for $1,000. Being lowest in the pecking order, the merchant is now missing a laptop from inventory and also missing the $1,000 it expected as payment. To add insult to injury, a chargeback fee is then levied, amounting to anywhere between $20 and $100. And the initial merchant processing fee, perhaps 2 percent or $20, still sticks. On this one transaction, the criminal gets a free laptop, the consumer feels no immediate pain (that can come later), the banks make between $40 and $120, and the merchant is out a $1,000 laptop and the fees.

The exact same procedure is used for credit card fraud committed over the phone. Both situations are known as "card-not-present" or "signatureless" transactions in the industry. There's no way to verify the cardholder's signature, as there is in retail store transactions, where clerks are supposed to glance at the back of the credit card and file a signed receipt. Under the standard contracts virtual merchants must sign with their banks if they want to accept credit cards, they are the guilty party when fraud occurs. They were supposed to spot the fraud and stop it; so they must eat the loss and pay the chargeback fee. There is no other option, aside from not accepting credit card payment—a virtual impossibility for web sites and catalog companies.

A lawsuit filed by three small Internet companies in May 2002 accuses Visa, MasterCard, Discover, and American Express of collecting $383 million in such chargeback fees during 2001. It's a rough calculation based on an estimate—disputed by the credit card firms—that 1.4 percent of all card-not-present transactions were fraudulent that year. Visa claims during 2001, only one-fourth of 1 percent of all Net transactions were fraudulent. But independent surveys, including one sponsored by the credit industry in 2003, indicate fraud rates were as high as 2 percent during that year.

The lawsuit goes even farther, accusing the associations of actually encouraging fraud in some cases. When a database of credit card numbers is put at risk by an Internet merchant with a security flaw—such as the theft of up to 8 million credit card numbers from Data Processors International in February 2003—the credit card associations could immediately instruct issuing banks to cancel the cards, but they don't. Instead, they monitor the accounts for evidence that they are being used for fraud, and only when a criminal spending spree emerges do issuing banks begin closing the accounts. The reason is simple: Canceling and reissuing cards can cost a bank up to $25 for each card. The industry claims that fraud either shows up immediately after a security breach or not at all.[12] The problem is, the policy permits the first few thefts, ultimately at the expense of a merchant. The wait-and-see strategy sacrifices the merchants hit by the initial frauds as guinea pigs. They then face chargeback fees and loss of merchandise.

This wait-and-see strategy violates federal racketeering laws, says attorney Mark Ishman, who filed the suit on behalf of the three web sites. The credit card companies put merchants at risk, all in the interest of avoiding a massive reissuing of plastic. Three of the four card associations at the time declined to comment on the lawsuit; MasterCard issued a statement saying it was "confident that our practices with respect to our Internet merchants are lawful and appropriate and have served to benefit not only consumers, but these merchants as well."[13]

Ishman and his clients have since withdrawn the lawsuit from the North Carolina court; he plans to refile it in another jurisdiction.

There are certainly other examples of the credit card associations acting passively in the face of fraud. For example, every day private investigators and web enthusiasts find caches of stolen credit cards on the Internet. But if you browse the Visa or MasterCard web sites, or call their 800 numbers, you'll spend a lot of time trying to find some way to report the stolen information. In fact, there has never been a simple mechanism to report such exposed credit card numbers. It almost seems as if the associations don't want to know.

Merchants, on the front lines of this battle, also regularly come across stolen card numbers—and have no idea what to do with them. "Citibank Visa in South Dakota recently told me that their "security department" would not take calls from merchants. What good are they?" asked merchant Bill Crane.[14] Another merchant, Gary Howell, regularly tracks down those who try to pass stolen credit cards at his store and attempts to initiate criminal prosecutions. The credit card firms are no help.

"We have never been able to get a credit card company to help prosecute any credit card crime," he said.[15]

***

It's not fair to claim the credit card associations have done nothing to stop fraud. In fact, consumers are quite familiar with the industry's most successful fraud-fighting tool. Many have received one of those alarming calls from a fraud expert at an issuing bank with a question like, "Are you really buying expensive jewelry and staying in an expensive hotel room in London right now?" Ingenious "neural-network" software called Falcon is the source of those calls. The software analyzes consumer buying habits and sets off alarm bells when something very out of the ordinary happens, such as a sudden out-of-the country spending spree. Developed by San Diego-based HNC Software, Falcon stormed the credit card industry during the 1990s after it was introduced in 1992.[16] Perhaps the most successful fraud-fighting product ever built, in 2001 the software was gobbled up by credit-scoring formula firm Fair Isaac for $800 million.[17] In 2003, it monitored nearly 65 percent of all credit card transactions for fraud, according to Fair Isaac.[18] Some card issuers and merchant acquirers have their own in-house equivalent, and others supplement Falcon with their own fraud detection software.

That kind of pattern recognition and neural-network programming is behind the credit industry's most promising identity theft-fighting effort to date, a technology being developed by San Diego-based ID Analytics. The firm's executive team is largely made up of the same people who built Falcon for HNC in the late 1980s and early 1990s.

Identity thieves follow predictable patterns once they grab a person's digital information. Often, the criminals buy gasoline first, get a cell phone, order a computer, and then escalate to larger purchases. They tend to use similar pseudonyms, or addresses that are slight variations of one another, in an attempt to evade simplistic antifraud software. By convincing a wide cross-section of creditors, from credit card issuers to banks to cell phone companies, to share their transaction data and analyzing the broad spectrum of credit applications, ID Analytics is developing statistical models that can detect an ID thief in progress. Warnings can then be issued across industries, which can prevent the extension of credit to the person using that digital dossier.

ID Analytics' first crack at developing such statistical models in 2003 uncovered remarkable data that revealed creditors really have been enabling identity theft. This rare peek under the hood of American's creditors showed that in an overwhelming number of cases, 7 out of 8 times, lenders miscategorized identity theft as a "credit loss"—dejargoned, simply an unpaid bill. ID theft has grown so far, so fast, because financial institutions and other lenders have missed it.[19]

In a massive study of 200 million new credit cards, checking accounts, and cell phone accounts opened during 2001—with participants like Citibank, Dell, Bank of America, and T-Mobile—ID Analytics revealed that identity thefts were miscategorized by lenders as simple credit losses 83 percent of the time.

The study, really the first of its kind, included 100 million credit card applications and follow-up data from 2001 supplied by some of America's largest credit card firms: Bank of America, Capital One, Citibank, Diners Club, and Discover Financial Services. The study included another 100 million accounts from other credit granters such as Dell Financial Services, JP Morgan Chase, Sprint, and T-Mobile, along with Circuit City's instant credit arm, First North American National Bank.

Here's how far off the mark the credit firms were. Participating lenders had attributed $85 million in losses to ID fraud in 2001. The after-the-fact study of the year-old data uncovered ID theft losses at $1.07 billion that year for the companies.

In the best possible light, the miscategorizations can be explained as mere accidents. To lenders, most identity theft cases simply look like unpaid bills. It's not until months later, when the identity theft victim discovers the problem and calls to complain, that the lender finds out fraud is involved—and then, the money has already been written off in company financials as a simple credit loss, a deadbeat customer. There's no easy way to refile it as a fraud loss. That's one reason financial institutions haven't reacted more quickly to the identity theft crisis: they just didn't see it.

"I had this sense that the problem was bigger than people suspected it was," said Martin Abrams, former chief privacy officer at credit reporting agency Experian. "I believed the fraud numbers were too low. This study begins to show why that's the case."[20]

In a more sinister light, there's another explanation. Fraud makes financial investors nervous, and banks have a long-standing tradition of burying fraud within their balance sheets. Avivah Litan, a Gartner analyst and internationally renowned credit card fraud expert, said it was possibly a happy accident by the banks and other lenders.

"The question is: Are they doing that intentionally? Maybe they don't have much incentive to stop," she said. "Wall Street would frown on the high fraud losses. If they start reporting all this loss as fraud loss, their stock would take a hit."[21]

The study confirms the idea that the faster that credit is available, the more vulnerable it is to ID theft. ID Analytics found incredibly high rates of identity fraud in certain segments of credit—with on-the-spot credit grantors being the most susceptible to ID fraud. So-called faceless, instant credit grantors, like web-based wireless phone sellers, face average fraud rates of 7.5 percent. Fully 1 in 15 approved applications were identity thieves at work.[22]

"Immediacy is the enemy of accuracy," says Abrams, now an analyst with Hunton & Williams, which coauthored the study. "ID thieves are successful because we have a marketplace based on immediacy."

"We can't move away from instant credit, but it is the enemy of good authenticity."[23]

***

Abrams was describing the credit market of 2003, but his statement could easily apply during any time of the march toward the credit culture. The credit industry has always been willing to sacrifice safety for expediency, to trade high fraud rates for market share. After all, as long as profits outpace fraud, it might seem to be a solid business decision. A 50-year pattern of behavior by credit card companies reveals this easy trade-off, one that constantly exposes consumers to higher rates of fraud in exchange for higher profits.

The credit card era was largely ushered in by the emergence of BankAmericard (eventually, Visa) in the 1950s as the first truly universal credit card. In those land rush days, which also saw the emergence of Carte Blanche, American Express, Diners Club, and Chase Manhattan, BankAmericard pioneered a marketing method that seems absurd to 2004 ears—the bank simply mailed out millions of active credit cards to prospective customers, whether they wanted them or not. As mailboxes filled up with what was essentially $300 or more in free money, fraud was rampant. Bank of America lost about $20 million on its BankAmericard during its first 15 months, an undisclosed amount the result of fraud. But the misguided distribution plan continued unabated. Consumers had trouble resisting the lure of seemingly free money sitting in their mailbox. After sending 2 million cards to California residents during one 13-month stretch in the late 1950s, Bank of America had a lock on the market.[24]

This credit card carpet bombing, an ingenious tool for gaining market share, marked the next two decades of furious competition in the credit card business. By 1967, 30 million live credit cards had been mailed home to consumers.

In 1970, after a wave of bad publicity, Congress finally banned this mass mailing of unsolicited credit cards. Undeterred, credit card firms developed the next-best thing—preapproved applications. Still widely used today, preapproved applications are now an identity thief's best friend. These unsolicited blank forms do require identity thieves to take an extra step—filling out a form—before obtaining a stolen credit card. Still, that's often a mere formality.

One might imagine an intelligent force double-checking credit card applications for potential trouble signs. And in fact, once upon a time, some banks initially had extensive, common-sense procedures to verify applications, says Martin Biegelman, a former U.S. Postal Inspector who specialized in credit card fraud during those early years. At the time, some small banks even inspected applications by hand. One application investigator Biegelman worked with became expert at spotting Nigerian handwriting on applications submitted from New York City. Knowing that Nigerian-based credit crime rings were common in the city, the expert pulled the applications and processed them by hand.[25]

But that's no way to quickly ramp up market share. Big credit card companies were hard at work building automated processes for approving the applications; they just couldn't provide personal service. As the shoddy security procedures evolved, Biegelman implored credit card firms to simply add one single step to their application process—a phone call to the employment phone number listed on the application, to verify place of employment and identity.

"They wouldn't do that," he said. It was too expensive.

Today, billions of preapproved applications are scattered willy-nilly across the nation. One family in Hamilton, Ohio, received 217 of the applications in 2002, with offers of credit totaling over $8 million. The head of the household was a 65-year-old retired teacher.[26]

Scant attention to the data listed on preapproved credit card applications has resulted in several celebrated cases of five-year-olds or pets receiving the plastic money. The stories prompted Federal Reserve Chairman Alan Greenspan to remark during a renomination hearing before the Senate Banking Committee in January 2000: "Children, dogs, cats and moose are getting credit cards."[27] Children, dogs, cats, moose, and identity thieves. That's what happens when the nation is carpet-bombed each year with 4 billion credit card applications.[28]

***

The record of recklessness in the face of rampant fraud, of choosing speed, profits, and market share over security, has far more severe consequences than unnerved consumers and financial harm to merchants. As federal authorities began to unmask terrorist groups in the aftermath of September 11, 2001, the role of credit card fraud in terrorism emerged as one of the biggest lessons. Put simply, easy credit has made funding terrorism easy. It enables organizations like al-Qaeda to send single agents or small groups into the United States with little or no assets, as they have learned they can subsist on petty credit card fraud alone. Millions of dollars have been stolen by terrorists operating in the United States, Canada, and Europe using credit cards, according to congressional testimony, court documents, and published reports.

In the days after September 11, many news accounts presumed identity theft played an important role in the hijacking of four airplanes destined to strike at the heart of America. It was reported that as many as nine of the hijackers used fake names to board the four airplanes. When the FBI released the list of the 19 names, there were countless stories of unlucky men in Saudi Arabia with similar names, pleading innocence, blaming any association with September 11 on identity theft.

The news reports were premature; we now know that, surprisingly, the hijackers didn't bother to disguise their identities when they boarded the planes that terrible morning. But that doesn't mean identity theft had no role in September 11 or in other terrorist activity around the world. False ID papers were probably used by the September 11 hijackers to enter the country and have been used by other convicted terrorists to cross U.S. borders.[29] Financial experts will repeat to anyone who'll listen that America's system of easy credit and easy identity theft means easy funding for terrorists working to quietly blend into the American way of life. Congressional testimony in the aftermath of September 11 repeatedly pointed the finger at credit card fraud as a major tool for financing terrorism. Dennis Lormel, chief of the FBI's Financial Crimes Section, told the House Financial Services Committee in October 2001 that some of the 19 hijackers from the September 11 attacks had used false identities and engaged in credit card fraud prior to the attack.[30]

"The ease with which these individuals can obtain false identification or assume the identity of someone else, and then open bank accounts and obtain credit cards, makes these attractive ways to generate funds," Lormel said to the committee.

A Spanish judge who presided over the indictment of eight suspected al-Qaeda members for involvement in September 11 says the group financed itself largely through credit card fraud.[31] The terrorist cell, thought to be a financing hub for al-Qaeda, used stolen credit cards and false identities to move money and people around the globe. Perhaps $1 million was raised and moved out of the country by couriers to Saudi Arabia, U.S. investigators say.[32]

France's top terrorism fighter, Jean-Louis Bruguiere, told the *New York Times* identity-based fraud was a key al-Qaeda tool. "They do not need orders from Osama bin Laden to carry out the jihad. They finance their own operations with credit card fraud and theft."[33]

It's even been suggested that credit fraud is a standard operating procedure for Osama bin Laden's band of terrorists. "We have an al-Qaeda training manual that talks about financing terrorist operations through credit card fraud," said Secret Service Special Agent Jim Mackin. "It's a whole new ball game."[34] In Europe, al-Qaeda's Algerian agents are suspected of raising approximately $1 million a month through credit card fraud and other frauds committed with organized crime racquets.[35] French probes have shown al-Qaeda operatives can rake in up to $17,000 a month in credit card fraud.[36]

That's more than enough to finance serious attacks on American targets. Police believe the 2000 *USS Cole* attack, in which 17 U.S. servicemen died, cost $50,000.[37]

"Identity theft—credit card theft, bank fraud—is hugely important to al-Qaeda, as it is to many terror groups. I've been astonished that there's been so little attention paid to it," Magnus Ranstorp, director of the Center for the Study of Terrorism and Political Violence at the University of St. Andrews in Scotland, told *Newsweek* in 2001. "The pattern was very clear within the North African contingent of al-Qaeda members operating in Europe. Every time you arrest one of them he has 20 different identities and 20 different credit cards."[38]

Congressional testimony reveals that credit card fraud had become an essential tool for terrorists targeting the United States long before September 11. In February 1998, a top U.S. secret service official named Richard A. Rohde told the Senate Judiciary Subcommittee on Technology, Terrorism and Government Information that two Middle Eastern terrorist groups involved in massive credit fraud cases bilked $21 million from U.S. financial institutions.[39] And credit card fraud was a primary source of funding for what was almost America's worst pre-September. 11 terrorist attack, the Millennium Plot, a harrowing tale worth reviewing in detail.[40]

U.S. authorities say in 1998, Algerian national and now-convicted terrorist Ahmed Ressam met Mokhtar Haouari in Montreal. Ressam heard Haouari paid for simple financial data, the starting point for identity theft. Ressam gave Haouari a stolen Social Security number, a driver's license number, and three bank cards and got $60 in return. Later, Ressam gave Haouari a stolen passport and got $110 in return. That began a fraud relationship that eventually almost resulted in the destruction of Los Angeles Airport on New Year's Eve 1999.

Soon after their initial meeting, Ressam went to an Afghanistan-based terrorist training camp for six months. He returned to Canada determined to do something terrible to the United States. He settled on a New Years' Eve plot to blow up Los Angeles Airport.

But first, he needed quick access to spending power. Ressam told authorities he was given $12,000 of seed money to set up his operation. When he asked for more cash, he was advised to finance himself by credit card fraud.

Ressam quickly sought out his old friend. He knew Haouari had the ability to encode credit cards on his own, right in his small Montreal apartment. Haouari would steal account information from diners at local restaurants and other retail stores, then encode the data onto the magnetic stripe of other cards using a computer at his apartment. It seemed almost a license to print money—all Haouari needed was ready access to stolen account numbers—an ideal way to fund the terrorist's preparations. The two discussed creating a front business just to skim credit card account information from consumers.

A third accomplice, Abdelghani Meskini, developed an even more elaborate idea: Buy a gas station and use it to hoard credit and debit card account information, including PIN numbers. According to the FBI, the plan involved placing a camera in a location where it would be possible to watch people punching in their PIN numbers. The group had its eye on a gas station being sold in New Jersey, but before they could buy it, the plot unraveled and Meskini and Haouari were arrested, according to the *Chicago Tribune*.

On December 14, 1999, Ressam boarded a ferry in Canada bound for Port Angeles, Washington, in a car loaded with 130 pounds of explosives. There was plenty of firepower to destroy an entire building at Los Angeles Airport. Fortunately, he never got farther than the border. An alert inspector spotted the suspicious cargo in Ressam's trunk, and he was arrested. Haouari and Meskini were arrested soon after, and authorities pieced together the plot. Ressam later testified that identity theft and credit card fraud played a key role in the plot.

What little public documentation there is concerning the more intense September 11 prosecutions draws the clearest link yet between credit card fraud and the death of Americans at the hand of terrorists. Ali Saleh Kahlah al-Marri, authorities say, may have directly funded the September 11 attack with credit card fraud. His case has been shrouded in secrecy since his designation as an "enemy combatant," which moved the proceedings out of the public arena of the U.S. court system and into a military tribunal. Before that the government had accused him of lying to the FBI about his relationship with alleged September 11 paymaster, Mustafa Ahmed al-Hawsawi. Al-Hawsawi is suspected of helping finance the attacks by transferring tens of thousand of dollars to the 19 hijackers before September 11, 2001.

Al-Marri had been indicted by a federal grand jury for fraud before his case was transferred to the military tribunal, and the indictment provides stirring details concerning his alleged use of credit card fraud.[41] When authorities caught up with him, there were over 1,000 credit card account numbers on his laptop computer. Most of the cards had been used for fraud, said the complaint signed by FBI agent Nicolas Zambeck. Also on the computer: bookmarked Internet web sites relating to, among other things, computer hacking, fake driver's licenses and other fake identification cards, buying and selling credit card numbers, and processing credit card transactions.

The indictment alleged that from July 2000 to August 2000, al-Marri used false identification to open bank accounts so that he could deposit and withdraw funds under an assumed name; that during this time, he rented a room at the Time Out Motel in Macomb, Illinois, in the name "Abdulakareem A. Almuslam" so he would have a local address to receive documents related to the bank accounts he intended to open; and created a fictional business called "AAA Carpets" using the hotel address as the business address. The indictment also alleged al-Marri used a faked Social Security number to open fraudulent accounts with three banks in Macomb.

Court documents alleged a direct link between al-Marri and the September 11 hijackers. During interrogation, al-Marri told

FBI agents he had never called al-Hawsawi's phone number, when in fact he had dialed the number using a calling card on several occasions between September and November 2001. The same number was a point of contact for lead September 11 hijacker Mohamed Atta and alleged attack coordinator Ramzi Binalshibh, investigators said.

***

Two years after the clear national interest in the credit card fraud problem had been demonstrated by the September 11 attacks and subsequent investigations, little had been done to correct it. Congress spent a good part of 2003 debating an update to the federal law that governs the way America's credit reporting industry operates, the Fair Credit Reporting Act. Hours of scathing testimony made clear just how lax most credit card application procedures are, even today, even after September 11. In fact, some credit card issuers still grant new accounts to applicants as long as the Social Security number in the application is valid—even if virtually all the other information in the applications is wrong. Even if the applicant's address lists the wrong state and the birthday is 50 years off.

When suggested, commonsense provisions such as simple address verification have been resisted by the industry. In his testimony urging improvements to the system, Edward Mierzwinski, consumer program director at the Public Interest Research Group, urged a more commonsense approach:

> Well, I think the credit bureaus need to match credit card applications to credit reports on four or five items rather than simply on the Social Security number. That's the big problem. If I get your Social Security number off the Internet, I can get credit in your name very easily. They need to match on my previous address. They need to use some out

of wallet identifiers, something that an ID thief wouldn't know. And, they need to use several identifiers in concert together rather than only the SSN.[42]

Mierzwinski was echoing an idea that had been floating around since at least 1997, when the California state legislature debated an identity theft prevention law that would require retail firms to make sure at least three items listed in a credit card application matched three items in a consumer's credit report. The law was certainly simple enough. It indicated the "categories of information may include, but are not limited to, first and last name, month and date of birth, driver's license number, place of employment, residence address, and social security number." The credit bureaus repeatedly fought the provision. At the time, they "dismissed the identity-theft issue as a quixotic do-gooder's cause" that they hoped "would just go away," wrote the *Wall Street Journal*'s Kathryn Kranhold.[43] Later, after the California bill passed and was signed into law, Maxine Sweet, an Experian vice president, described the provision as "onerous." [44]

Fraud experts suspect the law has since been largely ignored, given the celebrated cases of underaged credit card holders. Verifying three data points would require complex computer upgrades, and more importantly, slow down the entire credit granting process—a result the industry could not allow. It prides itself on breakneck speed. In a white paper that appeared on Experian's web site late in 2003, the firm bragged it could offer response to preapproved credit applications in fewer than two seconds.[45]

It has taken nearly a decade for the credit card industry to implement the simple safety measure of not printing account numbers on paper receipts. The 2003 version of the Fair Credit Reporting Act finally mandates such a baby step. But other recommended provisions in the bill, provisions as simple as California's recommended three-point matching, were effectively kept out of the law. And in fact, in 2003 the South Carolina Supreme

Court stood behind this right to sloppy verification of credit card applicants. In a unanimous decision, the court ruled that banks have no duty to protect noncustomers from identity theft. In other words, banks can issue credit to an imposter in any consumer's name, and the consumer has no right to sue if they aren't a customer of the bank. The court held that Citibank, Capital One Bank, and Premier Bankcard couldn't be held responsible for giving credit cards to an imposter who had acquired them in the name of victim P. Kenneth Huggins because the banks had no existing business relationship with Huggins.[46]

The industry also resisted significant improvements to the only instrument that can help identity theft victims while their crime is ongoing. Debate surrounding observation of so-called fraud alerts illustrates just how obstinate the credit industry can be and how slowly it accepts changes that will make American credit safer and more secure.

The first piece of advice given to any ID theft victim is to call the three credit bureaus and place a "fraud alert" flag on their accounts. The alerts are supposed to tell potential creditors they shouldn't grant credit in the victim's name unless some extra step is taken, usually a phone call to the applicant's home for verification. It's a simple enough idea: Stop issuing credit to a Social Security number known to be in the hands of an identity thief. But the system has largely been a failure, because inexplicably, the alerts have been largely ignored. There are endless reports that, long after a person reports their identity is actively being used to open fraudulent accounts, and a fraud alert is applied to the account, creditors grant new credit cards to the ID thief anyway. Documents obtained from the FTC under a Freedom of Information Act request reveal the pattern is clear: In a sampling of identity theft complaints filed by consumers against credit card firms and credit bureaus, victims repeatedly indicated creditors had neglected to honor fraud alerts on their accounts.[47]

In fact fraud alerts, the industry's most significant measure to stop ID theft, have been at times completely useless, according to congressional testimony supplied by consumer Sallie Twentyman. In September 1999 she received a bill for $12,000 in cash advances and convenience check payments she never made. She immediately placed fraud alerts on her credit reports. But during the next six months, her imposter moved almost every month to four different new addresses. From Falls Church, Virginia, to Brooklyn, New York; to Sea Port, Georgia; to Chicago, Illinois, and Pleasanton, California. And credit reports showed the imposter succeeded at opening several new credit card and bank accounts at each address. "And this is all after I had placed a fraud alert on my name file," she said.[48]

Part of the reason the alerts are ignored is because they are misnamed. "Alert" implies some kind of large red flag that would appear at the very top of a credit report or at least a warning label as substantial as the one consumers now find along the side of cigarette boxes. This is not the case. An alert is often as simple as a mere entry in the "100-word statement" box in credit files that's made available to consumers who disagree with an entry made in their credit file.[49] It can look like just another entry on a credit report, another line item next to all those credit cards opened in Brooklyn, Sea Port, and Pleasanton. They're very easy to miss, particularly when the economics of the situation make everyone much more eager to grant the credit card application than deny it. Firms that rely entirely on a simple credit score, rather than a full report, never saw the alerts. The system is so weak that known criminals just couldn't be stopped from obtaining credit cards in their victim's name.

The new Fair Credit Reporting Act mandates observation of the alerts, promising an end to this maddening practice of granting credit to imposters using personal information known to be stolen, but the mechanism for doing so is unclear. Credit industry officials fought strict legislative language, arguing that consumers would be frustrated by burdensome requirements to prove they are who they say they are once they place a fraud alert on their account. Consumers will stop using the fraud alert system if it is too cumbersome, the industry argues. Lawmakers bought that line of thinking, so credit firms are merely mandated to use "reasonable" procedures to confirm the identity of an applicant. Of course, it's unclear who decides what "reasonable" is, and experts fear the measure will be watered down so much as to be useless. A reasonable measure might be as simple as requesting a glance at a driver's license, for example. As we will see in Chapter 5, rarely has the requirement to produce a license stopped any criminal.

"A careful balancing has to be done with regards to stopping ID theft but not strangling the credit system," said Joe Rubin, executive director of technology and e-commerce at the U.S. Chamber of Commerce, an advocate for retail America. "If a consumer applies for credit and can't get it because of a fraud alert, if they want to get their 10 percent off at Macy's, but can't, they will be frustrated with the system. It will be harming them instead of helping them."[50]

Norm Magnuson, spokesman for the Consumer Data Industry Association, which lobbies on behalf of the credit bureaus, said he thought legislators managed to strike a good balance with the bill.

"You try and implement a system that restricts incidence of fraud without restricting consumer habits," he said. Stricter provisions, such as some antifraud measures tried in states like California, "might be more tedious than consumers originally envision."[51]

Identity theft victims were never given the choice: Would you surrender the ability to get a new credit card at a moment's notice for a guarantee that your imposter couldn't either? The credit industry made that choice for them.

***

The industry's favoring of market share over consumer safety has been consistent across the decades. Even as federal regulators get around to insisting on new safeguards, clever marketing types inside the industry continue to develop ingenious new instruments that place consumers at risk. Having been prevented from sending out unsolicited credit cards, facilitating the fraud wave of the 1960s, the industry seemed bound and determined to find another aggressive way to market their lending. And as the century drew to a close, it had been found.

Once the market for new credit card consumers had all but dried up—by the 1990s, Americans were averaging 10 credit cards per consumer—financial institutions had to find a new way to gain market share. Outside of seducing 18-year-old college students, stealing account balances from rivals seemed the only way. Enter convenience checks.

Convenience checks work almost like cash. Cardholders get them in the mail, and with the stroke of a pen, they can shift balances from one credit card to another, usually with the enticement of a lower interest rate, at least temporarily. They seem the ideal instrument for a revolving debt holder who is starting to run out of time to pay down a high-interest rate card. The checks can also be used to make a single, large payments for high-ticket retail goods.

But when stolen from a mailbox, convenience checks are exceedingly convenient for identity thieves. Unlike credit cards, convenience checks don't usually require consumers to call an 800 number to activate them—American Express being a notable exception.[52] Banks don't follow up on the checks and don't miss them when they are gone. A thief hits the jackpot when he or she finds a convenience check packet inside a mailbox. There are 30 days of free money inside. Industrious criminals can even score additional convenience checks simply by calling the credit card issuer and asking it to send more, then watching for the valuable mail to arrive.

Yet financial institutions can hardly keep themselves from mailing them out; a U.S. attorney who prosecutes ID theft cases relayed a story recently of his dogged efforts to convince his credit card company to stop mailing them to his house, as he fears ID theft. After months of calls, he says, the bank simply told him, "We can't. Another department sends those out."[53] A Washington state legislator discovered the same thing when she asked that convenience checks stop filling her mailbox. "I've asked for them to stop, but those little checks keep coming," said Senator Margarita Prentice, D-Seattle. "That's the reason I got a shredder."[54] State legislators have attempted to limit credit card firms' ability to send out the blank checks; and, of course, the industry has battled those efforts. Privately, even bankers often don't like the checks. At a meeting of bank fraud fighters in Gleneden Beach, Oregon, investigators conceded that they face the daily nuisance of the almost perfect crime—a checking account opened by an identity thief with a few dollars, then bolstered by a stolen credit card convenience check, turned into cash by daily withdrawals from an ATM machine. Criminals using this scheme often have 30 days or more until the consumer reports the fraudulent transaction.[55]

The convenience check, the credit card industry's latest reckless market share trick, is perhaps the least secure financial instrument ever designed. In fact, the industry expects consumers to supply the security device. Fleet Bank once bragged to its customers in a mailing that its FastLoan checks were so easy to use that they were literally "live" checks. Sign them on the front, endorse them on the back, and deposit them at any bank with whatever identification the bank may require. The notice came with a caution: "If you choose not to accept this loan offer, please write 'VOID' across the attached check and destroy it."[56]

But even more alarming for consumers than being left to secure the checks themselves—legally, consumers could be left paying the bill for fraud. Credit card convenience checks lack the protections of the credit cards themselves, according to a Federal Reserve advisory panel. There is no $50 liability limit, a staple of consumer protection with plastic. The fraud-ready paper checks have no such legal limit. The distinction is only spelled out to cardholders in small print.[57] Meanwhile, using the check is just like making a cash withdrawal—interest charges start racking up right away, along with an automatic cash advance fee of 2 to 5 percent. While in celebrated cases of identity theft, consumers have not been held liable for convenience check spending by imposters, and refunds have been issued, it's not clear what happens in the uncelebrated cases.

"When consumer rights are dependant on the good will of the company, and dependent on who can sit on the phone for an hour, and dependent on who can speak good English, I'm concerned," said Consumers Union's Gail Hillebrand.[58]

***

Convenience checks are simply the latest in a long line of choices made by America's credit industry to push more and more borrowing toward Americans, with little regard to the security of the devices. Whether it's the mass mailing of live credit cards, the reluctance to cancel accounts exposed in Internet chat rooms, or the prevalence of convenience checks, credit issuers do what any MBA student would expect them to do—as long as losses from fraud rise slower than market share gains, the aggressive marketing tactics will remain, at least until Congress prohibits them, or the fraud becomes so widespread that it starts to eat into profits, or the tide of consumer goodwill really begins to turn.

But the credit-granting industry is only half of the identity theft story. While readers may be thoroughly unimpressed by the security measures put in place by the credit industry—such as asking consumers to write VOID across convenience checks— billions of dollars have been spent to create the world's largest database of information to keep dibs on consumers and how well they handle their debts. The credit reporting system is the most complete set of information in the world—far more thorough than any government census. It is designed exclusively to create the perfect actuarial tables for credit issuers, allowing them to carpet-bomb just the right people with their credit applications and cut out whole clumps of people who might be risky. But while this dataset is enormous and powerful and has served the credit industry incredibly well, it is also perhaps the world's "dirtiest" database, riddled with so many errors some surveys say half the consumer reports in it are wrong.

While credit card issuers have recklessly shoved easy access to money at consumers, putting millions of consumers at risk of identity theft, it's the credit bureaus—the other half of the unholy alliance that keeps America's credit system rolling—that preserve the problems. The national archivists of financial sins, the credit bureaus record every interaction consumers have with the credit firms, and don't let go. If the data were accurate, perhaps most would think that fair. But it's the credit reporting system that turns all these momentary crimes, the misspent convenience checks, the stolen credit cards, into a permanent false record attached to victims' names. It's the credit reporting system that is really to blame for the fact that America's identity theft crisis won't go away. The industry is the true author of the Kafkaesque novel 27 million Americans have found themselves playing an unexpected role in during the past 5 years.

4

THE TRIAL

The credit industry simply refuses to accept change. It is a reckless dinosaur, much like a 100-year-old who refuses to stop driving a car.

—Consumer attorney David Szwak

Every identity theft starts with a mistake. Someone fails to verify the identity of a credit applicant at a gas station, retail store, cell phone shop, or bank. Criminals who have a good enough story, either on paper or in person, get away with it. Mistakes happen; the consequence of a momentary lapse of reason. A few stolen items later, the fraudulent account is closed, and eventually, the ID theft linked to that identity is stopped. The criminal's trail quickly grows cold. Some retailers lick their wounds, write off their losses, and move on. Consumers have that disappointing feeling of violation that comes with being impersonated, but quickly, it fades.

And it would all end there if not for America's great database of mistakes.

The credit reporting agencies track the financial moves of virtually every citizen who participates in the economy. Any fiscal mishap, such as late payment of a credit card bill, is likely to find its way into this database of financial sins. The data is accumulated with incredible diligence, or at least, in incredible amounts. The problem is, the database, like all databases, is dumb, and it never forgets. It can't tell the difference between you and your imposter. The database doesn't know the difference between a five-year-old unpaid credit card bill and a five-year-old identity theft attack. One is just as haunting as the other.

A single black mark on a credit report caused by an identity thief can prevent a would-be homebuyer from obtaining a mortgage or stop a student from getting a student loan. As this chapter shows, God help those who try to erase that black mark in the financial sin database. For most consumers, the pain of identity theft is not caused by the criminals; it's caused by a system tilted so steeply against them that it simply isn't designed to forget, forgive, or even fix mistakes.

The credit reporting system was designed to rescue lenders from giving credit to consumers with a history of defaulting on loans. Today's systems were built to be digital private investigators, capable of sniffing out any delinquent accounts that might be lurking somewhere in an applicant's past—under a maiden name or an old address—and warning off potential creditors. They were designed to be thorough, not accurate, with a bias toward revealing more information about applicants, not less. Credit histories are often marred by a plethora of mistakes, even supplemented by information from other consumers who have similar names or Social Security numbers, all in the name of giving lenders the maximum possible information before they give money away. Better nine innocent people are denied credit than one guilty debtor be granted another loan, the thinking goes. For that reason, it's far easier to enter false information into the financial sin database than to delete it.

The emergence of identity theft into an electronic system designed to favor completeness over accuracy has been an unmitigated disaster. In the end, identity theft victims find themselves completely at the mercy of this system and the farcical process that's been designed to deal with inaccuracies and errors. Meanwhile, the credit bureaus, titans of American capitalism, continue to expand their domains and reap enormous profits—including profits from the crisis itself—even as they largely escape the responsibility they bear for enabling the identity theft epidemic.

***

Equifax, TransUnion, and Experian. Few Americans can rattle off their three names, yet these three companies have much more impact on their daily lives than any government office ever will. The firms hold data on nearly 210 million Americans, anyone who has ever received any kind of credit, virtually every adult in the nation.[1] When a consumer wants to buy a house, it's not really the bank that stands between buyer and money—it's the consumer's credit score, generated by the credit reporting agencies through a mixture of personal spending history and a proprietary formula that tries to predict the financial future based on past performances. The system is vast. Three million credit reports are issued every day. Two billion data points arrive at the bureaus every month.[2]

Consumers usually have little idea what the criterion are for good credit or bad credit or what can be done to fix any problems. Most don't even know they have a problem, until they are sitting embarrassed at a car dealership, until they receive a rejection notice from a credit card company, or until they miss out on a home in a fast-moving market because their mortgage application has been denied. They might be told their credit score was too low, that they failed the credit industry's test. More likely, they simply get a cryptic message, a "notice of adverse action."

Secrecy has always been the hallmark of the credit reporting industry. For years the credit score used to give a thumbs-up or thumbs-down was a carefully guarded secret. Car dealerships and banks were forbidden from sharing the results of a credit inquiry with customers, under pain of death by the credit reporting agencies—who vowed to shut out any business which violated that contractual obligation. Since no lender can work without access to the credit reporting system, keeping scores a secret was effectively the law of the land. Years of heavy consumer criticism eventually made the industry relent in the late 1990s, and now, credit scores are sold to consumers online. But the spirit of secrecy still shrouds the industry.

And secrecy always breeds mistakes. The massive national database of financial sins is perhaps the dirtiest database ever created. Study after study has shown that credit reports are riddled with inaccuracies. In December 2002, for example, a study by the Consumer Federation of America and the National Credit Reporting Association found that credit scores for one-third of consumers vary by 50 points. For 4 percent of them, the variation was at least 100 points. The study concluded that because of the variations, one-fifth of consumers, about 40 million Americans, are at risk of being misclassified into the subprime mortgage market. Over the lifetime of a 30-year, $150,000 mortgage, that could cost a consumer more than $124,000 in extra interest.[3]

Other studies suggest the situation is even worse. A 1991 Consumers Union study found 20 percent of credit reports contained a major inaccuracy that could affect a consumer's eligibility for credit, and 48 percent contained inaccurate information of some kind.[4] A year 2000 version of the same study found much the same, indicating more than 50 percent of credit reports contained inaccuracies that could lead to denial of credit or a higher cost of credit. The errors included mistaken identities, misapplied charges, uncorrected errors, misleading information, and variation between information reported by the various credit repositories.[5]

A 1998 survey by the U.S. Public Interest Research Group found that 7 in 10 of the 133 credit reports it surveyed contained errors of some kind; about 3 in 10 of the credit reports contained serious errors that could lead to a denied loan, the group said. Four in 10 had incorrect names, Social Security numbers, birth dates, or addresses.[6]

But perhaps the most damning study was published by the Federal Reserve Board in 2003, which looked at a quarter of a million credit reports and found that nearly 70 percent had some missing information and one-third had errors that could result in the denial of credit.[7] The researchers also found that among accounts reported with a major derogatory piece of information as the most recent addition, such as a significant delinquency, almost three-fifths of the reports were not up to date. In other words, when bad news tops your credit report, it's likely to stay on top.[8]

The credit industry denies these torrid error rates and rightly points out that the consumer group studies didn't utilize statistically significant samples. Consumers Union, for example, only studied a selection of consenting employee credit reports for privacy reasons. The industry claims "an extremely small percentage" of errors in its data.[9] But the industry had its chance to verify its claims in 2003 when Congress's investigative arm, the General Accounting Office (GAO), was ordered to do a study of credit report error rates and their impact. But the credit bureaus said they didn't keep statistics on accuracy and wouldn't give the GAO raw data to perform the test itself.

"While we asked the three major [credit reporting agencies] CRAs to provide data on the frequency, type, and cause of errors in credit reports, they told us that they did not have data that would specifically respond to our request," the GAO report said. "The CRAs also told us that they compete with each other on the basis of the accuracy and completeness of their credit reports and were reluctant to provide us with any data they considered proprietary."[10]

***

The problem of credit reporting errors has lurked just below the radar for decades, because it is a problem of class warfare.

America's better off—those with a FICO credit score of over 725, which includes about half of all Americans—have little to fear from the occasional credit report mistake. Knock a few points off that score with mistaken late payment entries, and an applicant will still get his or her house or car. No hassle, no one is the wiser.

For years, inaccurate credit reports really only hurt the fringe of America, those on the credit bubble. To consumers on the borderline, or below it, a single error or two on a credit report can be the difference between owning a home and renting. But these outliers didn't deserve special treatment, manual review of credit reports to spot such errors, or a real procedure for fixing them. America's credit-loving system perpetuates a "debtor's prison" attitude—once your credit is less than perfect, you deserve what you get.

But identity theft has changed all that. It has brought the glaring consequences of credit report inaccuracies into the mainstream. Now, the incredibly flawed system of the credit reporting agencies is an equal-opportunity nightmare.

Attorneys who work with consumers trying to help them clean error-riddled credit reports describe the credit reporting agencies as drunken godfathers, running the credit system with an iron fist, defending computer systems and procedures so arcane they can be incapable of fixing their own errors. And this incredibly flawed system has been entrenched since the 1970s, largely immune from scrutiny. How immune?

Participants in the system enjoy remarkable legal insulation from their errors. The Fair Credit Reporting Act of 1970 made the firms who furnish information to the credit bureaus immune from private lawsuits, whether the information is accurate or not. Only state and federal agencies can sue for inaccuracy. Credit reporting agencies, meanwhile, couldn't be sued for retelling wrong information, despite the devastating impact that can have on individual lives.

The immunity was granted to encourage full participation in the system—lenders who were afraid of defamation lawsuits might not want to share customer payment histories, the industry argued. Because the system was designed to tolerate errors, it was overrun with them. By 1990, consumers just waking up to the idea that they even had credit files were screaming about their inaccuracy.[11]

A 1996 update to the Fair Credit Reporting Act added in some consumer rights. Still, credit bureaus could only be sued for failing to follow "reasonable procedures" to maintain accuracy. Proving negligence only earns the victim actual damages and attorney's fees. Consumers must prove "willful" retelling of erroneous credit information in order to gain punitive damage judgments against the bureaus[12]—an extremely high legal barriers that's akin to pre-meditated violation of federal law. Still, that's the area where consumer attorneys have trained their attention. Lawsuits against the credit bureaus generally attack their procedures for guarding against and investigating mistakes. In a few celebrated cases, credit bureau procedures and computer systems have been deemed so faulty that judges found them in willful violation of the Fair Credit Reporting Act.

That same law gave consumers only one method to address the inaccuracies in the national financial sin database; they must take their case to the credit bureaus. They were not allowed to go directly to the furnisher of the error, such as the retail stores that reported an account as delinquent, thanks to the misdeeds of an identity thief. The consumer must report the issue to Equifax, TransUnion, or Experian. And until recently, when an update to the law provided some exceptions to this restriction, only at those three firms were identity theft victims given a chance to clear their ruined credit.

And there, they entered a digital kangaroo court. The bureaus are secretive about their dispute process, but consumer attorneys have managed to piece together much of it through a lengthy set of lawsuits and depositions of former and current bureau employees.

***

Credit reporting is big business. Atlanta-based Equifax had $178 million in net income on more than $1 billion in revenue in 2002, most from the United States and Canada. California-based Experian, owned by British conglomerate Great Universal Stores, said it had operating income of $290 million last year on revenue of $1.2 billion. Privately held TransUnion, based in Chicago, doesn't disclose financial information, but it is roughly the same size as its chief competitors.[13]

Yet the duty to care for consumer errors nets precious few resources from the billion-dollar firms. Court documents reveal that customer service representatives are often given less than five minutes to handle each consumer's identity theft crisis.

In a deposition taken during 2001, a TransUnion employee named Eileen Little revealed that while between 30,000 and 40,000 consumer disputes arrive weekly, they were handled by 80 "dispute investigators" in the dispute department—a tiny portion of the 3,600 employees who made up the company. Employees there were paid between $10 and $17 an hour and were expected to handle between 10 and 14 cases per hour. And their future prospects at the company, in addition to their bonuses and raises, were directly tied to how quickly they processed disputes.[14]

One representative at Experian explained in a deposition that when she began working at the firm, agents were required to handle 62 calls per day, but within a couple of years, the quotas had increased to 100 complaint calls per day, leaving them only an average of 3 to 4 minutes per call. The quotas were strictly enforced, and representatives were told they could lose their jobs for failing to handle an adequate number of daily calls.

During training, customer service representatives were specifically taught to mistrust consumers. Moreover, one customer service representative explained that Experian's call center would block an individual's number who called too many times.[15]

In response to questions about the deposition, given by former employee Vicky Thompson, Experian denied that it has a quota system, or that it controls the length of calls handled by customer service agents. In a statement, the company said it had "established standards . . . like any other business," but insisted those standards were flexible based on the nature of the consumer calls. A TransUnion representative said the same about Little's deposition, adding that the firm has 100 employees who work full time helping fraud victims.

Experian also denied that customer service agents were trained to mistrust consumers. They are trained to spot liars, however, the company said. It has to, because so many consumers and small businesses are actively trying to cheat the system, Experian claims. The firm says about one-third of all contacts into the company come from credit repair clinics, trying to convince the firm to remove accurate delinquencies on credit reports. The skepticism is necessary, Experian says, because "40 percent of all proof documents received from such repair clinics are actually fraudulent." And while it denies consumer calls are blocked, the company does place some consumers on a "write-only" basis if they are threatening, obscene, or abusive to call center operators.[16]

Either way, there is little disputing consumer dissatisfaction with credit bureaus. And prospects for renewed emphasis and spending on the dispute resolution process were dimmed by revelations late in 2003 that all three credit reporting firms were in the process of moving their dispute centers overseas. TransUnion had publicly stated that 100 percent of the mail it receives regarding customer disputes is handled in India, and it planned to farm out the dispute process to a third party there. Equifax used a vendor in Jamaica that performs the "very beginning" of the reinvestigation process, the company said. Experian publicly denied reports that it was "actively testing" an overseas vendor, but told the *San Francisco Chronicle* that it was "evaluating every option on the table, and offshoring is one of them."[17]

***

It's not hard to see why the credit reporting system is so riddled with errors that seemingly can't be removed once there is understanding of how the system works and why. Essentially, the credit bureau database was built to make sure no piece of potentially negative information about a prospective borrower would escape a lender. Mistyped Social Security numbers, women who change names when they are married, men who move frequently—clever software programs with names like Shark have been designed by the bureaus to hunt down these variations, to ensure no one can escape a potential black mark from the past.[18]

The problem is, the software often outsmarts itself, and has for years. And in its zest to uncover every stone in a consumer's financial past, it often lumps several people's pasts together.

To understand how credit bureau databases work, one must erase the obvious mental picture that comes to mind—a set of complete credit reports, one for each consumer, sitting in a virtual file cabinet in a very large computer. In fact, there really is no such thing as a standing credit report, according to consumer advocates. Equifax disputes that description, saying their systems do maintain individual files on consumers, but agrees they change daily, even multiple times each day.[19]

But lawyers who regularly sue the bureaus say their systems collect massive amounts of "credit events" one at a time. They are not sorted or separated in any way; they just lie en masse in a massive virtual bin. Only when a business requests a report are a series of credit events tied together to create a momentary snapshot of a consumer's financial life—the credit report. And that report is a one-shot deal. Once it is created and sold off, it disappears, and all the bits are separated and go back into the bin again.

That's important because there's really no way for a consumer to order the exact credit report a lender has used to deny them credit. All a consumer can do is order his or her version of the collection of credit events, called in the industry a credit "disclosure." Credit reports and credit disclosures are very different. When a bank or auto dealer asks for a full credit report, they get all credit events that might even closely match the information the applicant provides. For example, if an applicant has a name similar to another person who lives in that ZIP code, and seven of the nine digits in the Social Security number match, their two credit histories might become intermingled. The financial backgrounds of both people might be blended and presented to the creditor. When that occurs, the applicants can be denied credit because of black marks in this blended person's past. Similarly, if an identity thief uses a victim's exact Social Security number but with a different name and birthday, to obtain credit, the information will often be mingled into the victim's report.

The idea is to give the lender the most possible information, so no consumer can get away with hiding a defaulted loan underneath a maiden name or an old address. But what results is the source of a large part of the credit reporting nightmare, a so-called mixed file. Once a file is mixed, there's Hell to pay to get it unmixed.

But there's often no way for a consumer to know he or she is a victim of a mixed file, because consumer disclosures, like those ordered on Internet sites, usually don't mix such credit events. Disclosures are "cleaned up" versions of credit reports. They only include events that precisely match all information supplied by the applicant. Since the disclosures aren't used to make credit decisions, the credit bureaus need not dig so deep.

That's why consumers who are denied credit because of a mixed-file situation, when their digital twin has a bad credit history, often don't understand what's happened. If they ask the credit bureau to see the exact credit report given to the lender who denied their loan, they can't see it—it's gone. And the lender is, by contract, prevented from sharing its copy of the report. Meanwhile, the consumer's own copy, the copy he or she orders from the credit bureau, can contain none of these errors.

Identity thieves figured these system flaws out years ago. This is why thieves often hijack the identity of someone with a similar name. The trail is easily obscured in a database that is so easily confused. The identity thief's only goal is to submit a credit application that generates a favorable credit report or credit score, so the credit is granted. "Neighborhood" names and similar addresses often do the trick.

According to the Electronic Privacy Information Center (EPIC), in one instance, an identity thief applied for a credit card at Dillard's department store using her own name and address and the victim's Social Security number. The thief's first initial and last name were the same as the victim's. TransUnion provided Dillard's with the victim's credit report because the first initial, last name, and Social Security number on the application matched its credit report file. Dillard's approved the credit card, and the thief was issued a credit card under the victim's identity.[20]

Fixing a mixed-file situation can take years. In perhaps the most notorious case, Judy C. Thomas, of Oregon, spent six years battling TransUnion after the agency merged her file with that of a woman named Judith L. Upton, who was born the same year and whose Social Security number varied from Thomas's by only one digit. Credit bureaus sometimes tell their sorting programs to disregard differences in women's last names because they can change their name in marriage. Upton had a series of bad debts to her name, and they leaked into Thomas's credit file. Thomas, a 57-year-old real estate agent, said she repeatedly notified TransUnion of the erroneous information listed on her report in 1996, only to see some of the deleted accounts reappear again in 1999, when she applied for a mortgage. Even as late as December 2001, nearly 18 months after she had sued TransUnion, the firm still listed Judy Thomas's a.k.a. as Judith Upton.[21]

***

Thomas quickly became the poster child for anyone who'd ever faced an uphill battle fighting with the credit bureaus. Her struggle to have erroneous information deleted—and its continued reappearance in her file—is the trial many identity theft victims face, a problem known in the industry as *repollution*. Much like the game of Whack-a-Mole, those trying to clean up pockmarked credit reports find the errors just keep coming back.

A consumer's first step when disputing a listing in their credit report is to contact the credit bureau and initiate a reinvestigation. Under the Fair Credit Reporting Act, credit bureaus must hold these trials. But the law says nothing about making it a fair fight. In the world of credit reporting agency reinvestigations, consumers are considered guilty until they prove themselves innocent. In fact, in the most common form of hearing, called in the industry an ACDV, or automated consumer dispute verification, the consumer nearly always loses, by design. The name indicates exactly what this process entails. There is no review of documentation, merely a restatement of the accusation from the company that furnished the black credit mark in the first place. The system is designed to satisfy the absolute minimum letter of the law as set in the Fair Credit Reporting

Act, which says the agencies must act on a consumer dispute within 30 days.

The dispute process is so automated that it's virtually automatic. When a consumer files a dispute claiming that a certain credit furnisher, such as a credit card firm, has placed an erroneous demerit on his or her credit report, the process is straightforward. Consumers might be inclined to mail the credit reporting agency piles of documentation, notarized forms, or signed affidavits arguing their innocence. No matter what extensive paperwork the consumer submits, his or her entire case is boiled down to a tiny two-digit computer code.

When a credit bureau sends the automated query to the credit card firm, all that is being asked is: "Did you really send us this data once before?" The answer—another tiny electronic clip—comes back yes, nearly always. End of trial. As long as the computer screen on the credit furnisher matches the computer screen at the credit bureau, the customer—in this case, the credit card firm—wins. It is a kangaroo court, a rubber stamp process in which the lender is always right. Len Bennett, a consumer lawyer who has sued the credit bureaus repeatedly, described process this way in congressional testimony on June 4, 2003:

> The three bureaus collaborated through their trade organization to automate the entire reinvestigation process using an online computer program, E-Oscar. Upon receiving a written dispute, often in the form of a detailed letter with documents attached, the CRA assigns the dispute to its dispute department.
>
> The employees within the department are usually hourly employees and are minimally paid. In the case of Equifax, things are even worse. The CRA contracts out its FCRA responsibilities to a foreign company based in Jamaica

which uses only foreign labor for its "investigations." The job of a CRA dispute department employee, even if titled "investigator," is solely data entry. No matter how detailed the written dispute, the CRA will merely translate it into a two digit code and, usually by automated means (ACDV), send a message to the furnisher identifying the code its employee believes best describes the dispute. The employees of all three CRAs operate under a quota system whereby each employee is expected to process all of the disputes of an individual consumer in less than four minutes. Worse still, the "codes" used by both the CRAs and their subscribers (the furnishers) are limited in number and rarely describe the actual basis for the consumer's dispute. For example, in two of my recent cases, both identical, consumers Van Evans and Ray Bailey wrote dispute letters to all three bureaus. The disputes were conveyed in great detail and explained that the consumers were not responsible for the disputed accounts and that any signatures claimed to be theirs were forgeries. Each consumer dispute letter also enclosed copies of handwriting exemplars such as signatures on driver's license, military IDs and other credit cards. Van Evans had also obtained a copy of the forged note and included it in his dispute letter. When Equifax and TransUnion received the letters, their employees simplified the disputes to a code and the description "not his/hers." This was all the furnishers received. In a deposition taken in a Pennsylvania case, TransUnion's responsible employee explained the CRA's "investigation procedure."

Q . . . [T]he dispute investigator looks at the consumer's written dispute and then reduces that to a code that gets transmitted to the furnisher?

A. Yes.

Q. Does the furnisher ever see the consumer's written dispute?

A. No.

Q. Are there any instances in which the dispute investigator would call the consumer to find out more about the dispute?

A. No.

This is consistent with CRA testimony in every other case of which I am aware. The Bureaus do not convey the full dispute or forward any of the documents to the furnishers. As an expected result, nearly all consumer disputes are verified against the consumers. . . .

It is not an unfair characterization to describe the investigation process as a shell game wherein the CRAs and furnishers have worked in concert to protect one another from their already minimal liabilities under the FCRA.[22]

In fact, he went on to say, the credit bureaus actually train lenders such as credit card companies to do the least possible work and to merely make sure their data screens mirror each other, so that consumer disputes will be processed as quickly as possible. A Capital One representative, during a deposition, said she asked representatives of the three bureaus if she should have her staff go the extra mile and pull billing statements or do other research during a dispute. "In each case the bureau rep said, 'No, we want you to verify it. We want you to make our system look like your system. So that's what we've been doing.'"[23]

But even if an ID theft victim is successful in convincing one of the bureaus that an entry should be removed from his or her credit report, the battle is hardly won—because credit black marks are like computer viruses. Until they are all stamped out simultaneously, there is a chance any error could maddeningly reappear. Furnishers, such as credit card companies, regularly send massive credit event data via tape or other electronic means to the credit bureaus for inclusion in the "bin." Even if a credit agency removed the information, that doesn't necessarily mean the furnisher has removed the entry. So it can easily reappear when the furnisher supplies a new batch of data to the credit bureaus, repolluting the credit report. Identity theft victims have seen this error occur again and again. That's precisely what happened to Judy Thomas and thousands of Americans who think they've cleaned up their credit reports, only to find, like a bad cold, the black marks keep reappearing. The 2003 update to the Fair Credit Reporting Act includes provisions designed to stop repollution. In addition, an ad-hoc group of credit industry firms calling itself the Financial Services Roundtable plans to introduce a simplified identity theft reporting system that allows victims to call just a single firm, such as their local bank, which then will spread the bad news out to all companies in the credit system through an Identity Theft Assistance Center.[24] Theoretically, that could end the repollution problem, but it remains to be seen how well the system will work.

***

The firms' reticence to invest in new systems and employees that would ensure accuracy is understandable, and predictable, when viewed as a business proposition. After all, the firms make money selling credit reports whether they are accurate or not.

Ensuring the accuracy of the credit reports is in reality a volunteer effort at the moment. And in fact, the very inaccuracy and sluggishness to fix errors that has led to the identity theft crisis has opened up a new revenue stream for the credit reporting agencies.

Through a sudden change of heart in the late 1990s, the secretive credit reporting agencies now have a consumer face, and sell some of their services directly to consumers. Identity theft, the firms realized, was a great opportunity to boost profits.

Now, they all make good money on ID theft. The sale of credit reports online, direct to consumers, is one of their fastest-growing businesses—and why not, with nearly every consumer advocate and government official recommending regular credit report check-ups in the wake of the identity theft crisis? Experian was the first to recognize the potential of direct-to-consumer sales, and the firm is very proud of its Experian Consumer Direct division. More than 30 million consumers visited its family of credit reporting web sites in early 2003.[25] Under brands like Free-CreditReport.com, ConsumerInfo.com, CreditExpert.com, and CreditMatters.com, the company delivered more than 1.5 million scores in 2002 and in 2003 more than 1.6 million members belong to its credit monitoring service,[26] offered under the various Internet brands.[27] Subscriptions cost $89.95 annually for the Experian service, suggesting the firm could be earning at an annual clip of $100 million for it—an estimate that's reasonable, considering it paid $130 million to acquire ConsumerInfo.com in 2002 from Homestore.com.[28] Alarmed consumers concerned about ID theft have rushed to sign up and pay $89.95 to get late notice that they've already been victimized by an identity thief and to have access to their own data, which now legally must be given to them for free. Those same credit reports cost credit furnishers a few pennies each.

Experian is even trying to profit from the dispute process, mandated as a consumer right by Congress. In the firm's marketing materials for ConsumerInfo.com, Experian says subscriptions to the service offer "Improved! Credit Dispute Forms and Tips. Easily correct mistakes that could be hurting your credit rating."[29] The obvious implication is that paid subscribers have better access to Experian's dispute-resolution process than nonsubscribers.

During 2003, EPIC filed a complaint with the FTC that Experian's sales tactics for ConsumerInfo.com were unethical.

The heavily advertised free credit reports offered all over the Internet and on television weren't free at all, EPIC wrote, but instead were sneaky "free-to-paid" conversion products, designed to seduce people into signing up to Experian's pricey credit monitoring services. Furthermore, EPIC charged, Experian was trying to profit off its own mistakes.

"The company markets their service with an advertisement that plays on consumer fears of inaccurate credit reports and pushes their credit monitoring service as necessary to maintain accuracy. In other words, here is a credit reporting agency promoting its subscription service by capitalizing on its own failure to adequately fulfill its statutory responsibility to maintain the maximum possible accuracy of credit reports," the complaint alleges.[30]

Equifax and TransUnion are also making money off ID theft; Equifax said it saw revenues of $22 million in the fourth quarter of 2002 from its direct-to-consumer offerings, though that figure includes other products besides its scores and reports.[31] It offers e-mail alerts on possible fraudulent activity, $20,000 in identity theft insurance, and unlimited access to credit reports for $9.95 a month. TransUnion sells credit reports from all three bureaus for $34.95 and ongoing credit monitoring for $10.95 a quarter.

The industry defends these new profit centers. "Any criticism of this nature is like criticizing the software industry for making anti-virus software," Equifax said in a statement. The comparison would only make sense, however, if the antivirus software firms wrote computer viruses, too.[32]

***

In addition to the new consumer face, the credit bureaus have sought to extend their empires in a number of other directions in recent years. The unholy alliance between credit card companies and credit bureaus saw the card companies begin peppering bureaus with more and more frequent requests for information—some pull credit reports as often as once a month in search of hot leads, adding nicely to bureau profits. But such repeated requests for reports have also been profitable for the credit card firms, too. By 2003, consumer credit experts spotted a new, disturbing trend: Credit card companies would notice if consumers had made late payments on other credit cards and use that opportunity to raise the interest rates on their card. In fact, credit reporting agencies now offer daily account reviews, with names like notification services and risk triggers, allowing the credit card companies to raise rates the instant any late payment is noted.[33] In other words, cardholders with a teaser rate of 9 percent could suddenly find themselves paying 22 percent interest, even if they hadn't missed a single payment on the card—because the credit card firm had given itself the right to raise the interest rate if the consumer was late on any of his or her other bills. The move has been explained by credit card firms as a natural step taken against consumers who demonstrate they are a credit risk, but consumer advocates complain this is just a good excuse to squeeze higher interest rates out of consumers; after all, it's hardly automatic that late payment of one credit card means late payment on all others.

Credit reports are also being used by the auto insurance industry to squeeze consumers. Insurers now regularly pull credit reports when new customers arrive and charge higher rates to consumers with bad credit. The link between bad credit and the likelihood a driver will suffer a car accident or car theft has only been tenuously established by the auto insurance industry. But drivers with bad credit have few options. Homeowner's insurance underwriters are pulling the same stunt with home fire and theft insurance policies, as well.[34] A number of state legislatures have attempted, so far unsuccessfully, to limit or bar the practice.

Meanwhile, the big three credit bureaus have moved far beyond credit-related industries, into areas such as employment screening. But use of America's history of sins for such purposes can have unsavory consequences. Employee screening was the cause of legal run-ins for Equifax in the early 1990s, after the firm had been hired by Delta Airlines to help background 600 former Pan Am employees who were job applicants. The New York attorney general charged that while checking Pan Am employees' personal references, Equifax illegally asked the job candidates about possible psychological problems or disabilities, physical problems, drugs use, excessive drinking, arrests, and activity in community service. Equifax settled a class-action lawsuit related to the incident in April 1993 for $4.6 million. Without saying it did anything wrong, Equifax settled with the New York attorney general's office by aggreeing to stop asking certain personal questions, and removed them from questionnaires.[35]

***

The 1993 settlement was hardly the first, or last, run-in that the credit bureaus have had with the law. The firms certainly haven't established reputations for being good corporate citizens. In fact, it's hard to find an industry with a longer rap sheet than the credit reporting business, exemplified by the long-standing battle the industry has enjoined with the Federal Trade Commission. The FTC has dragged the industry to court on dozens of occasions and has taken eight enforcement actions against the industry between 1996 and 2003, directly or indirectly related to credit report data accuracy.

In the most significant of these, the big three agencies agreed in January 2000 to pay a $2.5 million Federal Trade Commission fine to settle charges that they violated the Fair Credit Reporting Act.[36] In a 1996 amendment to the act, Congress ordered the agencies to provide toll-free telephone numbers at the bottom of credit reports so consumers could call the firms with complaints.

The law also required that the firms hire adequate staff to answer consumer questions. Instead, just as the identity theft epidemic had begun, the FTC found that the big three often simply didn't bother answering the phone. Millions of consumers who called received a busy signal or a message telling them to call back later. Other consumers were put on hold indefinitely.

With electronic crimes like identity theft, time is of the essence. As every day passes, criminals armed with fraudulently obtained Social Security numbers can wring more and more money out of the financial system and wrack up more and more headaches for the victim. But just as criminals were discovering how quickly they could work the system, the credit bureaus were providing permanent busy signals to consumers. Equifax agreed to pay $500,000 and Experian and TransUnion both paid $1 million to settle the charge; the firms admitted no wrongdoing.

The substantial fines weren't enough to drive the lesson home, however. In 2003, Equifax was fined another $250,000 by the Federal Trade Commission for essentially the same problem and for violating the terms of the 2000 settlement, which mandated that the bureaus answer consumer calls within 3.5 minutes on average and ensure 90 percent of callers don't get a busy signal.[37] Again, Equifax admitted no wrongdoing, in agreeing to the settlement.

Just how persistent the credit bureaus can be at misbehavior is evident from a 10-year battle the FTC had with TransUnion over the selling of consumer information to direct marketers, catalog companies, and other firms, in violation of the Fair Credit Reporting Act. The credit agencies are only allowed to share the data with businesses that have a pressing need to know the credit history of a consumer. But TransUnion found another revenue stream, selling all manner of personal financial data to marketing firms hungry for solid leads.

It's a long-standing practice for all three credit bureaus to "monetize" their rich databases by selling marketing data, compiled from credit reporting information and supplemented with outside data. Experian, for instance, sells a "bladder control" problems marketing list. You can buy that list for $150 per thousand names.[38]

But TransUnion went one step farther than targeted marketing lists. The firm was selling what are called tradelines in the industry—which include credit events, such as the granting of a new credit card, along with critical personal data such as Social Security numbers. This meant anytime consumers applied for credit, competitors would find out and immediately flood them with pitches for similar products.

Among the data being sold, according to the FTC: estimates of consumers' annual income, calculated from an individual consumer's credit data; the presence of an open mortgage, presence of a second open mortgage, and the open and closed dates and high credit amounts of both mortgages; and lists indicating the number of open automobile loans, loan type, the open and expiration dates for the lease or loan, and the high credit amount of the lease or loan.

In 1992, the FTC began legally attacking the sale of tradeline data. After an FTC order to discontinue to practice, which was honored by Equifax and Experian, TransUnion persisted. The firm argued it had a First Amendment right to sell the information. And it kept arguing—after a 1993 administrative judge upheld the FTC's order, after a second order by the FTC in 1994, after a 1998 trial verdict that sided with the FTC.[39] Finally, in 2002, the U.S. Supreme Court refused to hear the case, signaling the end of the 10-year fight. TransUnion says it finally stopped selling the data sometime in 2000—but not before it had earned eight more years of income on the fire sale of data while it strung out the legal battle.[40]

The FTC eventually shut down TransUnion's target marketing business, but the bureau was never penalized for selling the lists in the first place. It simply profited from the illegal venture until it had played the legal system as long as possible, says David Szwak, a consumer attorney and frequent critic of the credit bureaus. "TransUnion never had to disgorge any of the money it made by breaking the law repeatedly. There's a lot the bureaus get away with that FTC never touches them about," he said.[41]

Meanwhile, the companies still find ways to make money selling credit information anyway. Experian is now selling summarized credit statistics by ZIP code. According to Experian's fall 2003 Lift Services catalog, the service allows marketers to "Locate neighborhoods with recent and/or heavy credit purchase activity. Activity may indicate families in new housing developments and neighborhoods undergoing revitalization where households have diverse product and service needs."[42]

As the nation's protector of the consumer, the Federal Trade Commission is more aware of the problems with the credit bureaus than any other federal agency. According to figures obtained by a Freedom of Information Act request, identity theft-related complaints about the credit bureaus have skyrocketed since the FTC started keeping statistics. While 9,700 people filed complaints with the FTC about credit bureaus in 2001, nearly 13,300 complained in 2002, and almost 14,000 filed complaints in the first nine months of 2003.[43]

There's not a lot reason to believe the all the fines and government scrutiny will really cause the three bureaus to change their multibillion-dollar business strategies. Similar government censures and trivial fines have been issued before, but the bad habits appear to be entrenched. In 1992, the big three were the target of a Federal Trade Commission lawsuit, which was eventually taken on by attorneys general in 18 states. The firms were accused of failing to maintain accurate records on consumers. The states received settlements of $300,000 from TRW (now Experian), $150,000 from Equifax, and $222,000 from TransUnion to pay for investigation expenses. And the bureaus agreed to set up a toll-free number to answer consumer problems. They admitted no wrongdoing.

"Consumers throughout the country have complained that their credit reports are riddled with errors and that their attempts to correct these errors have fallen on deaf ears," New York state Attorney General Robert Abrams said at the time, in a statement that rings just as true 10 years later. But he added an optimistic prediction that now drips in irony. "This settlement will compel Equifax to maintain reasonable procedures for clearing up these inaccuracies and preventing them in the future."[44]

***

Who are these three companies with so much influence on our lives and our financial fortunes? The system is so entrenched in American capitalism, it might seem the three credit bureaus have always been a part of our lives. In fact, they are a relatively recent phenomenon.

Credit bureaus have their place. Economists say technology that lets lenders automatically assess risk before they lend money has dramatically increased the free flow of capital and was at least in part responsible for the economic boom of the 1990s. Credit histories and credit scoring gives banks and other firms more latitude to lend money to applicants on the fringes. Lending is entirely a risk-based business; armed with mathematical models that predict risk, many banks are able to push the edges a little more, putting capital in the hands of would-be borrowers who might otherwise not get their loans. At least, that's how it's supposed to work.

Founded in 1899 as Retail Credit Co., Equifax is the granddaddy of the bunch, the first major credit reporting company in the country. When brothers Cator and Guy Woolford opened the firm in Atlanta, they compiled credit records of local residents into their Merchants Guide, which they sold to retailers for $25 a year. The company grew steadily, and by 1920 had offices across the United States.[45] Hundreds of other credit bureaus imitated Retail Credit's success. But while the credit business and the credit bureau industry grew up together during the next five decades, the bureaus quickly gained an ugly reputation for using illegal methods to dig up dirt on potential borrowers.

By late 1960s, abuse in the industry was rife. Investigators were required to fill quotas of negative information on data subjects. Some fabricated negative information. Others collected lifestyle secrets on data subjects, including their sexual orientation, marital situation, drinking habits, and cleanliness. The agencies were criticized for maintaining outdated information, and in some cases, providing the file to law enforcement and other unauthorized people. Public outcry led to congressional inquiry and, eventually, the Fair Credit Reporting Act of 1970.[46] The law served to legitimize the industry, and even as it was being debated, the other two major credit bureaus would be born.

Retail Credit certainly had its run-ins with the federal regulators. In 1973, the FTC filed an antimonopoly suit against its consumer credit division and a complaint against its investigative practices, which allegedly included the use of field investigators to probe people's backgrounds. In 1976 the company changed its name to Equifax, short for "equitability in the gathering and presentation of facts," in an attempt to shed its reputation.[47]

Through the 1980s, the firm made aggressive worldwide acquisitions, and it now boasts a database of information on 400 million people, including the largest collection of such information on Latin American residents.[48]

***

Chicago-based TransUnion actually began its life, as its name might suggest, as a railcar leasing operation, then called the Union Tank Car Company. In 1968, the firm created a parent holding company called TransUnion and the following year acquired a local credit reporting firm called the Credit Bureau of Cook County. At the time, credit data was still maintained by hand—3.6 million card files in 400 seven-drawer cabinets, according to the company. But TransUnion spotted the power of automation and the opportunity that a national credit reporting agency created. TransUnion-affiliated offices sprung up around the country. Within 20 years, the firm boasts, this former railroad-oriented company had full national coverage and was now "maintaining and updating information on every single market-active consumer in the country."[49]

The most mysterious of the three credit bureaus, TransUnion is the only privately held company of the three—its financial results are a secret, and the firm doesn't have to file quarterly reports or answer reporter's questions like public companies do. It was purchased in 1981 by the Pritzker family of Chicago, perhaps the closest thing to the Rockefellers that our era has. Along with TransUnion, the family owns the Hyatt Hotel chain, the Royal Caribbean Cruise Line, and the conglomerate Marmon Group, with about 100 subsidiaries. The family name has a permanent place on the Forbes 400 list of richest Americans—in 2003, current Marmon Group CEO Thomas Pritzker was 22nd on the list, with an estimated $7.6 billion in assets himself. He's tied on the list with family patriarch Robert Allen Pritzker, who has about the same-sized bank account—a few steps above well-known billionaires like Amazon.com's Jeff Bezos and News Corp.'s Rupert Murdoch.

The Pritzker empire began with Ukrainian immigrant Nicholas Pritzker, who according to family legend taught himself to read by translating the *Chicago Tribune*.[50] He earned his law degree by age 30 and founded his own firm in Chicago in 1902. Nicholas' son A.N. Pritzker pushed the family away from practice of law and toward real estate speculation, but it was Nicholas's grandson Jay who, in the racy 1950s, turned the firm into an investing and acquisition powerhouse. In 1963, Jay and brother Robert acquired the Marmon Herrington Company, renamed it the Marmon Group, and put most of its subsidiaries under that single name. After a brief foray in the stock market as a public concern, Jay Pritzker took control of the firm again through a series of stock purchases and delisted the company in 1971. The family has continued to go on corporate spending sprees ever since. At the same time it acquired TransUnion in 1981, it was eyeing concert and sports ticket broker Ticketmaster, which it purchased in 1982 and later sold to Microsoft billionaire Paul Allen. In 1984, it acquired Braniff Airlines and later attempted to buy Pan Am. In 1999 and 2000, the Marmon Group spent $1 billion to buy 60 more companies.[51]

The Pritzkers are well-heeled philanthropists, with dozens of multimillion-dollar donations to universities and Chicago-area arts to their credit. But all the while, the fact that the Marmon Group is private has helped keep the family clear of the kind of scrutiny people like Microsoft CEO Bill Gates receives.

That is, until the death of Jay Pritzker in 1999 set the stage for an ugly and very public inheritance dispute among surviving children. In 2002, with Jay's brother Robert now the remaining patriarch, Robert's 18-year-old granddaughter Liesel Pritzker sued the family, saying surviving members had conspired to split up and sell off the $1 billion she had coming to her. The story has plenty of romance; in Hollywood, Liesel is known as Liesel Matthews, a budding young actress who played Harrison Ford's daughter in the 1997 hit *Air Force One* and also starred in *The Little Princess* in 1995.[52] Two months later, another member of the youngest Pritzker generation, 20-year-old Matthew Pritzker, a student at American University, also sued his family, alleging his $1 billion had been split up and sold off as well. Trust accounts had been "bled dry" and "completely emptied," he said.[53] The suits claim that essentially family members got together and signed a secret agreement to split the $15 billion family fortune among 11 relatives, each getting $1.3 billion—deftly done before Matthew and Liesel were of adult age, so they would be cut out of the money.[54] The family, of course, maintains the lawsuits are baseless. But that's the kind of family that controls data on "every single market-active consumer in the country."

***

Experian humbly began its existence as a tack-on business at Cleveland-based manufacturing conglomerate TRW. While the firm's main business was building aerospace, automotive, and defense industry products, a brilliant executive named D. Van Skilling was growing a small division called TRW Information Systems. In 1996, as Skilling reached near retirement age, he convinced TRW to spin off the now-burgeoning credit reporting business as its own company. It was sold to a group of investors, who left Skilling at the helm and changed the name to Experian.[55]

But the independence was short-lived. Within a few weeks, the investors sold the Orange County, California-based company to British retailing megacompany Great Universal Stores PLC—a famous European catalog sales firm whose most prominent brand name is Burberry. Experian, along with Equifax, now had a global presence. Great Universal saw Experian as a logical twenty-first-century extension of its worldwide marketing and sales business, and Experian quickly became the top performing group within GUS.[56]

Thanks to its marriage with GUS division CCN, Experian now had customers in 40 countries. And it was part of a conglomerate devoted to accumulating more and more business intelligence—personal data—for power and profit. Soon after the Experian purchase, for example, GUS gobbled up Metromail, a Lombard, Illinois, company that compiles public record information, in a deal worth nearly $1 billion. Metromail culls data from telephone directories and county real estate records and tracks, such as how long a person has lived in a home, the property's current assessment, and whether there are liens against it. The firm even tracks state certification licenses—for hunting and fishing, for example, or for occupations like beautician or manicurist.[57]

***

Global conglomerates with information on as many as 400 million people, with details as minute as manicurist licenses, have a lot of power—particularly if they have earned themselves congressionally blessed immunity from state law and earned their partners immunity from lawsuits. Still, consumer rage after decades of inaccuracies, along with the growing identity theft epidemic, has led to a surge of courtroom showdowns in recent years. The barrier to win damages is enormous—proving factual credit file errors isn't enough. Plaintiffs in credit bureau cases must prove the firms negligently or willfully violated the Fair Credit Reporting Act. Mere mistakes, however painful, aren't enough. But in recent years, there are indications that judges and juries are now poised and ready to penalize the big three. And some litigators believe attorneys who specialize in suing credit bureaus and credit furnishers may be sitting on the next tobacco-industry-scale litigation.

In 1998, a Mississippi federal court awarded $4.5 million to Terry Cousin after TransUnion confused his credit history with his brother's, then failed to correct the error for nearly 15 years—even after Cousin sued. "There has never been a reported case involving a credit reporting company that acted with such callous indifference toward a consumer and whose conduct was so reprehensible," said the judge who heard the case. But a federal appeals court rejected the award, saying Cousin had not presented enough evidence to prove that

TransUnion willfully violated the credit act.[58] Still, the case was a shot across the bow at the credit bureaus, signaling a new willingness for consumer attorneys to take such cases to trial. Lawyers say the bureaus are generally quick to settle such cases, fearing the predictable ire most juries feel for the credit industry.

That same year, Oregon resident Barbara Jorgensen won a $600,000 jury award for actual damages against TRW, now Experian, for the harm and aggravation that resulted from its failure to fix inaccurate credit reports for six years.[59]

Then in 2000, Portland lawyer Michael Baxter, who argued Jorgensen's case, brought Judy Thomas's six-year mixed-file odyssey to an Oregon jury. It sympathized with her plight, awarding her $300,000 for harm to her reputation and $5 million in punitive damages to send a message to the industry.[60] Months later, a judge lopped $4 million off the jury's award.[61] But the case is still seen as a potential watershed moment for private litigation against the credit bureaus and their mistakes.

"The message is continuing to be sent to these people at the national credit reporting agencies that people are tired of this," said consumer attorney Szwak, one of a cottage industry of consumer lawyers who specialize in bringing credit report lawsuits.[62] The emergence of such an industry suggests the easy days might be over for the credit bureaus, says James B. Fishman, a prominent consumer lawyer in New York City. He believes change ultimately will come through litigation, just as it did with the tobacco industry.

"It's really the possibility of punitive damages that would keep these companies in line," he said.[63]

5

THE DOCUMENT PROBLEM

"Need a fake ID to get into the nude bar? Come to www.fake idman.org"

—E-mail Advertisement

Master counterfeiter Youssef Hmimssa sat behind a seven-foot panel wall, completely blocked from public view, and spoke hidden-camera style. His gentle, self-assured voice wafted over Room 50 on the ground floor of the U.S. Capitol building on that chilly September day, essentially the second anniversary of 9/11. He was there for pure shock value.

Hmimssa was testifying before the Senate Finance Committee on Homeland Security issues. His appearance at the hearing was an unannounced surprise, and security was tight. As he spoke, chamber doors were closed and guarded, so no one could enter or leave. Media cameras had to be turned off and pointed down when he entered and exited. The former suspected terrorist who turned state's evidence is a marked man, the government believes, and a fully public appearance could have endangered his life.[1]

Hmimssa was one of the first suspects arrested in America's war on terror, picked up just days after September 11, 2001, when his name was found in a Detroit apartment used by a suspected terrorist cell. Also found in the apartment that day: plans to attack some of America's most important landmarks, according to the government. Authorities say they found literature denouncing the United States and calling for the mass murder of Americans. "Kill them all and don't keep any of them alive . . . take away all the Jews and Christians," the paraphernalia said.

Abdel-Ilah Elmardoudi and Karim Koubriti were taken from the apartment and arrested that day; two years later, they were convicted of aiding terrorist plots against the United States. Hmimssa maintains he renounced the alleged terrorist cell's radical version of Islam and divorced himself from the group when he discovered its intentions. Still, Hmimssa says he supplied Elmardoudi and Koubriti with Social Security cards, driver's licenses, visas, passports, and other documents they needed for colleagues to enter and move about the country. He eventually pleaded guilty to 10 counts of fraud and agreed to be a government witness in the terrorism cases against Elmardoudi and Koubriti.

Their convictions have not been without controversy. Defense lawyers argued all along that Hmimssa was a liar who cooperated with the government in exchange for a lesser sentence. And six months after the celebrated trial, the Elmardoudi and Koubriti convictions were in danger of being overturned. The federal prosecutor on the case, Richard Convertino, allegedly withheld evidence that might have cast doubt on Hmimssa's testimony—a letter written by his jail cellmate saying Hmimssa planned to lie to the government.

But while Hmimssa's accusations against Elmardoudi and Koubriti may have been cast in doubt, there's no reason to believe he wasn't telling the truth about his own forgery methods and the counterfeit document underground when he testified in the Senate building that chilly morning, two years after the September 11 attacks.

At a hearing largely dominated by bureaucrats discussing the finer points of driver's license security and Social Security card reform, his was the sober voice of realism. America's paperwork system is hopelessly flawed, he said, and incapable of even slowing down a determined criminal or terrorist.

"It's very easy" to get everything from fake birth certificates to foreign passports to driver's licenses, he told the committee. Hmimssa even managed to create a special ink for birth certificates that would stand up to ultraviolet light tests that are administered by more security-minded agencies.

But he demurred at the idea that he was an expert. "There's a lot of people out there who . . . are more expert than I," he said.[2]

As any 19-year-old who's ever snuck into a bar knows, America's paperwork identification system is a farce. In fact, it is often harder to get into a bar as a teenager than it is to open a bank account as an imposter or to enter the country as a terrorist.

Today, in the United States, ID papers are nothing but a placebo. Any illegal immigrant can easily obtain a Social Security card. Any identity thief can manufacture a birth certificate. Any terrorist can buy a driver's license—or, as we'll see later in the chapter, simply ask their local department of motor vehicles office for one.

The system is so weak, it's almost too scary to think about the implications, so many people and government agencies simply don't, even in the wake of September 11. Instead, we all go through the motions, acting as if these documents mean something, giving busy work to thousands of government workers, and merely adding pointless hassle to our everyday lives.

For example, every single person who boards an airplane must show a photo ID. And after September 11, 2001, in most cases, fliers have had to show ID at least twice. All that effort is essentially wasted.

Just ask Youssef Hmimssa. His appearance was the theatrical moment in a hearing designed to embarrass government agencies about their shoddy document procedures. Papers are easy to come by, he said.

"Overseas, it's very easy. You have to have the right connection. You can get any passport, you know, French, Italian, or any passport from Europe," he said. In the United States "it's the same thing. You just have to have the right connection. You can get birth certificates. You can get the Social Security card of someone who is not using them or someone dead."[3]

Speaking from behind the seven-foot-tall protective wall, his faceless voice wafting over the room, he spat out casual indictments of the system. It had the intended effect.

"It's very easy," he kept saying again and again, when asked how he supplied Elmardoudi and others with visas designed to get associates into the country. Hmimssa just scanned the documents into his computer, made a blank template, and then pasted the new name and other information onto the screen. Using a high-quality printer, he produced documents that were nearly foolproof.

In fact, at one point during the hearing, Patrick O'Carroll, of the Social Security Administration's Office of Inspector General, admitted "in many cases, the counterfeit passport or counterfeit document looks a lot better than the genuine."[4]

The plot Hmimssa was wrapped up in was scary stuff. The government says his alias was found in a day planner that included the layout for İncirlik U.S. Air Force Base in Turkey, along with a layout for a shoulder-fired missile attack on airplanes taking off and landing there. The day planner was discovered during a raid on September 17, 2001, just days after the 9/11 attacks. Also discovered was a videotape that included "casing" information on U.S. landmarks—close-ups of garbage cans at Disneyland, the front door of the *New York Times*, various locations around Las Vegas. The Detroit terrorist cell meant business, prosecutors say.[5]

***

At first, Hmimssa was just another black market document customer who wanted entry into the United States, like millions of other illegal immigrants. A Moroccan, he simply bought a

French passport in Romania for about $700 and flew into the country. His identity now Patrick Vuillaume, he entered his new life without incident. Armed with the passport document and the right immigration forms, Hmimssa next got his hands on a Social Security card. Now, he could work and get a driver's license. He attended school and got a license to drive a taxi. When it was time to visit home, he was worried about reentering the country, so he created an entirely new identity, Edgardo Colon. Colon, conveniently, was a U.S. citizen from Puerto Rico. After he obtained a passport in Colon's name, he had no trouble going home to Morocco and reentering the United States. And despite the fact that he spoke little English and no Spanish, he was able to get a driver's license under Colon's name from the state of Illinois.[6]

The Internet turned out to be his Counterfeiter's University. There, he learned how to "skim" credit cards while driving a taxi. A small device stuck under the driver's seat of his cab let him swipe customers' cards in an instant, copying all the information contained on the card's magnetic stripe. Later, using a device called an encoder, he would take the stolen magnetic stripe data and write it onto his own plastic—thereby using his credit card to spend other people's money. He also learned how easy it was to falsify identification papers using simple software tools he could download from the Web.

When the credit card fraud was discovered, Hmimssa fled to Detroit to get another fresh start. Almost immediately, he met Karim Koubriti and other alleged cell members and began sharing an apartment with them. They were radicals who hated America and complained constantly about sinful U.S. cities like Las Vegas, Hmimssa said. They knew Hmimssa was a forger now, and they tried to convince him to help their cause by creating false passports and visas for cell recruits who wanted into America. But Hmimssa was spooked; he refused to make fraudulent documents for the group, the government says, and soon moved out after a heated altercation and headed back to Chicago.

But the alleged Detroit cell tracked him down. Hmimssa says that once he was established in Chicago, and had become a professional forger, he was approached by a man he knew only as Abdella. Abdella was a great customer, with big plans to help move friends into the country. Hmimssa complied, not knowing that Abdella was really Abdel-Ilah Elmardoudi, a key figure in the alleged Detroit cell. Despite his intention to leave the radicals behind him, Hmimssa's artwork ended up helping the Detroit group anyway. Abdella started bringing immigration forms and visas to Hmimssa that he could alter to make fraudulent immigration documents. Using a computer scanner, he created templates for foreign passports, often French or Moroccan passports, and would simply plug in the requested names and other biographical data.

In part of the scheme, would-be immigrants sent their picture and information to Hmimssa by fax. He would make a visa for them and mail it back to include in their passport.

It's not clear how many aliens actually entered the country thanks to Hmimssa's work. And he might have faced more serious charges, if not for an order he says he disobeyed from Elmardoudi. When September 11 hit, Elmardoudi told Hmimssa to destroy everything. But Hmimssa saved the paperwork in a storage locker instead. And when he was arrested, he had something to bargain with—a box full of fake IDs he'd made allegedly to help terrorists enter the country.

***

Government officials have repeatedly acknowledged that terrorism goes hand in hand with identity theft, and the procuring of fraudulent identification paperwork is almost always the first step in terrorists' web of deceit.

The September 11 terrorists were certainly well-versed in the art of fraudulent paperwork. About a month before the hijackings, Abdulaziz Alomari and Ahmed Alghamdi paid a Virginia lawyer to fashion residency certifications for them. Using the false documents, Alomari and Alghamdi obtained Virginia state IDs, used to board aircraft on September 11. Five other hijackers also got fraudulent Virginia ID cards, and authorities believe that, at one time or another, each of the 19 terrorists may have used false Social Security numbers.[7] There have even been reports that two of the hijackers, Abdulaziz Alomari and Salem Alhazmi, used passports stolen in common burglaries to enter the United States. A former Saudi exchange student named Abdulaziz Alomari reported his passport stolen while at the University of Colorado in 1995. The Alomari who boarded the first flight to hit the World Trade Center on September 11 shared a birthday with the former exchange student.[8] Another Saudi citizen, Salem Alhazmi, said his passport had been taken by a pickpocket in 1998.[9]

If true, it raises the likelihood that at least two hijackers entered the United States using false papers—in one case, papers that were stolen on U.S. soil. In an age where web sites are capable of tracking every move an Internet surfer makes, why weren't the terrorists stopped at the border?

It is in the realm of document forgery that terrorism, illegal immigration, and identity theft meet and become the same cause célèbre. Simple paper documents, like Social Security cards, are all that stand between a criminal and a new bank account in a consumer's name. A driver's license is all that stands between the next Mohammed Atta and an airplane. Such flimsy documents are the way we prove who we say we are in America. Once upon a time, when the means of producing such documents was naturally constrained by expense or access to equipment, pieces of specially marked paper or plastic with a simple magnetic strip on the back had a place. Today, they are completely out of place. Laser printers make creation of fake papers as easy as printing a resume; and black magnetic encoding on the back of a credit card is no longer the mystery it once was. Criminals now rewrite the black stripe as easily as they forge a signature.

In the digital age, a stolen identity is every criminal's favorite tool. It can be a get-out-of-jail-free card—imposters know they can give an arresting officer a fake driver's license, make bail, and flee, no questions asked. In fact, a stolen identity can be permission to commit the perfect crime. ID theft is the twenty-first-century equivalent of Star Trek's cloaking device, allowing financial criminals and terrorists to operate almost completely out of sight.

It is America's obtuse and complex paperwork system that enables this cloaking device. There are nearly 10,000 legitimate agencies that issue birth certificates,[10] and decent fakes cost only about $10. In 2002, the Social Security Administration issued 18 million Social Security cards. An audit by the Social Security Administration's Office of Inspector General estimated that in 2000, 63,000 Social Security cards were issued to noncitizens based on fraudulent documents.[11] There are 240 formats of driver's licenses issued by the various state agencies, every one just as valid as the next.[12] No airline agent or bank teller could possibly be expected to recognize all of those valid driver's license formats.

That's why it's so easy to make fakes. Driver's license sales on the Internet are a cottage industry, aimed innocently enough at would-be teenaged drinkers. ("Buy beer! Drive again!" the ads say.) But the seeming legally-immune existence of web sites like FakeIDMan.org stand as testimony to how badly the system works. In fact, fakes work so well that in 2001, 10 million fake identities were confiscated by authorities.[13] There's no telling how many were produced. With the continued improvement in quality and reduction in price of sophisticated computer graphics programs and printers, falsification of paperwork is clearly exploding. One lawyer who manages liquor licenses for national chain restaurants says the increase in the use of fake IDs to buy liquor from 1999 to 2003 was "unbelievable."

"Some of the locations actually received almost 40 percent fake IDs," said attorney Vince Paragano. "And the quality of the IDs is remarkably good."[14]

Why? The Internet makes it easy, and not just for Youssef Hmimssa. Anyone who wants to make or obtain false identification papers can find ready help online.

"I know someone who knows someone who has a program that makes fake IDs," writes one would-be underage drinker. "I've seen it on his computer . . . they enter in the information and . . . they have the little reflector thingies too, then they stick it in their laminator in his basement and it's good to use . . . they can make driver's licenses, permits, birth certificates, Social Security cards, work permits . . . all kinds of stuff for every state in the US and I think one of the Canadian provinces."[15]

Meanwhile, real documents—not the Youssef Hmimssa counterfeit kind—can be just as easy to come by. All around the country, ID thieves have learned how easy it can be to steal blank forms used to create identification paperwork. Birth certificates are known as "breeder documents" in the ID theft trade. They are the key to obtaining everything from a new driver's license to a new Social Security number or passport. And every month, across America, petty burglaries of blank breeder documents go by almost unnoticed: 3,300 taken from a locked safe at the Texas Department of Health[16]; 700 stolen at gunpoint by a man posing as a telephone repairman from the West Palm Beach Office of Vital Statistics[17]; 135 taken by a temp worker at the Waukesha County register of deeds office in Wisconsin[18]; 2,300 sheets of preprinted security paper used for birth certificates taken from Denver's Vital Records Office.[19] Small thefts that can easily lead to big trouble.

And states sometimes offer up the data necessary to create fraudulent driver's licenses for sale—making the job of an ID thief even easier. The practice drew unwanted attention in February 2002, when Oregon authorities arrested a 22-year-old woman named Jeanni Lee Rolfe, of Lake Oswego, for identity theft after she, ironically, had left her purse in a store. An alert clerk noticed it was full of checks in various people's names. When police searched her home, they found a computer disk labeled "2000–2001 EYE DEEZ/LICE ENDS." On the disk was the entire state's motor vehicle records database. In the file, which was updated through 2001, were the name, birth date, address, height, weight, and driver's license number for all Oregon drivers. The disk also included scanned copies of driver's licenses from every state; apparently templates that could be used to make out-of-state frauds.[20]

This wasn't the first time authorities found the state's entire driver's license database in the hands of an ID thief. Three months earlier, authorities arrested Jody Gene Oates, 44, and charged him with identity theft and forgery after he was fingered by a youth using a fake ID. When police searched Oates's home, they found four dozen compact disks with the state's driver database.[21]

Oregon discontinued the practice of selling its motor vehicles records in May 2001, but that hadn't discontinued criminals' practice of sharing the data.

Stolen IDs can be the result of an inside job, too. Bogus driver's licenses can be purchased directly from low-paid motor vehicles employees looking to make a fast few extra bucks. In August 2003, a Georgia Department of Motor Vehicles employee was arrested for allegedly issuing fraudulent licenses. He had worked for several years as a driver's license examiner, and was placed on administrative leave.[22]

Just how cavalier states can be with giving away driver's license documents was made clear in 2003 by the passage of SB60 in California, an ill-fated law designed to give the state's 2 million illegal immigrants legal licenses. Signed by Governor Gray Davis in the waning days of his recall election, it was a transparent political ploy designed to win Davis the Hispanic vote. Davis lost, and the law was repealed in the first few days of Arnold Schwarzenegger's tenure. But the case shone a spotlight on the thorny issue of illegal aliens and their ability to obtain legal documents. Anecdotal reports indicate other motor vehicles departments around the country regularly look the other way when an alien arrives with less-than-perfect paperwork, looking for a driver's license. A former Oregon department of motor vehicles employee, who requested anonymity, said his office gave special consideration to migrant workers, an important part of the state's economy.

"There was a large amount of pressure to issue licenses to migrant individuals. This pressure, from management! Not only from my direct office manager but from my district manager as well. We were encouraged to overlook minor discrepancies in ID presented to us, such as white out on birth certificates. Even if that white out was over name and date of birth."[23]

According to research organization FAIR, 14 states currently allow illegal aliens to obtain driver's licenses: Alaska, Connecticut, Idaho, Louisiana, Montana, Nevada, New Mexico, North Carolina, Ohio, Rhode Island, Tennessee, Utah, Washington, and West Virginia.[24]

Many of those states issue licenses relying on the so-called Mexican consular card – also called Matricula Consular – a form of photo ID issued by the Mexican government to keep track of citizens in other countries. While the card has been issued for 130 years, its importance spiked in the early part of the decade when U.S. banks, eager to court favor with an exploding Hispanic population, began accepting the cards as proper identification to open new accounts. The cards are controversial, because they are generally used by Mexicans unable to obtain any other form of identification, often because they are undocumented aliens. To receive a card, applicants only pay $29 and provide a birth certificate, another photo ID, and some kind of proof of residency. The Mexican government issued more than 1 million of the cards in the United States between January 2002 and October 2003.[25]

Debate over the consular cards is a high-stakes game. Mexicans living in the United States were expected to wire $14.5 billion back to Mexico during 2003. Nearly 1 in 5 Mexican residents receive money from outside the country, making it the largest remittance market in the world—a market jealously eyed by U.S. banks.[26] In May 2002, Bank of America launched a service called "SafeSend" designed to attract some of that business. At about the same time, the bank announced it would accept consular ID cards as identification.[27] Encouraged in part by the wide participation of U.S. banks, municipal governments around the country are increasingly accepting consular cards as identification for community services.

But the FBI says the cards aren't reliable and shouldn't be accepted as legitimate ID. In fact, they are an open door both for criminals and terrorists, the agency says, because the Mexican government does no due diligence before the cards are issued.

"[C]onsular ID cards are primarily being utilized by illegal aliens in the United States," said FBI Agent Steve McCraw, before the House Judiciary Subcommittee on Immigration, Border Security, and Claims on June 23, 2003. "The U.S. Government has done an extensive amount of research on the Matricula Consular, to assess its viability as a reliable means of identification. The Department of Justice and the FBI have concluded that the Matricula Consular is not a reliable form of identification, due to the nonexistence of any means of verifying the true identity of the card holder. . . . As a result of these problems, there are two major criminal threats posed by the cards, and one potential terrorist threat."[28]

The Mexican consular card is just another thorny issue in the thicket that is America's complex immigration problem.

Immigrant rights organizations correctly point out the reality that millions of out-of-status visitors and workers in the United States need somewhere to put their money, and some way to obtain necessary health care and government services. If banks and other institutions didn't accept the Mexican consular card, the lot of immigrants already facing inhumane work conditions and other unfair treatment would be much worse. They'd be forced to perform all transactions in cash, for example, making them much more likely targets for robbery and violence. U.S. banks argue with merit that accepting the cards is the right thing to do. Still, the quagmire that is the consular card controversy reveals just how unworkable America's identification system has become.

But if you are a terrorist or an identity thief in need of a driver's license to do your dirty work, you need not risk a late-night burglary, download forms from the Internet, or even fill out paperwork at a Mexican consulate. A terrorist can just walk into almost any department of motor vehicles agency and simply ask for one.

***

If you are a government bureaucrat, the last thing in the world you want to hear is that Ron Malfi has been to your office. Stocky, dark, and armed with a New York cop's accent so thick it belongs on a network sitcom, Malfi runs the office of Special Investigations at the Congressional General Accounting Office (GAO). The GAO is an intriguing agency, perhaps the only government body with true credibility inside Washington, D.C.'s, beltway. It's the nonpartisan arm of Congress, set up to do sober, nonpolitical audits of government spending programs. Its work is generally beyond reproach. Malfi's unit is one of the plum assignments at the GAO.

He does undercover work, exposing critical vulnerabilities, oversights, and waste within government programs. Picture a crack investigative journalism team that has the power of congressional subpoena, along with legal immunity for their exploits. Journalists go to jail for bringing weapons onto airplanes in undercover tests; Malfi's team does it, then simply embarrasses people.

In the security field, Malfi's work is called penetration testing or "red teaming." A group of government good-guy experts go undercover as bad guys and see how much havoc they can wreak. If we can do it, certainly the bad guys can, the thinking goes. If this had been a real attack, here's how bad it would be. One embarrassing lesson, the thinking goes, can save a lot of money and lives down the road.

In 2002, Malfi and company decided to test agencies around the country that issue driver's license ID cards, the main document used to verify identities around the country.

The nation's motor vehicles departments failed the test with flying colors. In all eight states tested, GAO investigators armed with fake birth certificates, out-of-state licenses, and other paperwork scored a real driver's license. If Hmimssa was the lightning of that September 9, 2003, hearing, release of this damning GAO investigation report was the thunder. Much of the investigation was removed from the public version of the GAO report; but below are many details from the "law enforcement sensitive" section issued only to Senate Finance Committee members.

GAO agents actually went out of their way to give the driver's license offices a chance. They used documents that were obviously faked—such as birth certificates printed on regular paper, without any government seal. Some of the documents didn't even have matching birthdays.

Many motor vehicles employees did indeed spot the problems; but not once did they follow protocol and ring the alarm bell. Supervisors weren't told; law enforcement wasn't notified. At one office, a polite DMV employee even "apologized for being unable to assist" the GAO investigator, then handed the fake documents back.[29]

The test was extremely realistic. Criminals normally have a try, try again mentality. So that's what the GAO did. And in every case, the GAO investigators simply walked out, fixed whatever the problem was, when back into a DMV office, and got the license.

In Virginia, the first state tested, an undercover agent was at first turned away because the birth date on the fake birth certificate didn't match the birthday associated with the fraudulent Social Security number. Six days later, the same agent went to another motor vehicles office with a new set of paperwork, making sure the birthdays matched. He got the license.

Getting a Maryland license proved a bit trickier, but agents were able to beat the system there on their third DMV visit. On first attempt, the DMV clerk noticed that the fake birth certificate did not include a state or county seal, and the texture of the paper was suspicious. But again, the fake documents were returned to the agent—in direct violation of a Maryland DMV policy that tells workers there to confiscate such documents and send a Teletype within 15 minutes alerting all state offices of the suspicious transaction, the GAO report says.

A week later, agents were turned down again by a Maryland DMV because employees there said the agent didn't have the required documents to establish Maryland residency. On the third visit, armed with a utility bill, the agent got a license.

But the most serious vulnerabilities appeared in California, where agents managed to complete the process to receive three temporary state driver's licenses within two days using the same fake information.

On one occasion, after one agent failed the standard eye test, a second agent stepped in for him, passed the eye test, then handed the successful results to the first agent, who had his photo taken for the license.

Simultaneously, a third investigator was using the same data in another line in the same office; he also was issued a temporary license.

"No one at the DMV noticed that two individuals were simultaneously using the same fictitious name and same fraudulent supporting paperwork," the report says.

And perhaps more troubling, that same undercover agent had already received a temporary license a day earlier from a different location, using the same name. On August 20, 2002, the agent supplied a fake out-of-state West Virginia license as verification of identity and managed to get the California license. On August 21, using the same name but a fake Texas license, he got a California license again, even after the clerk noticed the agent had received a temporary license the day before. The GAO agent simply said he'd lost the first license, and the DMV clerk issued a second California license "without questioning the story further."

Other locations that ultimately failed the GAO test: Washington, D.C.; South Carolina; Arizona; Michigan; and New York.

***

The presentation, almost exactly two years after the onslaught of high-security measures driven by the September 11 attack, should have been shocking. After all, with so much security based on driver's licenses, could the system really be such a sieve? Yes, said Linda Lewis, president and chief executive officer of the American Association of Motor Vehicle Administrators. "Neither I, nor any of my members, are surprised by the findings of the investigation," she said.

But the story told that day by the General Accounting Office was not one of simple single-agency neglect. In fact, the GAO's havoc-wreaking team has been finding such casual care with documentation during a string of stings for three years—both pre- and post-September 11. The results haven't changed over time.

In April and May 2000, agents claiming to be law enforcement officials discovered how easy it was to get red-carpet treatment and get around security measures. Investigators wearing bogus badges claiming to be law enforcement officials had no trouble breaching security at 19 federal offices and two commercial airports. The agents were waived around magnetometers and managed to cart guns onto airplanes and into Cabinet secretary offices.[30]

The courtesy "waive around the magnetometer" issue didn't change after September 11 in many locations—even in New York City. On July 23, 2003, that cost New York City Council member James Davis his life. During a regular business day, while attending a council meeting with political rival Othniel Boaz Askew, Davis was gunned down. They entered city hall together that day and were allowed to skip the metal-detection tool. That allowed Askew to bring his gun into City Hall without facing any questions. Moments later, he shot and killed Davis.[31]

In 2002, GAO agents gained armed access to more federal office buildings, despite the recent lessons of September 11 and the Oklahoma City bombing. Using counterfeit law enforcement credentials, they got real building passes and again were waived around magnetometers. Eventually, they even got an after-hours access code by presenting their building passes.

Also that year, the GAO exposed the weakness of firearms background checks. Agents were able to buy a firearm from a Virginia sporting goods company and have it shipped—using a counterfeit federal firearms license. One year later, agents with counterfeit driver's licenses bought firearms from sellers in five states—Virginia, West Virginia, Montana, New Mexico, and Arizona. In all five states, the applicants passed background checks required by the Brady Handgun Violence Prevention Act. Since the identities were all counterfeit, there was no negative information in the Brady database to stop the sale.

Guns purchased with fake paperwork have been involved in notorious crimes. James Kopp used the name B. James Milton on a fake Virginia driver's license to buy a Russian SKS rifle from the A-Z Pawn Shop in Nashville, Tennessee, on June 16, 1997. Kopp was later arrested in France after a two-and-a-half-year manhunt in the slaying of abortion provider Dr. Barnett Slepian. Investigators say Slepian, 52, was killed in the kitchen of his Buffalo, New York-area home by a single shot from the high-powered rifle on October 23, 1998. Kopp was later convicted of second-degree murder and sentenced to 25-years-to-life in New York.

From September 2002 to May 2003, GAO agents using counterfeit licenses and fictitious names and posing as travelers from Jamaica, Barbados, Mexico, and Canada had no trouble slipping by immigration officials and entering the country.

And in May 2003, the GAO showed how easy it is to obtain Social Security cards. Posing as parents of a newborn, armed with a fake birth certificate and baptismal certificate for a bogus baby, GAO agents were given a Social Security card after a visit to an Social Security Administration (SSA) field office. Mailing the documents worked just as well; officials obligingly mailed the fraudulent Social Security card to the agents.

Worst of all, the GAO exposed that federal offices still don't understand what a ready supply of fraud data the dead can be. Using the Social Security Administration's Master Death file—which is publicly available—investigators managed to get driver's licenses in two states for a dead person. This is hardly an exaggerated game of "What if?" Identity criminals know about this flaw and take advantage of it. An audit of one month's transactions at one of the offending states showed 41 other licenses had been recently issued by that agency to a dead person.

Given the ease of obtaining essential documents like driver's licenses and Social Security cards, it doesn't take long to play the game of "What If?"

What if a terrorist could obtain security clearance at a U.S. airport? On June 25, 2002, U.S. Attorney Paul J. McNulty told Congress that his office had conducted a review of 28,000 people who had security badges in five major airports in eastern Virginia. Of those, 75 had used a false Social Security Number to gain their security badge.[32]

What if a terrorist could impersonate a U.S. soldier? In November 2003, Maria Ramirez, an enlisted sailor aboard the San Diego-based aircraft carrier *Nimitz*, was accused of using her access to personnel records on shipboard computers to steal information that allowed her husband and others to create phony military identification cards.[33]

What if America's identification system is useless to stop both terrorists and identity thieves alike?

It's clear that driver's licenses and Social Security cards, the basis of virtually all identification in this country, are regularly issued to dead people, illegal immigrants, and thirsty teenagers. In the post 9/11 era, it's also clear how important proper identification can be. That September 9, 2003, hearing, the one dominated by Youssef Hmimssa, began with Sen. Chuck Grassley saying simply that, "identity theft and document fraud are far too easy to commit for us to be safe. . . . How easy is it to make counterfeit documents that work? I don't think anyone here is going to like the answer." It was punctuated by Sen. Jim Bunning complaining that he's spent 10 years telling the Social Security administration it had to change the way it issues tax ID cards, after hearing how easily Youssef Hmimssa got his. But even as the outside experts began to chime in with their dramatic solutions to this apparently dire problem, the room slowly emptied. And when the final consultant offered the only obvious solution—nationwide standardization of identity documents like driver's licenses—only one senator remained on the dais, along with a handful of aides who'd hung around to be polite.

A paltry crowd of 20 remained in the audience. The bold pronouncement was made to a largely empty room—after all, Paul Wolfowitz was testifying across the building about expenditures on the war in Iraq. The identity theft paperwork hearing, with all its sober warnings and foreshadowing, was completely overshadowed.

6

WHERE ARE THE COPS?

I went to the police to file the report, where I was almost laughed at because I could not name the person against whom I want to file the report and I did not know where the "crime" had occurred, and since most likely it was not in Sarasota County, Florida it was not likely to be investigated. I feel like I'm living in a country where the crime is unpunishable.

—Anonymous Victim

This time the victim was a woman named Sheri Knudson, but every day, in every city across America, it's someone. Charles Rutherford stood in his small cell phone shop in Minnesota's Twin Cities, eying an application that was an obvious fake. This "Knudson" wanted a family phone for her 16-year-old daughter, but a credit check of the real Knudson indicated she was only 27 years old. Criminals committing high-tech crimes don't necessarily have high-tech minds. In fact, often a sprinkle of common sense and a dash of thoughtfulness unmasks digital imposters in a heartbeat.[1]

Rutherford, who ran his shop for years, used to get these badly faked applications all the time, and it became a sport to stop them. He couldn't afford to have four or five imposters steal cell phones every week. But he didn't just stop at foiling the attempts. He knew behind every bad application was a good person whose financial future was currently at risk. Instinctively, he took the time to hunt down the real Sheri Knudsons of the world, to warn them about what was happening, and even helped compile evidence for potential prosecutions.

But as the real Sheri Knudson, Charles Rutherford, and so many others around the country have discovered, ID theft seems most unstoppable when law enforcement authorities seem most disinterested.

More Americans are victims of identity theft than any other crime in America now, and there's a reason: For criminals, the rewards are high, and the risks are infinitesimal. By one estimate, only 1 out of every 700 identity theft crimes are ever prosecuted.[2] Those are some odds—getting away with identity theft is as sure a bet as there is.

As the owner of a local cell phone dealership, Rutherford was on the front lines of the ID theft war. Ordering a new, untraceable cell phone is often among the first tasks for criminals who have just obtained a stolen identity. It's akin to setting up an office before opening for business. ID thieves need to have a working phone number to put on credit card applications and other loan forms. So once they get the numbers they need, they usually head to the cell phone shop quickly.

Rutherford knew the drill, and he saw right through the Sheri Knudson application. He tracked down the real Knudson, who lives in a suburb of Minneapolis, and gave her the bad news. She was disappointed, but not shocked—one year earlier, her car had been burglarized and her purse stolen. She had been waiting for a phone call like Rutherford's. But there was good news, too. Rutherford's sleuthing provided a hot lead on her identity thief, who perhaps was the criminal that had broken her window and stolen her purse. Rutherford even had an idea to catch her thief.

Rutherford had no walk-in retail store and wouldn't ship to a P.O. box. So the imposter had to supply a real shipping address with her order. If that weren't her home, it would at least be a drop-off location where investigators could arrange a simple sting and arrest whomever showed up to receive the package. It seemed like a foolproof plan. But instead of bagging a criminal, Knudson and Rutherford entered the world of identity theft bureaucracy.

In quick succession, Rutherford contacted the police in Minneapolis, where the suspect had asked for the phone to be delivered, and then the police in New Brighton, where his Twin Cities Wireless office was located. Meanwhile, Knudson called the sheriff's department in Anoka County, where she lives. Then Rutherford called a special fraud unit of the St. Paul Police Department. All of them said there was nothing they could do. The crime was in someone else's jurisdiction, or wasn't large enough, or wasn't a crime at all, they said. After all, the fake Knudson hadn't received any stolen merchandise.

This open-and-shut case was closed immediately.

The unlikely crime-fighting duo got another break two months later, when the same criminal brazenly made a second attempt to purchase cell phones through Rutherford's shop. This time New Brighton police came to the store and filled out a report—and even taped a phone conversation Rutherford had with the imposter. But the investigation stalled there.

All the while, the real Knudson knew full well that someone had her name and her credit, and that someone was making repeated attempts to spend money in her name. No one seemed interested in stopping it.

With her frustration reaching a boiling point, Knudson took the dangerous step many ID theft victims have been tempted to take. Against all the advice of friends and family, she tried to contact the imposter herself.

First, she called her imposter at the number on the cell phone application. She disguised her voice, just hoping to hear what her imposter sounded like. It was a brief phone call, just a chat designed to sound like a wrong number. But Sheri had heard the voice of her tormenter and perhaps the voice of the woman who had broken into her car and stolen her purse.

The voice sounded young, indifferent, nondescript. And certainly not guilty. Her tormenter was living a perfectly happy life, Knudson thought. That whet her appetite and fueled her passion for justice all the more. For weeks, she considered stopping by her imposter's house herself. She plotted the home on a map, drove to the area, and realized it was in a bad section of town. She considered driving by the house fantasized about running up to the door, ringing the doorbell, and screaming at this woman for all the frustration and pain she had caused. But then she heard the voices of her friends and decided against it.

But as she did she thought to herself, "Why aren't the cops doing this?" If it were so easy for her to find the suspect's home, why wouldn't the police do that?

"At least call these people and scare them so they'll stop doing it. Anything would have been better than nothing," she said.

***

That may sound reasonable, but it's hardly legal. Police can't bully people into becoming solid citizens. In the world of law enforcement, ID theft is a devastating catch-22. Even though the crime of ID theft often leaves a thick electronic trail in its wake, following those electronic cookie crumbs can be incredibly complex—particularly for investigators who are far better trained to take fingerprints and track murderers. The average ID theft case takes 100 hours to research, and complex cases can take 500 hours.[3] And even when victims do much of the research and show up with all the requisite paper trails—as is customary with this crime, where victims learn quickly that justice in ID theft cases is largely self-service—cops still must retrace their steps.

All that time might be worth it if there were guarantees that the criminal might actually end up behind bars, unable to victimize others. But that's rarely the case. Even when the evidence is iron-clad, many local district attorneys just don't have the time to prosecute single ID theft cases. To a DA with a docket jam-packed with assault cases and drug dealers, a small-time white-collar criminal seems hardly worth the bother.

That's even more true if the local judge doesn't understand the severity of the crime. Judges are more than willing to put repeat drunk drivers or armed robbers in jail. But district attorneys who do take the complicated ID theft cases, and go to the trouble to explain the case to a judge, often find it pales in comparison to everything else going on in the courtroom that day. Victims aren't bleeding, and often they aren't even out very much money, so what's the problem? Probation-only sentences are common, even for repeat offenders. That's why recidivism is nearly 100 percent among identity thieves who are convicted, say law enforcement agents who investigate ID thieves. They also know all about the catch-22: Why investigate when no one will prosecute, why prosecute when no one will throw the book at the criminal? Why not commit the crime?

And that's why, according to the most-often-cited statistic in the world of law enforcement and identity theft, criminals act as if they are completely immune from prosecution—because statistically speaking, they almost are. In 2000, according to Gartner analyst Avivah Litan, 699 out of 700 ID thefts weren't prosecuted. Many law enforcement agents interviewed for this book think the numbers were probably even worse in 2003. There is hardly a better bet anywhere on the planet than a bet that an ID thief will get away with committing his or her crime.

"This is the fastest growing crime today because the thieves know they can get away with it," said Linda Foley, director of the Identity Theft Resource Center. "An ID thief who finds out [he or she] can keep getting away with it is going to keep doing it."[4]

***

The problems of law enforcement run much deeper than a lack of manpower or willingness to chase after the criminals. In many cases, cops won't even give victims a good listen. Across the country, many police agencies often refuse to take the report of an identity theft crime unless there are obvious, immediate damages. A 2002 study by Congress's investigative arm, the General Accounting Office(GAO), reached this startling conclusion: Many police departments around the nation consistently see ID theft as "someone else's problem." Cops too busy with other things jump at the chance to push a case off on another jurisdiction, the report said. And since ID theft almost always involves multiple locations—a purse stolen in one state, used to open bank accounts in another—there's always someplace else to push the responsibility.

"Because identity theft is still a 'nontraditional' crime, some police departments may be unaware of the importance of taking reports of identity theft, much less initiating investigations," the report said. "Officials . . . told us that limited resources are allocated to priorities such as violent crimes and drug offenses and, thus, the number of investigators and prosecutors for addressing identity theft often is insufficient."

Victims can and should insist that a police report be taken, but often, they don't know any better. Statistics examined by the GAO indicated that in the year 2000, most victims were smart enough to call the police, but in one-third of the cases, they were unable to convince police to take a report of the incident. Publicity surrounding the crime seems to have helped on this issue—in 2001, only 18 percent said they couldn't get a police report. Still, 1 in 5 victims was unable to take even the first step to protect against further financial harm after facing an identity theft.[5]

Anecdotal reports suggest the real-life situation facing victims might actually be worse than that. The San Deigo–based Identity

Theft Resource Center says half the victims it helps have been unable to obtain a police report.

Both Knudson and Rutherford heard it was "someone else's problem" repeatedly when they tried to hunt down justice. You're not out any money, so there's nothing we can do, Knudson was told. No crime was committed because no stolen property was received, Rutherford heard from various agencies.

That's not true: Attempting to obtain credit in someone else's name runs afoul of federal law, specifically the 1998 Identity Theft and Assumption Deterrence Act. In addition, Minnesota is one of 44 states that had passed identity theft laws by 2002.[6] Like many other states, Minnesota's statute indicates clearly that, "A person who transfers, possesses, or uses an identity that is not the person's own, with the intent to commit, aid, or abet any unlawful activity is guilty of identity theft."[7]

By the time Rutherford hit his dead end with Knudson, he was already fed up with inaction on a host of other attempted frauds and decided he wasn't going to take no for an answer. So he wrote to his state attorney general's office and got no reply. Then he decided to ask the federal government for help. He sent an e-mail to the Social Security Administration. An official there responded quickly, but with a disheartening suggestion: Go to the press.

"In your shoes, I would start with a letter to the editor of the local newspaper to generate some public pressure," the official wrote in an e-mail.[8] Exasperated, Rutherford contacted MSNBC.com with a plea to have his story told.

"Everyone's heard about identity theft prevention, but it doesn't seem there is much identity theft prosecution," Rutherford said. "I've called and e-mailed police departments and news agencies, hoping to gain support for these very personal crimes. I fear these criminals are getting the impression that there are no consequences for their actions."

They are. Reliable statistics on nationwide identity theft prosecutions are hard to come by, but clearly they amount to a tiny fraction of the crimes. In the year 2000, the most recent year for which statistics are available, the FBI reported only 922 identity theft arrests. That same year, federal prosecutors filed only 2,172 cases—certainly only a trickle of the crimes.[9]

Mom-and-pop stores and consumers aren't the only ones complaining about the lack of prosecutions. Officials from financial institutions also say they can't get justice from the legal system that's supposed to protect them.

Oregon Bankers Association Chairman Mike Foglia thinks the lack of prosecutions is the real reason identity theft has exploded. Criminals know about prosecution "thresholds" and exploit them, he says.

"We have cases we tie up with a bow and give them to [federal authorities], and we can't get them interested unless the loss is at least $50,000," Foglia said. Criminals know this, he said. They know they can risk a $10,000 fraud with almost no fear of jail time.

"What if we could take all the millions we have lost in fraud in the past year and hire some prosecuting attorneys?" he asked hypothetically. "The fact that there are no prosecutions is deplorable, particularly when we know this stuff funds terrorism."[10]

***

While hometown police are an easy target for victims' frustration, they hardly deserve all the blame. Even when police do try, there are no guarantees that the wheels of justice will turn in favor of the victim. Detective Bill Sorter, who investigated the Sheri Knudson case in New Brighton, Minnesota, concedes that his work stalled because her crime is a low priority—not to him, but to the Minnesota court system. Police officers who undertake complicated identity theft prosecutions get buried under a mountain of paperwork and often find their cases neglected by prosecutors or courts, he said.

Last year, Sorter handled the cases of two criminals who impersonated over 200 victims. The criminals will likely end up only "doing time served," he said.

"These are very time-intensive cases. There were 200 victims and we had to call each and every one of those folks, we had to get them to file reports with their local police, then get all those reports," he said.

In another case, one identity theft suspect he arrested three months earlier hadn't even been charged yet by the local district attorney. The suspect was released on bail 48 hours after the original arrest and has been arrested twice more for identity theft since then. With only three detectives on staff, and mandates from city hall not to work overtime, it doesn't make sense for Sorter to spend time on cases that won't result in prosecutions.

"It's a catch-22. . . . It's extremely frustrating," he said. "In our area it will take one of the judges or legislators to become a victim so we get stiffer penalties."

And as for Knudson's case, Sorter simply hasn't had time yet to set up an all-day stakeout of the alleged criminal's home. And he said that however frustrating it might seem, he can't just knock on the suspect's door and harass her.

"I don't have a legal right to go there and run them up the flagpole," he said. "We're stuck between a rock and a hard place."

That's a familiar place for investigators around the country, the GAO found. An avalanche of ID theft cases is collapsing on them, many with hard-to-quantify or seemingly minimal financial losses, a death by a thousand cuts. One California deputy attorney general told the GAO that she was handling four active cases, and she commented that these were a "tiny drop in the bucket" of the caseload she could have. What's more—the four active cases had one thing in common: The number of victims was "in the hundreds" or even "never ending."[11]

So are the cases themselves: The Los Angeles Identity Theft and Credit Card Squad, one the nation's model identity theft crime squads, had over 8,000 cases arrive in 2001. And the agency only takes reports from Los Angeles residents.[12]

Dismal payoffs are also discouraging for investigators. Identity theft cases require highly trained detectives, require longer-than-usual efforts, and often end without an arrest. And even after arrests, criminals rarely have faced stiff jail time, partly because of the way sentencing guidelines administer justice, and partly because of the way judges view white-collar crimes. For instance, to get a minimum prison term of one year for an economic crime in Pennsylvania, a defendant probably would have to steal approximately $100,000. In contrast, a felony drug case conviction involving more than 2 grams of cocaine or heroin—an amount with a street value of about $200—has a mandatory minimum sentence of one year of imprisonment.[13]

***

Further complicating matters for local cops, chasing down the criminals behind the identity theft incidents can be as intractable as snuffing out drug users in their jurisdiction—and that's no accident. There's evidence the two are now inter-twined. Meth addiction is a powerful factor in the growth of identity theft, many police investigators say. ID theft ring bosses use meth addiction to keep their runners in line and to get new recruits, says Eugene, Oregon, Police Detective Steve Williams.

When Williams arrested career criminal Stephen Massey in 1999, he discovered an ID theft ring involving dozens of runners, and methamphetamine was the glue that kept his ring together. Massey knew where to find meth addicts, and he made them a simple proposal: I'll trade mail for meth. Massey had a small army of meth addicts prowling neighborhoods near Eugene, stealing mail out of hundreds of mailboxes and raiding the local recycling center for preapproved credit card applications. Recycling centers make for much cleaner identity scavenging work than traditional dumpster diving in trash. Others in the ring broke into cars to steal purses and wallets—not for the money, but for the ID papers.[14]

Massey knew how to turn the applications into cash. So he traded the stolen mail for a hit of meth and maybe a few bucks. Back in a hotel room, Massey would have a small network of laptop computers tracking the various elements of the crime. He had a real division of labor. One team went through the mail, cataloging the valuable documents. Others filled out the preapproved credit card applications. Still others used the information garnered to apply for credit cards online, or verify the value of a stolen identity through a free credit report web site.

Amazed runners, many teenagers and addicts in their early 20s, watched a bit like disciples as the charismatic Massey fooled the credit card companies again and again.

It's a typical case, Williams says.

"Ninety percent of our ID theft cases deal with drugs," he said. And it's usually methamphetamine, which is easy and cheap to produce in mass quantities. "You don't see a lot of meth users robbing banks. You see someone on heroin do that. Meth users are less likely to get themselves shot. Plus, they can make more money in a fraud crime than they can sticking a gun in someone's face. If you bring a gun in a bank, you can face life in prison. Or you can write a series of bad checks and score 10 times that amount and get parole."

Detective Jim Dunn of the Thurston County Sheriff's Office tells much the same story. Methamphetamine addicts are prolific check forgers and identity thieves, he says. His office, which handles fraud cases in far-flung parts of the Washington state county, says that perhaps 95 percent of his ID fraud cases are drug related. His counterparts around Washington state see much the same.[15]

"Meth keeps them up for so long, two or three days at a time. They have the time to sit and make counterfeit checks, counterfeit driver's licenses," Dunn said.

The work is detail-oriented and methodical—sometimes, addicts will spend hours piecing together shredded documents to glean information—but meth highs make such tedious efforts bearable, even enjoyable. Obsessive-compulsive tendencies, enhanced by meth, can be an identity thief's best asset.

Robert Maes, a Phoenix-area U.S. Postal Inspector, told *The Privacy Times* that the primary ID thieves in the Phoenix area are loosely knit circles of methamphetamine drug addicts, sometimes called "Tweakers." Raiding mailboxes for personal data and financial instruments fits their vagrant lifestyle, he said. "They have their own terminology. They don't work, they live in hotel rooms and stolen vehicles; they keep late hours. They love to gamble. When arrested, they usually don't have much because they've blown all their money. . . . Someone will know someone who will trade drugs for Social Security numbers, he said.[16]

***

Identity theft is truly a new kind of crime, involving anonymous, very mobile criminals capable of leaving the scene of a crime instantly. It also involves complex webs created by teams of well-trained criminals with a variety of specialties working together. To combat the crime, law enforcement must fight fire with fire. The only method that has seen true success thus far is the formation of cooperative tasks forces that combine law enforcement officers from a variety of jurisdictions and levels of government, who combine their expertise and together throw a big net around the web of identity thieves.

Veteran cop Mike Gray now spends his time roaming California trying to inspire as many agencies as possible to join such task forces. Gray spent 17 years working as an L.A. County sheriff, the last 10 as a detective, until he retired in 2001. The last several years of his tenure he became a student of car thieves, and he noticed a disturbing trend. Car alarms and other security devices had made brute force burglaries harder and harder for criminals, particularly those targeting high-priced automobiles. But as often happens in the world of crime, the bad guys didn't just go away—they started to adjust. When physically stealing expensive cars became too difficult and too risky, they started virtually stealing the cars instead.[17]

Known as vehicle theft by fraud, or fraudulent application, criminals quickly learned it had become easier to steal a $40,000 car from a dealership than from the street. In fact, Gray says, some of the same organized crime rings that gave the world the term "chop-shop" in the 1980s turned to car theft by ID theft. Other organized crime rings have taken to it as well. Rings from around the world regularly buy cars—particularly high-end SUVs, like Land Rovers—using phony data and have them shipped back to Russia in closed containers, he says. The profits can be staggering and the risks are low. And for the criminals, the merchandise is better—these are no longer the slightly used cars that were once stolen off the street. These are brand-new Western-style cars that sell at top prices.

Gray became fixated on the problem of ID theft—easy money, nearly impossible to prosecute. He made a training video in 1996, well before many law enforcement officers had ever heard of ID theft. When he retired, he kept on going, traipsing up and down California, training detectives around the state how to deal with complicated identity theft cases. Now he is known as program administrator for ID Theft Investigation Courses for the state of California. And he is a regular consultant to the five high-tech task forces sprinkled around the state, assembled to combat identity theft.

By mid-2003, some 600 investigators had been through Gray's classes. He tells all of them to be sensitive when victims call in, to understand that even an ID theft where there is no obvious financial loss can still be a devastating crime. Gray is, as those who work in the realm of identity theft say, a true believer.

He is hardly alone. For years, every winter, deep in northern Connecticut where they were sure to be snowbound, police officers from around the Northeast gathered at a casino on the Mohegan Indian reservation to attend the Internet Crimes Conference, run by Bob Doyle, founder of New York City's Electronic Crimes Task Force. Hundreds of officers took intensive training classes in techniques to follow e-mail trails and web site hosts. Thousands more took Internet Crimes classes on the road, as part of the now-defunct company's road-show training.

Federal prosecutors have their own annual computer crime training, at the brand-new National Advocacy Center, nestled away on the University of South Carolina in Columbia, just blocks away from the statue of Senator Strom Thurmond outside the state capital. Government lawyers from all 50 states, along with FBI agents, attend classes taught by Visa fraud investigators, postal inspectors, and a host of other experts, all designed to help them hunt down the kind of computer criminals who perpetuate identity theft. Most of these prosecutors are true believers, too.

But it's not enough. With some 80,000 separate local, state, and federal law enforcement bureaus around the country[18] trying to chase down the 10 million identity theft crimes committed each year, hundreds of faithful cops and prosecutors often feel they are simply sticking their thumb in a leaky dam. It's a numbers game: There are far more criminals than detectives who can put in overtime to hunt down an elusive culprit. And most law enforcement agencies have yet to plug into the one electronic tool that the federal government says might actually do more than just plug holes in this leaky dam.

Recognizing the need for a national agency to take the helm in the fight against ID theft, the federal Identity Theft Act of 1998 made the Federal Trade Commission (FTC) the government's lead agent in pursuing the crime. Within a year, the Identity Theft Clearinghouse had been created. It's a one-stop shop for both ID theft victims and investigators, who can call a toll-free number (1-877-ID-THEFT) or fill out a web form to add a crime to the database. Various law enforcement agencies can also sort through police records from around the country. Victims have jumped at the chance to populate the database, which amassed some 162,000 reports of identity theft just during the calendar year 2002.[19] They volunteer to complete the process, even though it almost never results in any kind of immediate satisfaction.

But the data is invaluable to local, state, and federal law enforcement officials who tap into it every time they investigate an ID theft. Few single ID theft crimes are worth a detective's time; but ID thefts are almost never isolated incidents. Criminals who succeed keep at it, following familiar patterns, using the same stolen Social Security numbers or fake names as they move from hotel to hotel. And often, the thieves work in teams, so the crimes seemingly grow tentacles. A clever investigator using the right search terms can stitch together hundreds of victims and hundreds of thousands in losses. Detectives who aren't allowed to pursue small-dollar cases can often meet their thresholds by tying together related crimes found browsing the data. Hunting an ID thief using the Clearinghouse is a lot more like surfing the web or hunting for an article on Lexis-Nexis than it is chasing a bank robber down an alley.

Officials at the Federal Trade Commission also comb the data, looking for patterns themselves. With the help of the U.S. Secret Service, the FTC hopes to tie together crime rings from a national perspective that local law enforcement would never notice. During 2002, a few dozen such top-down cases had been initiated.[20]

Cops and other law enforcement agencies access the ID theft data using a front end called "Consumer Sentinel," which also includes data on other consumer scams. Sentinel continues to be refined by geeks at the FTC. It now includes an alert capability, so an officer can flag a certain incident and receive an e-mail if new data comes in related to that crime, such as an additional report of credit being issued in a victim's name. There are also special tools to warn investigators in different jurisdictions if they are working on an overlapping case.[21] And FTC officials have a traveling road show, where they offer free training to anyone who will listen, in a dogged effort to gain attention for Sentinel. Jay Miller, the FTC's program director for Sentinel, was at the National Advocacy Center in 2003, offering training courses to about 100 U.S. attorneys.[22] Using Consumer Sentinel is free, and easy, over the web; the only requirement is that participating agencies sign confidentiality agreements.

But despite all the efforts at exposure, only a tiny fraction of America's police agencies are wired to use it. In Texas, for example, less than 1 percent of all law enforcement agencies were participating by the end of 2002. Uptake was so slow that by 2003, only a few hundred of the nation's 18,000 law enforcement agencies had connected to Sentinel.

That limits Sentinel's effectiveness. Without comprehensive crime data, and comprehensive participation, it's easy for ID thieves to slip through the cracks and evade even the most creative searches for crime patterns. The 2002 GAO ID theft report concluded that the single most effective step the federal government could take to combat ID theft is greater participation in the Clearinghouse.[23]

***

Ironically, participation in another nationwide crime database, however, is a very different story. Not only does the National Crime Information Center, or NCIC, demand nearly 100 percent participation, it is the single most alarming cause of trouble for identity theft victims.

Hardly a car is pulled over in the United States today that its driver is not subject to a search through the NCIC database. Nearly every arrest warrant, every missing persons report, every stolen car is in there. So are names and other information about known gang members, terrorists, and fugitives and even reports of stolen guns and boats. All this crime-related data makes its way into the NCIC courtesy of participating agencies, which constantly populate the database. And for every arrest of a wanted criminal, picked up after a routine motor vehicle stop, the amazing, comprehensive NCIC database is to thank.

The NCIC was founded in 1967 by J. Edgar Hoover's FBI. And the agency is now beaming with pride about the system, which got a $182 million overhaul in the late 1990s. It's now capable of providing near-instant mug shots and fingerprints of suspects to any point in the country.[24] On March 15, 2002, the FBI announced the system had achieved a record, processing 3.3 million requests for information in a single day. It can return a response to a cop on the beat in less than a quarter of a second under ideal circumstances.[25]

And it means that the NCIC can spread mistakes around the country just that fast. Most cases of criminal identity theft, such as California resident Clay Henderson, who spent a week in jail because of an imposter's arrest warrant in the mid-1990s, can be traced to bad data in the NCIC database. Unlike Consumer Sentinel, it's nearly impossible for criminals with outstanding warrants to slip through the cracks of NCIC. And it's almost as hard for an ID theft victim to clear his or her name from the NCIC, once it's been entered in error.

In a sense, it is impossible. Once a criminal uses a name as an alias, the alias lives in perpetuity in NCIC. There's really only three ways an ID theft victim can find out if he or she has a criminal record in NCIC—to face a surprise arrest, to be rejected for employment because of a surprising criminal record, or to befriend a police officer and ask quietly for a criminal background check. If there is a mistaken entry, the best the victim can do is convince the jurisdiction where the warrant was issued—even if it's on the other side of the country—to move his or her name from the primary name field into the alias field in the NCIC database. Police agencies simply won't remove aliases from the data. A criminal record in J. Edgar Hoover's database is for life.[26]

Many privacy advocates fear the situation will be made worse by an administrative order issued quietly by Attorney General John Ashcroft in March 2003. In 1974, Congress passed the Privacy Act, which mandated that law enforcement agencies do their best to ensure information entered into NCIC was accurate. But in the interests of fighting terrorism, Ashcroft issued an administrative order in 2003 declaring the NCIC exempt from the Privacy Act.[27] Accuracy requirements might prevent beat cops from entering unconfirmed tidbits into the database that might prove useful in later terrorism investigations, the Justice Department argued. More than 5,000 citizens and 90 organizations complained about the decision, which wasn't reviewed by the Bush administration. The Electronic Privacy Information Center described its concerns this way:

> The lack of data quality obligations for the NCIC increases the likelihood that individuals will be wrongly stopped and detained, perhaps even placed in dangerous law enforcement interdictions, because of errors in the most important criminal history record system in the United States that the Department of Justice no longer feels obliged to keep accurate.[28]

It is troubling, but true: Just as the nation's largest crime database has been made more susceptible to the worst kind of identity theft nightmare; the nation's other large crime database, the one designed to help consumers, has been left begging for takers.

***

Yet such borderless policing, aided by technology and not stifled by jurisdictional border fights, is the only real hope to keep up with the marauding band of high-tech criminals abusing our financial systems. For now, multiagency task forces full of true believers are left to stick as many thumbs in the leaky dam as they have.

One of the model interagency cooperatives is the Los Angeles County ID Theft Task Force. There, 10 agents from the L.A. County Sheriff's Office, the U.S. Postal Inspector's Office, the Secret Service, and the California State Department of Consumer Affairs work exclusively on identity theft, cooperating to string together cases and track down criminals through cyberspace. Since its creation in 2000, the task force has handled 12,600 cases, 5,600 in 2002. That year, it made 114 arrests and succeeded in 51 prosecutions.[29]

"That doesn't seem like a big number," admits Sgt. Bob Berardi, the heavy-voiced police veteran who runs the task force. "But with 10 people on the task force that's a busy crew for the year."[30]

In Los Angeles, before the creation of the identity theft task force—and in many other parts of the country today—untrained officers with an old-fashioned view of identity theft would brush off victims, he said.

"In the past, since the victim was not responsible financially, they carved the victim out of the equation and said it was up to the finance companies to prosecute," Berardi said. "And they don't want to waste the money. So nothing happened. But the victim is still being impacted."

While plenty of crimes still remain unsolved, at least L.A.-area victims know they have somewhere to turn, and they can speak with officers who understand the severity of the crime. Identity theft victims deserve to be taken seriously by law enforcement, no matter the size of the police agency, Berardi said.

"They don't want to be ignored," he said. "It can be a matter of resources, but the general public . . . expects you are going to provide them a solution when this happens. And we should at least try."

However, few hometown departments have the resources of major urban centers like Los Angeles County. The truth is, ID theft is a national crime, almost always sprawls across multiple jurisdictions, and rooting it out ultimately requires investigation and prosecution by federal agencies capable of chasing criminals across borders.

***

Sean Hoar is hardly the perfect image of a federal prosecutor. There's nothing hard about him. Soft spoken, with soft eyes and quiet wit, it's easier to imagine the former college baseball catcher comforting a rookie pitcher on the mound than it is fighting to put a murderer behind bars. That's probably why he's found a home as a computer guru in the Justice Department and, more recently, as one of the top identity theft prosecutors in the Pacific Northwest. Working out of his office in Eugene, Oregon, Hoar has uncovered the secret that many prosecutors around the country have yet to unearth—very few identity thefts are isolated incidents.[32]

Hoar operates a working group of detectives and prosecutors in rural Southern Oregon who've taken an interest in computer crimes. Like many such working groups around the country, they are filled with participants who are the accidental geek of their department. A spark of interest in a piece of software led to some volunteer overtime in the past—for Hoar it was the use of Microsoft's PowerPoint to steer juries toward convictions—and that leads to a quick nomination as computer guru. Hundreds of volunteered hours later, the computer cop is an expert in things he or she never dreamed about: tracing digital breadcrumbs, finding web site owners, backtracking anonymous e-mails, sitting in Internet relay chat rooms. Many police departments around the country have one or two true believers, who now get all the geek cases.

Hoar, as a U.S. attorney, has a privileged spot. Many identity theft cases slip off the side of the train because they simply aren't big enough, they don't meet the dollar threshold. Federal guidelines dictate to U.S. attorneys which cases they can take; depending on whom you ask, prosecutors in the Pacific Northwest can't touch a case where the identifiable losses aren't at least $40,000—and some say the minimum is as high as $100,000. Few individual ID theft cases meet that threshold. That leaves a local police detective with a hot ID theft case holding the bag; if his local district attorney isn't interested, certainly the Feds wouldn't be interested.

But Hoar, as a true believer, sees things differently. Almost no ID theft is an isolated incident, he says—investigation almost always reveals a spider web. The purse might have been stolen by a runner, who works for a ringleader, who employs another 20 runners. Getting paperwork from every victim is a laborious process. But in the end, a single ID theft arrest can, and often does, open the door to a network of ID thieves who have taken far more than $100,000. Local district attorneys often can't extend their tentacles around the country to pull together such cases. The sheer expense of investigating, much less flying in witnesses from all corners of the United States, makes a local prosecution of such a nationwide crime nearly impossible. But Hoar, and other federal prosecutors like him, has that reach.

***

There is another nationwide U.S. law enforcement agency which has that reach, an agency most Americans don't know much about: the U.S. Postal Inspection Service. Postal police officers conjure up images of the Unabomber and the anthrax scare, and not much else. But theirs is a massive agency. The nearly 4,000 postal inspector agents work silently for the most part, and carry a big stick—they may provide the biggest hope for stopping ID theft-criminals. The agency possibly owns the record for ID theft-related arrests in the nation. Between October 2002 and June 2003, postal inspectors made 2,264 identity theft-related arrests stemming from mail theft investigations. In one recent month in one midsized western city, there were 20 arrests and 14 prosecutions. In that city, one team of postal investigators has four of its six investigators dedicated solely to identity theft.[33]

Its reach is nearly as broad as the FBI's. It has jurisdiction over any crime that has any connection to the U.S. mail. What's more, postal inspectors are familiar with both complex networks and complicated jurisdictional relationships. One might say the U.S. mail system was the first Internet—and today it deals with 200 billion pieces of mail a year heading for 138 million addresses.[34] So the Postal Inspector's Office has been dealing with cross-border criminals and jumpy local authorities since it was founded by Benjamin Franklin. It's been devoted to hunting nationwide scammers since the Civil War. The last known stagecoach robbery in the United States was solved by postal inspectors in 1916. When the nation's gold reserves were moved from New York to Fort Knox in 1937, U.S. postal inspectors managed the process—the gold was actually sent registered mail.[35]

When the FBI shows up in a small town sniffing around for tips on a crime, local police often bristle. But postal inspectors, who often aren't strangers, tend to get a warmer response, and agents are generally well schooled at making productive offers of help.

While much identity theft happens with the help of a computer and the Internet, the U.S. mail is almost always at the core of the crime. Fraudulently ordered credit cards must be intercepted at someone's mailbox. Almost every piece of paper that Americans receive with account numbers or other private data arrives via the mail—if it's not stolen outright from the mailbox, it's stolen from a dumpster or recycling center later. That makes identity theft largely the Postal Inspector's problem. And the agency has been fighting the crime for at least 30 years.

Martin Biegelman spent some 25 years working as a postal inspector in New York City during the 1970s, 1980s, and 1990s. He was fighting identity theft a full two decades before the crime even earned its name. A deep-chested, deep-voiced New York Yankee fan, Biegelman now conducts secret internal audits at Microsoft. But 30 years ago he began researching a rash of student-loan fraud around the country committed by a ring of thieves led by Nigerian nationals. At the time, in the early 1970s, credit card distribution had just about reached the tipping point, and the American people were getting used to spending what they didn't have. The Nigerians, who had perfected the art of assuming other identities to obtain fraudulent U.S. student loans, quickly realized the potential of credit card fraud. The first ID thieves, Biegelman says, were Nigerians who had been master imposters all along—over half the cases he prosecuted in those early days were against Nigerians. "They always find a way to beat the system," he said.[36]

Today, most Internet users know Nigeria as the birthplace of millions of spam messages imploring recipients to help some crestfallen government official sneak millions of dollars out of the country, the so-called Nigerian scam. The Nigerian government has taken great pains to remove the stigma attached to the country's name. But for Biegelman, Nigerians have always been on the forefront of identity theft—and technology-related crimes. And there's plenty of evidence that he's right. The largest ID theft crime ring that's been busted to date, Philip Cummings's alleged Long Island-based ring, involved a set of

Nigerian nationals who bought, sold, and traded the data, prosecutors say. James Jackson, the diamond identity thief, was initially trained by a Nigerian.

It often all starts with mail theft, which is still the agency's biggest concern. With 650 million pieces of mail delivered each day, much of it to residences where no one is home, mailboxes are still an easy mark. In 2002, nearly 6,000 suspects were arrested for stealing mail.

Investigations into simple mail thefts, just like Hoar's investigations into individual street-level ID theft cases, often lead postal inspectors to uncover enormous fraud schemes. This is just a sampling of cases from the Postal Inspection Service's 2002 annual report of investigations:

- Postal inspectors from the Washington, D.C., division caught a man who stole more than a quarter of a million dollars with a butter knife. They began surveillance of a Fairfax, Virginia, apartment complex on July 16, 2002, and watched a Nigerian national exit his car, grab a butter knife from the trunk, and enter an apartment building. He then forcibly opened several apartment mailboxes and stole numerous pieces of mail. Inspectors arrested the man as he returned to his vehicle and recovered stolen U.S. mail, stolen credit cards, and the knife. Losses from the scheme exceeded $250,000.

- Investigations in the Gulf Coast area exposed a crime ring that turned stolen business checks into $1.5 million. Ten people were sentenced in April 2002 after complaints that high-dollar business checks had been stolen from the mail. Inspectors learned the suspects had deposited the stolen checks into brokerage accounts and later wired money from the accounts into bank accounts they controlled. Prison sentences for ring members ranged from 6 to 84 months.

- Detroit postal inspectors caught a gang of mail thieves who were recruiting street people to obtain cash advances from banks and casinos via credit cards. In January 2002, investigators recovered more than 180 documents listing victims' personal IDs. The gang's ringleader was arrested with more than 700 car rental applications with names, dates of birth, Social Security numbers, and credit card accounts of potential victims. Total fraud losses exceeded $700,000.[37]

In late 2003, after the Federal Trade Commission revealed that incidence of ID theft was 10 times what had initially been suggested, that some 10 million people a year were being hit, the Postal Inspection Service launched a nationwide public awareness campaign. Posters are plastered all over post offices around the country now, warning residents to carefully guard their mail.

The campaign featured NBC drama *Law & Order* star Jerry Orbach, himself a victim of identity theft, as a poster child for victims. "If it can happen to me, it can happen to anyone," says Orbach, in posters placed in many of the 38,000 post offices around the country.

Along with the posters, 3 million notices were mailed to consumers at home with tips on how to avoid becoming a victim. Advertisements also ran in major newspapers at 17 cities around the country. Among the tips issued by the post office—abandon the time-honored tradition of leaving outgoing mail in the mailbox with the red flag raised. If you can't directly hand the mail to your postal carrier, make the trip to the post office, the agency says.[38]

Such warnings, which may sound paranoid to some, should be filed in the same place as twentieth-century urban-dweller advice not to leave the keys in the car or to lock the doors at night. The Postal Inspection Service's message was clear: We must all learn to act in our own digital self-defense. In the twenty-first century, our digital innocence is now long gone. However creative law enforcement agencies around the country may become, they will never be able to guarantee the safety of our identities, or offer absolute protection from our evil, digital twin.

7

THERE OUGHT TO BE A LAW

My health insurance card, which I'm required to carry, has my spouse's SSN, name, and address on it. I removed my SSN card long ago (as has she), but now that gesture seems somewhat irrelevant. My student loan, being serviced by the U.S. Department of Education, uses my SSN as my account number, and they print it prominently at the top of every statement that's mailed to my house. In what seems incredibly naive, on the payment stub they make the following request:
"PLEASE WRITE YOUR ACCOUNT NUMBER ON YOUR CHECK OR MONEY ORDER."
This makes it most convenient for identity thieves—now they can have my name, address, bank account number, and my SSN all on one document.

—Anonymous

It seems a simple enough question: Who's really opening that bank account? After all, every crime, whether for personal gain or political agenda, requires money. And that money nearly always touches the financial system in some way. Contrary to conventional wisdom and perhaps common sense, terrorist funds and criminal proceeds are often stored in U.S. banks, using traditional accounts. That keeps forensic accountants busy.

Forensic accountants do the dirty work of tracking down criminals through the breadcrumbs they leave in the financial system.

In the days after September 11, 2001, every available forensic accountant began poring over credit card receipts, bank statements, and wire transfers, all on the hunt for a warm trail that might lead to the people who financed the hijackers.

Such trails grow quickly cold if criminals are allowed to open bank accounts under false names and pretenses. Long before September 11, federal banking regulators embarked on efforts to require that banks find out exactly who their customers are— who is leaving the bank with that stack of blank checks each time an account is opened. And for the past half-decade, regulators' expectations for banks to "know your customers" have continuously slipped. By 2003, banks had largely escaped requirements that they add any safeguards to their new account procedures. This, despite two domestic crises—identity theft and terrorism—which demonstrated a crying need to do so. Identity thieves and terrorists alike now know their ability to open American bank accounts has been protected by the bureaucracy. A review of the know-your-customer saga is a case study in the federal government's flaccid efforts to exert any influence over private industry as it flails about in its efforts to protect citizens' identities.

But it's much more than an academic exercise. There is evidence that lack of identification procedures at U.S. banks made funding the September 11 attacks easier for the terrorists. Federal investigators eventually found quite a bit of their financial trail. According to a report published in the *New York Times* 10 months after the attacks, the September 11 hijackers managed to open 35 accounts at a variety of U.S. banks using fake Social Security numbers that were never verified. In fact, the numbers weren't even obtained through some form of identity theft— they were make-believe numbers invented by the hijackers. Hundreds of thousands of dollars used to support the attacks were moved into the United States from the Middle East using these accounts, including $325,000 dropped into 14 accounts at

SunTrust Banks.[1] It's not fair to pick on SunTrust, however, for much more than having bad luck. It just opened the accounts using the same procedures that all U.S. banks use.

***

The days immediately after September 11 were heady days for conservative lawmakers. It's hard to imagine legislation more grandiose than the Patriot Act, which largely bundled together wish lists from all corners of conservative, law enforcement America. The massive legislation was passed with hardly any informed public debate. Ideas that had died on the vine years ago, unthinkable in a civil-liberty conscious America, now seemed quite palatable in post-September 11-scared America. Emboldened legislators plucked proposals out of dusty old files and jammed them into the Patriot Act—such as one element that gave law enforcement agents the right to look at e-mail headers without a court order—and rammed them through a Congress that felt the need to do *something* in the aftermath of September 11.

As with all federal agencies, banking regulators had their wish list, too. Three years earlier, their proposed know-your-customer rules had been beaten back by the finance industry and privacy advocates. But the idea was still hanging in the air when September 11 arrived. Striking a very different chord, with a different strategy, Know Your Customer (KYC) was downsized into a customer identification program, which became federal law in Section 326 of the Patriot Act.

A Congress aghast at the idea that terrorists were fully capable of storing money in U.S. financial institutions—even using their own names and even when those names were on FBI watch lists—had no qualms about passing a law mandating banks make a good-faith effort to positively identify all their new customers. Section 326 demands that any financial institution which has an ongoing relationship with customers must go to "reasonable" lengths to confirm the true identity of its new customers. The law is far reaching, covering banks, credit card issuers, securities brokers and dealers, credit unions, and other institutions. The legislation left the nagging details for implementing Section 326 to the Treasury Department. The devil certainly would be in those details. Some five years earlier, a similar effort by bank regulators had quickly turned into a debacle.

The Know Your Customer proposals in December 1998 went much farther than the Patriot Act required and came well before either terrorism or identity theft were a part of the national consciousness. KYC was aimed squarely at trapping money launderers. It forced financial institutions to track customer transactions in order to detect unusual patterns, which could indicate criminal laundering activity. Under the rules, financial institutions were required to keep records on the spending and savings habits of every client, with any deviation being reported as suspicious to the Internal Revenue Service, the FBI, the Drug Enforcement Administration, and other government agencies. The regulations, largely the brainchild of the Treasury Department's Financial Crimes Enforcement Network, were quickly torpedoed by widespread criticism from both industry and consumer groups. Consumers were disturbed at the sound of the rules, which evoked worrisome Big Brother images; industry leaders said they were overly burdensome and impractical. An embarrassed Federal Deposit Insurance Corporation, which oversees the nation's banks, withdrew the requirement within three months, after receiving 300,000 comments and massive bipartisan opposition.[2]

September 11 changed that atmosphere dramatically, and in the days after the attacks, federal officials repeated the mantra that banks were on the front lines of the war on terror. Section 326 was born, but with considerably less-onerous requirements than KYC. As one expert put it, the Patriot Act wasn't "Know your customer" it was simply "Identify your customer."[3] By fall 2001, the agendas of identity theft fighters, terrorism fighters, and money-laundering experts were neatly aligned, and all three would be served by financial institutions doing a better job of positively identifying their new customers. The provision itself attracted little controversy. That came later.

***

The Treasury Department was directed to implement the customer identification program 12 months after the passage of the Patriot Act, to give the agency time to solicit industry comments. As the banking industry flooded the Treasury Department with practical concerns about implementing the Customer Identification Program, proposed regulations were slow to emerge. When they arrived in July 23, 2002, they had already been watered down somewhat. The crux of the proposal: Banks would have to view some kind of documentation from new and existing customers as proof they were who they said they were, and the institution would have to store a copy of the document as proof it had done its duty.[4]

A firestorm ensued. Practically speaking, this was a terrible idea that was dead on arrival. In a typical scenario, a new customer would be asked to provide a driver's license to prove his or her identity when opening a new account. A bank account manager would photocopy that license and drop the copy into a file cabinet for record keeping. Immediately, banks balked at what they saw as an expensive requirement to keep mountains of file cabinets full of photocopied driver's licenses. Privacy advocates worried that these file cabinets would be an easy mark for identity thieves. There were even questions about the legality of storing copied licenses in some states. By the time the October 26, 2002, implementation date arrived, the Treasury Department hadn't even finished its review of the public commentary.

Even as banks scrambled to meet the October deadline for whatever rules might eventually be published, Treasury decided at the eleventh hour to offer a reprieve—a temporary delay of Section 326 implementation.[5]

The delay would last six months. When April 2003 arrived, the American Bankers Association had already managed to convince the Treasury Department that maintaining file cabinets full of photocopies was simply a bad idea. The final Section 326 rule, issued the next month, would be even more watered down: Banks and other financial institutions simply had to keep some record that they had inspected an ID-related document from a new customer. A glance at a driver's license or passport would do, along with some kind of notation in a database indicating that glance had taken place.[6]

The rules were to be implemented by October 2003. But already, bankers were indicating that in reality, there was nothing to implement. "At the end of the day, the changes reflect current practice for banks," said John Byrne, the American Bankers Association spokesman. Consumers would see notices on bank windows indicating tellers might ask for a driver's license, but that would be about it.[7]

Now, it was Congress's turn to be aghast. House Judiciary Committee Chairman F. James Sensenbrenner Jr. charged that Section 326 had been whittled down to nothing. In fact, it could be worse than doing nothing at all. "The intent of Congress in directing the Treasury to write new regulations was to raise the bar on the difficulty with which terrorists can move money through the U.S. banking system. As written, this regulation appears to lower the bar," he wrote.[8]

In an unusual move, he convinced the Treasury Department to reopen the comment period on Section 326, allowing more discussion of the proposed rule. Some 34,000 comments arrived, almost all of them supporting the watered-down version.

The comments included yet another request from the industry to stall implementation.[9] In a letter to the Treasury Department, Byrne went . . . out of his way to describe how burdensome even the watered-down Patriot Act was:

> [The] ABA respectfully recommends that the regulatory agencies and the Treasury Department formally acknowledge that as long as an institution has begun the CIP process, there will not be any formal criticism of failure to comply with all aspects of the Section 326 obligations until after a reasonable period beyond the end of this Notice of Inquiry process. We urge the Treasury Department to follow the clear legislative directive that the requirements of Section 326 be both "reasonable and practicable." Flexibility regarding the compliance date is the only appropriate response to the Notice of Inquiry.[10]

Finally, in September, two weeks before it was to take effect and almost two years after the Patriot Act had passed, the Treasury Department made the regulations official, dismissing Sensenbrenner's complaints. Essentially, the new Customer Identification Program maintained the status quo.[11]

A law originally designed to keep terrorists from opening bank accounts, a law that offered the potential to at least slow down identity thieves at one of their most critical points of attack, had become a regulation that now required a new customer to flash only a driver's license or birth certificate when he or she arrived at a bank. Any effort to rigorously identify new bank customers had been effectively pocket-vetoed by the banking industry.

Peering at the practical effect of Section 326, what could be called a sincere effort to *do something* by Congress, it's easy to understand why the banking industry stalled until the law was effectively filibustered.

As has been well established, criminals have little trouble obtaining fake licenses. Asking a bank teller to be expert in all 240 state driver's license formats, and thus be able to spot a counterfeit, is far fetched. Government investigators have proven that criminals have little trouble obtaining real driver's licenses anyway. At any rate, the September 11 hijackers had state-issued identification cards. Most used legitimate passports and visas. Nothing in Section 326 would have prevented September 11 or stopped the terrorists. Asking bank tellers to spot terrorists—anointing them as de facto homeland security officers and document experts—was from the beginning a silly idea.

The circle was now complete. The end of the five-year journey that began with the Know Your Customer idea had ended with, quite clearly, nothing accomplished.

***

It's only natural for identity theft victims to see the mounting crisis and wonder aloud to anyone who will listen, why doesn't the government do something? As the Section 326 saga demonstrates, it's a wonder the government is ever able to do anything. Both privacy and security are incredibly hard to legislate, because such laws require that government bureaucrats nit-pick the operational details of a private industry. Naturally, industry bristles at the idea, and why not? Private citizens do, too. Americans, unlike their European counterparts, are prone to trust private industry far more than the federal government when it comes to protecting privacy.

One of the federal government's key roles is to regulate capitalism when it gets out of hand. Car makers can't cut costs so much that they unnecessarily endanger drivers. Likewise banks can't be so reckless that they endanger privacy or consumers' rights to a fair financial future. As hard as it was, and is, for Congress to stay in front of the auto industry, it's nearly impossible for Congress to keep up with the fallout of the digital age. The privacy provisions of the Gramm-Leach-Bliley Act, also known as the Financial Modernization Act of 1999, offer another example of a simple idea enacted through federal legislation that simply hasn't been put into practice, perpetuating a devastating kind of identity theft.

Perhaps the easiest way identity thieves like James Jackson, who stole the identity of the CEO of Coca-Cola and bought diamonds with his money, get a hold of private financial information is to simply call banks and ask for it. Thieves armed with the slightest information about a potential victim call customer service lines, pretend to be an account holder at the bank, and simply talk their way into the rest of the pieces of the puzzle. Just by having a good story to tell, they con phone operators into sharing account numbers, balances, even Social Security numbers. It's called pretexting—calling a financial institution under a false pretext. Kevin Mitnik, celebrated computer hacker and author of *The Art of Deception*, calls it "hacking the person." A good pretexter can get any information that the real account holder can get. Once the criminal has convinced a $10-per-hour customer service clerk into believing he or she is the real account holder, the sky is the limit.

Electronic-savvy private investigators picked up on this a decade ago and regularly sell information they obtain through pretexting over the Internet. Hundreds of advertisements can be found offering access to anyone's cell phone records, home telephone bill, or bank statements, usually for around $100. The friendly name for such digital private investigators is "information brokers."

In 1998, Rep. Jim Leach and his staff were shocked to learn that no federal law made such activity explicitly criminal. So a provision was added to the sweeping Financial Modernization Act designed to protect consumer privacy. Not only was pretexting declared illegal, but the Federal Trade Commission (FTC) was ordered to enforce the law, prosecuting firms and web sites offering such information for sale.

With all good intentions, the law was designed to stop the burgeoning pretexting industry and all the while put a crimp on the ability of common identity thieves to call banks and get the information they want.

Four years later, the law had done nothing to put a dent in either practice. The Internet is still jam-packed with advertisements hawking such data, far more than in 1999, when the Gramm-Leach-Bliley Act became law. Identity theft consultant Robert Douglas, who trains banks and their employees to comply with the law, says most banks remain completely vulnerable to this kind of attack.[12] In 2001, a *Washington Post* reporter was able to get account balances, transaction records, and even account numbers from a major bank after supplying only a name, Social Security number, and mother's maiden name. Identity thieves continue to use pretexting as their best method for gaining access to personal information. [13]

Industry's response: Consumers want it that way.

"We don't want to make it difficult for customers to get access to their accounts," Robin Warren, once privacy executive at Bank of America Corp., told the *Washington Post.* "Customers get irritated."[14]

***

Why has so little been done by the government to stop pretexters or identity thieves? The Federal Trade Commission, the federal agency charged with hunting down pretexters, has to date only announced four lawsuits against information brokers. All four have been settled by payment of fines. [15] Gramm-Leach-Bliley has had no deterrent effect on the data intruders; private e-mail lists devoted to the industry are full of digital sleuths hawking their ability to gain access to bank records.

Meanwhile, the other privacy provisions of Gramm-Leach-Bliley, designed to put a burden on financial institutions to stop leaking such information, were strikingly slow getting out of the gate. The law required federal regulators to set new security standards by July 1, 2001. That year, the FTC for example asked for public commentary on a so-called Safeguards Rule it authored, designed to "ensure the security and confidentiality of customer records and information . . . protect against unauthorized access to, or use of, such records or information that could result in substantial harm or inconvenience to any customer."[16]

A full year later, on May 17, 2002, the final rule was published in the *Federal Register*. But it wasn't designed to take effect for another year. When it finally did, in May 2003, nearly four years had passed. And companies with third-party contracts were given an additional year—totaling a full five years from passage of the legislation—to pull their partners into compliance.[17]

Are banks and other institutions reacting to the various agencies' new rules? The FTC did promptly issue a show of force, sending notices out to car dealerships demanding evidence that they were in compliance with the regulation.[18]

The FTC's Safeguard Rule doesn't stipulate any fines, though the agency theoretically can bring an unfair and deceptive trade practices case against a company and impose fines of $11,000 per day.

But by the end of 2003, no financial company had ever faced a regulators fine for non compliance with the Gramm-Leach-Bliley Act. In fact, there hadn't been a single notice of any action taken by regulators under the provisions of the new privacy rule. To both criminals and financial institutions, nearly five years after its passage Gramm-Leach-Bliley has so far been a toothless tiger, providing no relief to consumers victimized by the most obvious vulnerabilities enabling identity theft.

***

There have been plenty of government officials—from small-town city council members to U.S. senators—who have made honest efforts to preserve U.S. citizens' privacy rights and protect their identities, evidenced by the fact that privacy was even part of the Financial Modernization Act of 1999, a law largely designed by the financial industry to allow bank megamergers such as Citicorp's acquisition of Travelers Group. When viewed from a distance, state legislatures around the country have responded with great haste and efficiency while dealing with the problem of identity theft.

But a funny thing happens in America when citizens look to the government for help, particularly on the issue of privacy. In deep contrast to their distant relatives in much of Western Europe, where the citizenry is usually much more trusting of the government than private industry, the great tradition of American independence means U.S. citizens fear the government above all else—even above multinational corporations. In Europe, for example, private firms face far stricter regulation over the data they can gather from web site visitors. Meanwhile, there has been little hue and cry from the body politic as laws even more invasive than the Patriot Act have been passed by European legislatures to help investigators in the wake of September 11. Here's one illustrative example. In an attempt to cut down on credit card fraud, many U.S. web sites employ a system called AVS—address verification. It checks to see if the billing address entered by a customer really matches the billing address on file with the credit card holder's bank. In reality, the system checks merely the first few characters of the address. American-based Internet merchants say it cuts down on fraud. But web sites with international clientele have a big problem with AVS—it's illegal in much of Europe for a company to disclose to a customer's address to a third party.[19] Hackers know this; that's why they like shopping at European e-commerce sites; there's no pesky problem of tricking the AVS system. In the U.S., fraud-fighting systems get the nod. In Europe, privacy gets the nod, even if it's at the expense of greater fraud.

The subtle but critical difference has a major impact on the government's ability—inability, really—to deal with identity theft. This was evident during the summer and fall 2003, as Congress debated a necessary update to the Fair Credit Reporting Act (FCRA). Consumers likely have heard about this far-reaching law because it is cited on every credit card bill, every piece of junk mail that has to do with lending, and on most paperwork they receive from banks. The enormous law has been freshened up many times since 1970, when it was first passed to rein in an out-of-control credit reporting industry. Prior to 2003, the most recent comprehensive update to the law was in 1996; that version included a set of controversial provisions which relieved the credit industry from the burden of obeying certain state laws. In seven essential areas of law, most governing consumers' rights and credit bureau data, the federal Fair Credit Reporting Act superceded all state laws—such state laws were declared null and void, a process called "preemption." A traditional states' rights versus strong central government argument broke out during debate over the provision, and it remained in the legislation only after an amendment that it expire in eight years. The compromise was designed to force Congress to reexamine the preemption in eight years to see if it was working.

Supporters of the preemption say it worked like a charm. By 2003, consumer credit was flowing at unprecedented speed, liberating Americans to buy televisions, couches, even cars, on a whim. The impulse buy had reached its golden era. Free from the constraints of various state regulations, which could create a hodge-podge of laws requiring expensive and complex system updates, a single, national law helped the entire credit system operate more smoothly. The credit industry was able to make money available cheaper and quicker than any time in history. The Fair Credit Reporting Act might as well be known as the Consumer is King Act. With the buying power it granted to consumers, this thinking goes, the law has been given credit for the economic boom of the late 1990s.

But there was a flip side to this era of instant gratification. Consumer advocates say the megalithic credit companies—both the credit grantors, such as credit card companies, and the credit historians, bureaus like Equifax and Experian—were trampling on consumer rights. The industry enjoys remarkable immunity under federal law. Citizens have virtually no rights to sue furnishers for libel, while the firms can say anything they want about a consumer's payment history, such as "This consumer has defaulted on an account," to the credit bureaus with little fear of being sued. And if consumers turn to credit bureaus, they can only sue for actual damages, unless they can somehow prove willful violations of the Fair Credit Reporting Act. Simple accidents, no matter how devastating to victims, are insulated from liability.

Liberated by the generous legislation, both sides of the credit industry have created a number of systems that easily fail the commonsense test, discussed in Chapter 4. With 27 million victims of identity theft between 1998 and 2002, it hardly needs to be argued that the credit system was badly broken. Consumer advocates think of the 1996 Fair Credit Reporting Act as the Identity Theft Enabling Act of 1996.

When the time came to revisit the law, some legislators and most consumer advocates seized the opportunity to fix the identity theft crisis. They immediately set their sights on the preemption benefit enjoyed by industry. State legislatures, far more deft and agile than Congress, had already passed numerous creative laws aimed at stemming the tide of the crime and bringing to bear the credit firms that have enabled it. At the same time, lobbying groups from the credit bureaus and the retail industry geared up to win their top prize—permanent establishment of a state law preemption. To do this, they offered free annual credit reports and even adopted many of the identity theft prevention provisions that states around the country had passed.

But that was not enough, consumer advocates argued. It took eight years for Congress to reopen the Fair Credit Reporting

Act. In the 1990s, the former version of the law sat on the table for four years, from 1992 to 1996, while legislators and lobbyists bickered over the preemption provision. Such delays are common when Congress debates new laws, and that slow-moving legislative process is no place to fight identity thieves, who change their tactics hourly. States must have the right to tinker with the credit system as time goes by, passing new laws as needed. That's how the better identity theft–fighting ideas arose, from creative state legislators working to protect their constituents.

During the summer 2003, a seemingly endless march of identity theft victims and their advocates took the trip to Washington, D.C., to tell their sorry tales and plead their case. Don't let the industry off easy, they warned.

Industry giants appeared as well, offering their key argument: Letting states micromanage the credit industry would crush America's credit system, lead to more expensive credit cards and mortgages, and could ultimately cripple the economy. A patchwork of state laws requiring varying ways to verify a credit applicant's identity, for example, would be overly burdensome. A single, national law was needed for a single, national system.

It certainly mattered that the U.S. economy was still teetering on the edge of a fledgling recovery. But it also mattered which side of the Atlantic the legislators lived on. Overregulation is an argument that plays well in Washington, D.C., as does the boogey-man of higher interest rates and an economic collapse. In the end, Congress not only granted the credit industry the permanent state preemption it sought over the original seven areas of credit law, but also extended the preemption to several new areas of law. In the face of the biggest digital crisis ever created and the easiest financial crime ever invented, and at the apex of its outbreak, Congress granted even more leniency to the industry largely responsible for the problem. Essentially, any area of credit bureau operations governed by federal law or regulation were declared permanently exempt from any state law that might impose higher standards.

With a single stroke of President George W. Bush's pen on December 4, 2003, as he signed the Fair & Accurate Credit Transaction Act (Fact-Act) of 2003, a wide swath of state laws from around the country were either wiped out entirely or thrown into a state of vagary, leaving consumers at the mercy of the courts, which will no doubt spend years deciding which provisions are preempted and which are not. In many areas, more lenient federal requirements now supercede state laws. On that list are:

- California laws requiring credit bureaus furnish identity theft victims with one free credit report each month while they go through the ordeal of fixing their files. They will likely be entitled to only one free report each year now.
- An Illinois law requiring creditors to make reasonable efforts to verify a consumer's identity after a police report has been filed indicating an ongoing identity theft. It's unclear what standards federal regulators will institute in this area.
- A Louisiana law insisting that creditors make available to the victim information, such as any monthly billing statements, necessary to undo the effects of the identity theft within 10 days. The new federal law gives creditors 30 days to comply with such requests.
- A Texas law that a security alert must be placed on an identity theft victim's credit report within 24 hours of a consumer request—since speed is of the essence when an electronic thief is on the loose. Federal regulators will develop their own time frame. The Texas law also stipulated that a credit reporting agency must provide the consumer with a copy of the credit file each time a security alert is set to expire. Most alerts expire within 90 or 180 days unless consumers take some additional action.[20] That provision is effectively nullified.

Meanwhile, the 1996 preemptions have now become law forever. Unless Congress acts to reverse itself, state legislators will never be able to mandate additional responsibilities toward those creditors who furnish information to the credit reporting agencies, or mandate additional duties on those who deny a consumer credit, or require a better, more fair process for those who dispute credit report errors. That part of the law is now effectively set in stone.

Even some of the key givebacks the credit industry granted came with strings attached. The law finally acknowledges that credit grantors must actually pay attention to fraud alerts—flags identity theft victims currently attach to their credit reports as they are in the middle of an identity theft attack. The alerts are supposed to force creditors to contact applicants before granting credit, as an extra security step, to ensure additional accounts aren't opened by an imposter. But for years, the alerts were ignored by lenders, which maddeningly continued to grant credit to imposters long after fraud alerts had been placed in the consumer's files. The FACT-Act mandates that the credit bureaus make the alerts obvious and that they are available even when a lender simply asks for a credit score instead of a full credit report.

Still, there's wiggle room in the provision. Lenders need only take "reasonable" steps to verify the identity of the credit applicant. That could be as simple as a single e-mail message—which might end up being sent to the imposter instead of the victim.

There are many reasons why the error-riddled credit reporting industry thumped identity theft advocates in the Fair Credit Reporting Act debate. The chief reason is simple, and not really sinister. With consumer spending responsible for two-thirds of the nation's economy, no one in Washington, D.C., had an appetite in 2003 to do anything that might somehow slow it down. Free flow of credit is the cornerstone of capitalism; even Alan Greenspan, maven of the Federal Reserve and the nation's symbolic economic president, fell on the side of credit speed over identity theft precautions, even as the crisis continued to unfold. [21]

But there is another, deeper reason: The U.S. government seems an unlikely ally for most Americans as they fight for their privacy. After all, particularly in the era of the Patriot Act, the government hardly had much credibility on the issue with most Americans. Disclosure of John Poindexter's Total Information Awareness (TIA) Program in 2002 sent chills down the spine of all civil libertarians, and frankly, all Americans who took the time to read about the program. TIA, by happenstance the Spanish word for aunt, was the Big Brother George Orwell predicted. The brainchild of Poindexter, late of the Reagan-era Iran-Contra scandal, TIA would have married government and corporate databases in intricate ways, then searched for patterns in an attempt to predict terrorist acts before they happened. For example, if a terrorist used his checking account to pay for flight lessons, applied for a pilot's license, then purchased a suspicious amount of chemical agents with a credit card, an alarm bell would go off at the Pentagon.[22] Most security professionals saw through this the way they see through shoe inspections at airports; reactive security measures rarely help much. What is the likelihood that the next airplane terrorist will try a shoe bomb while the rest of us walk with stockinged feet through airport metal detectors? As John Markoff, longtime high-tech reporter at the *New York Times* put it, TIA might have identified people who buy the same things terrorists buy.[23] But it's doubtful the software would have been very effective at predicting terrorist acts. Under public pressure, Congress killed the funding for TIA in 2003. But similar projects are still being developed all over Washington D.C.

The FBI has had its data collections debacles, too. In the digital age, computers are often the most illuminating source of information for federal and local agents examining a crime scene. The moment they show up to arrest a suspect, at least one agent heads for the computer, making sure to preserve the incredible resource of digital records. Computer forensics is one of the fastest-growing fields in law enforcement. Criminals often keep spreadsheets, correspondence, diaries, and, of course, e-mail in their computers. The files, when the proper chain of custody is maintained with special software to preserve their evidentiary value, can be the closest thing to incontrovertible evidence that the government has.

Of course, getting to the computer's hard drive is a serious barrier. Generally, a judge must issue a court order; and agents need to know where the computer is. Wouldn't it better, the FBI thought, to get copies of e-mail destined for a suspect? Much like a wiretap, e-mail peeking would give law enforcement agents unprecedented access to ongoings in the criminal world. In fact, not since the birth of the wiretap has law enforcement come upon such a powerful new crime-fighting tool.

And Carnivore was born. Built both inside and outside the FBI by contracted software developers, Carnivore does exactly what its name suggests. Federal agents show up at an Internet service provider and either install a special computer or add a program to an existing computer. Once in place, the program slurps up all bits of data headed for a certain Internet address. The data is stored and, after a search warrant is received and the information covered by the court order is separated out, the FBI reads everything headed for the criminal.[24]

Carnivore is perhaps the least-thoughtful name ever given to a controversial government project—particularly one designed to expand the powers of crime investigators by utilizing mysterious new technology. Disclosure of the existence of Carnivore led to widespread complaints. Freedom of Information Act (FOIA) requests flowed freely as lobbyists at the Electronic Frontier Foundation and the Electronic Privacy Information Center tried to figure out how Carnivore worked and if it really worked as advertised. In 2003, despite congressional hearings and more

FOIA filings, there were still critical open questions. Chief among them: Can Carnivore really avoid trapping innocent citizens' e-mails while slurping up bits of data destined for alleged criminals specifically covered by a court order? The FBI isn't really saying. It did, however, change the name of the software to the intentionally innocuous DCS1000.

But before that controversy had come under control, a related storm appeared. Perhaps the most important, if wonky, civil rights argument of the 1990s revolved around private citizens' rights to encryption technology. Governments hate secrets; they like being in the know. They don't like citizens being able to keep information buried deep within their private homes or computers. Such secrecy, this line of thinking suggests, will ultimately be a tool used against the country by terrorists or a foreign government. Once upon a time, only large governments with a lot of money could afford complicated schemes to scramble data and make it unreadable to anyone without the proper key to unscramble it. But the age of cheap, fast computers make such scrambling, called cryptography, available to everyone.

Steven Levy's book *Crypto* explores the decade-long struggles of digital heroes like Phil Zimmerman to fend off government efforts to block cryptography from getting into the hands of the masses. The debate consumed much energy from the Clinton administration, which realized simple encryption programs like Pretty Good Privacy could easily be used by criminals to keep secrets from the government. A techno-hip bad guy could use Pretty Good Privacy, rendering his computer hard drive useless to investigators. Without the encryption key, it's just garble, the treasure trove of evidence now useless.

For a while, the Clinton White House favored a system that insisted software makers give a spare key for all its programs to the government or a trusted third party, just for emergencies. After all, if there were a secret that the government needed access to, perhaps a terrorist plan to destroy a bridge or a mobster's list of clients, the government didn't want a pile of useless scrambled data on its hands.

Technologists eventually won the day, convincing the administration that any such plan was foolhardy. Software knows no boundaries; domestic limitations on encryption could be easily skirted in the age of the Internet. The cat was out of the bag. Encryption was here to stay, for everyone—criminals, terrorists, and average citizens.

But that wasn't the end of the story at the FBI, which came up with a much more old-fashioned way to get encryption keys—breaking and entering. In 2001, during the investigation of alleged mobster Nicholas Scarfo, agents broke into his business and installed special software on Scarfo's computer to copy every single character he typed. The software is common on the Internet today, called spyware, or keylogging software. Scarfo was using Pretty Good Privacy to scramble a spreadsheet of clients in his gambling business. To unlock the scrambled files, Scarfo typed in a passphrase, or password, which told the software to decrypt the message. Once the FBI keylogging software copied Scarfo's passphrase, agents could gain access to the encrypted files on his machine. They arrested Scarfo, seized the computer, and accessed the files. That's fair in the digital age, proclaimed U.S. District Judge Nicholas Politan, when Scarfo's defense argued this was unfair search and seizure.[25]

Emboldened software designers at FBI headquarters decided to take the idea one step farther, and so was born Enhanced Carnivore and Magic Lantern. So also arrived a second public relations fiasco.[26]

Magic Lantern would allow agents to unlock encrypted files like Scarfo's from a distance—no break-in required. A developer who worked on the program says it was a kind of computer virus called a Trojan horse, similar to e-mail attachments computer users regularly receive. A suspect or other target of an FBI investigation would click on the disguised e-mail, become secretly infected, and suddenly, everything typed at that computer could be seen by investigators. Better still, even encrypted files could be viewed, remotely, because Magic Lantern knew how to gather pass phrases.

The program raises plenty of civil-liberties questions. Ultimately, it can be argued that reaching across the Internet to gather evidence, with appropriate court orders, is no different than walking into a criminal's house or business and seizing his or her computer. But as always, there was concern about mission creep, about how FBI agents could abuse such technology. And there was a question about why the government was secretly spending money developing software to steal encryption keys, when the nation had just gone through a torturous 10-year debate about private citizens' rights to keep such keys to themselves. The agency initially denied the existence of Magic Lantern, first disclosed on MSNBC.com. But as journalists around the world repeated the story, and the antivirus industry debated if it would detect and destroy the FBI's software, the agency eventually conceded the project did exist.

***

Perhaps many Americans appreciate the difference between the FBI and the FTC, but hardly all. One has the charter to protect consumers and, by extension, argue for privacy rights. The other, by charter, wants to pry. But to many Americans, it's all Washington. And it's hard to imagine the makers of Total Information Awareness, Carnivore, and Magic Lantern as champions of privacy. All that helps national industries when they throw up their arms and cry, "Too much regulation" in an exasperated-sounding press release. Americans may not trust major corporations, but they trust their government even less. It adds just enough confusion to the privacy debate that it's hard to imagine a government agency having the necessary bully pulpit to rein in any industry when it needs a crack of the whip to deal with identity theft. Instead, federal agencies are left to simply ask politely for help in the face of the crisis.

Meanwhile, the federal government has now legislated for itself complete ownership of the crisis. The credit industry has made a convincing argument that it shouldn't have to deal with 50 sets of state regulations ensuring citizen rights. It certainly can't deal with laws passed by thousands of municipalities. No, laws governing credit should only come from the federal government, industry says, and the 2003 version of the Fair Credit Reporting Act makes it so. That means the only hope for legislative relief from identity thieves comes from a federal government known for its own privacy issues and known for sleeping with the enemy.

In September 2002, for example, JetBlue Airlines gave the Transportation Security Administration and an overzealous defense contractor named Torch technologies a full dossier on 1.1 million recent passengers. The information was to be used in the development of CAPPS-II (Computer Assisted Passenger Pre-Screening Program), designed to help identify potential high-risk fliers from their travel and personal habits. The controversial data-mining project, being developed by the Transportation Security Administration's Office of National Risk Assessment, seeks to marry extensive commercial and government data—but the government was having trouble finding co-operative airlines who would share real data to test the system. Enter JetBlue.

When release of the data became public in September 2003, privacy advocates were aghast. The airline had promised its passengers in a privacy policy that it would never share such information. Here was a clear case of the government encouraging private industry to play fast and loose with its own privacy rules.

The database that could be developed from the data was alarming. In addition to basic flight booking data, JetBlue turned over entire "Passenger Name Record" entries in the airlines' reservation system, which can include a vast array of personal information details of car and hotel reservations, in-flight meal preferences, travel companions—even whether travelers stayed in a room with one bed or two. Married to that data were other private details like income and other indicators of economic status, occupation, specifics on residence, such as whether the traveler was an owner or a renter, the length of time lived at one residence, the number of children, the number of cars owned, and of course, Social Security number.[27]

At least some of the sensitive, private information released by the company made its way onto the Internet. The entire mess was initially disclosed on privacy crusader Edward Hasbrouck's personal Web site, called DontSpyOn.us. Hasbrouck had found a presentation about the system while surfing Torch Concepts' web site. The presentation included real consumer data, real names and Social Security numbers; certainly a treasure trove for identity thieves.

And JetBlue wasn't the only airline convinced by the federal government to reveal highly detailed, private passenger travel data in recent years. The Electronic Privacy Information Center released documents in January 2004 indicating that Northwest Airlines had shared similar data with NASA for a passenger pre-screening test project run by the space agency. In response to a request made only a few months after Sept. 11, Northwest gave three months' worth of travelers' data to NASA. The agency returned the data after the JetBlue dust-up.[28]

***

This is not the behavior of a government that can be expected to zealously protect its citizens from privacy violations and identity theft. But what likely gives Americans the greatest pause when looking to the federal government for help with identity theft are the close relationships between elected officials and the credit industry, one of the most powerful lobbying forces in Washington, D.C. The credit industry's largesse surrounding its massive efforts to convince Congress that it should rewrite bankruptcy laws is legendary. Consumer credit industry lobby groups gave, on average, more than $100,000 in political action committee (PAC) contributions to each member of the Senate from 1987 to 1998, according to an analysis by election watchdog group Common Cause. The biggest donor in the group was the American Bankers Association. Nations Bank gave just over $5 million. Lobby group America's Community Bankers gave $3.5 million. BankAmerica, Chase, Citicorp, and Beneficial all gave $2 million or more.[29]

Similar, if not as obvious, lobbying tactics were used in the summer 2003, when the credit industry's exemption from state laws was threatened by the looming expiration of parts of the Fair Credit Reporting Act. In an intriguing account by Washington watchdog publication *Roll Call*, reporter Sarah Bouchard describes the extensive and expensive schmoozing that took place while the House and Senate marked up their versions of the new Fair Credit Reporting Act.[30]

> Citigroup, TransUnion and Capital One have spent thousands of dollars flying key Congressional aides to a handful of conferences around the country to bring them up to speed on the issue. More than 10 staff members attended each conference, according to disclosure forms filed with Congress, most of which were aides working for lawmakers on the Financial Services and Banking committees.

> "It's a critical issue for our company and our industry," said TransUnion spokesman Jeffrey Junkas. About 20 staffers attended TransUnion's late-February symposium in Crum Lynne, Pennsylvania, costing the company about $650 a person, according to disclosure forms.

After introductory speeches and a tour of the facility, the staffers were treated to three panels: "Impact of FCRA Preemption Loss on Risk Assessment," "Impact of FCRA Preemption Loss on Consumer Credit" and "Impact of FCRA Preemption Loss on new applications of consumer report information," according to a symposium agenda.

Citigroup spent about $1,500 a pop to send Hill staffers to its conference, which took place at the end of January in The Lakes, Nev. The three-day tour included sessions ranging from an "Overview of Citi Cards and Role of Card Industry in Economy" to the "Importance of the Fair Credit Reporting Act."

Perhaps the most posh . . . was a conference sponsored by Capital One in early March at the Don Cesar Beach Resort and Spa in St. Pete Beach, Fla. Panelists included Lisa McGreevy of the Financial Services Roundtable, Floyd Stoner of the American Bankers Association and a group of Capital One executives.

Aside from the travel, the credit industry has pumped thousands of dollars into Members' reelection accounts and signed up a team of new lobbyists.[31]

Some of the connections between industry and federal legislators aren't even so gently disguised. Just a few days after Sen. Robert Bennett voted for changes to the Fair Credit Reporting Act that the credit industry wanted, Equifax threw a fund-raiser for him that brought in tens of thousands of dollars to the Utah Republican's reelection campaign. The Equifax political action committee event on September 26 at company headquarters in Atlanta raised roughly $25,000 to $30,000 for Bennett, who was facing a tough reelection challenge. In addition to supporting the preemption of state laws to help companies like Equifax avoid being responsible to state legislatures, Bennett also favored other not-very-consumer-friendly provisions that limited consumer access to free credit reports, barring requests made via telephone, for example. Equifax says the timing was a coincidence. The company told its employees, in a newsletter, sent a few days after the fund-raiser, that Bennett was a powerful force in the Senate. It said Equifax's PAC and employees were supporting a senator who has been "extremely helpful in our efforts to mitigate the impact of providing credit reports nationwide."[32]

It's hard to imagine identity theft victims were welcome at the party, even though; statistically speaking, about 1 in 10 of those who were there had already been hit with the crime.

8

THE INTERNET'S ROLE

I want to give you a good material for good news line. Very big and very well-known brokerage site has been hacked by our team and all personal information about their customers (over 25,000 people) has been stolen. We offered to the director of the company . . . to pay us money, but he declined this proposal. I think this info could be interesting for publicity.

—Mr. Zilterio

To anyone who received it, it would have felt like someone had just left a small bomb at the door—with no instructions on how to defuse it.

It was just an e-mail, sent through cyberspace. But it contained a powerful message. Attached to the e-mail was a large text file, and inside was one of the most thorough invasions of privacy imaginable.[1]

As a show of skill, the hacker had sent a pack of bank statements. Thousands of them. Not just names, account numbers, and balances—these were complete bank statements. Every check. Every deposit. Every ATM withdrawal—including time and place. And not just last month's statement. For each customer, there were about two-years' worth of monthly statements.

Armed with this much data, anyone could accomplish much more than simply steal identities. Someone with this much information could have written a novel about each customer. The hacker could have easily inferred when each consumer was low on cash, when their wallets were full, when they went on vacation, where they went, who their therapist was. It came from a Mr. Zilterio—his pseudonym—and he was trying to make a point, trying to prove his mettle, and ultimately trying to make a quick buck.

"Zilterio" said he was ringleader of a group of Russian hackers who, in hacker lingo, provided "security services." They regularly broke into web sites and financial firms, stole some data, then called the company and offered to fix their weak spots— for a fee. The offer always came with a "you can't refuse" message. Pay us and we'll go away; refuse, and we'll tell the world about your shoddy security measures. Banks, brokerage firms, and even web sites are particularly sensitive to this kind of bad news, so Zilterio knew how to hit where it hurts.

It's extortion, plain and simple. Zilterio said he would normally ask for $50,000 for his security work, and settle for about half of that. Nine firms paid him $150,000 in quiet money, he claimed, offering no proof. But a private investigator hired by one of his victims said that at least one company did pay up.

Mr. Zilterio was hardly shy about the havoc he wreaked at his computer. "Blackmailing is just a hobby for us, not a business. We like to be famous," he wrote. For over a year, Zilterio hacked into online companies and financial institutions, stealing data, and then demanding extortion payments. While the big-money claims may have been a fantasy, the crimes were quite real, and the FBI spent real time hunting for Mr. Zilterio.

"I do want fame only for one reason," he wrote. "To show our future clients, that we don't play a game, but all we offer is for real."

Zilterio certainly had the means to make his threats stick. When a company didn't pay up, he told its customers in a cold, calculating e-mail.

The e-mails always looked the same, as if cut and pasted by someone on an assembly line. The opening line "I hate to inform you that your account has been hacked." From 2000 to 2001, tens

of thousands of Internet users received a note beginning like that
from Zilterio, whose real identity remains a mystery. Included in
the rest of the unnerving e-mails were the recipient's personal
details, such as name, address, e-mail address, and credit card
numbers, and the name of the web site where the data was stolen.

"This site has a very weak security protection system and the
database with credit cards and other personal information is not
protected at all," Zilterio's e-mails continue, in a transparent
attempt to shift the blame for his crime. It's their fault, because
the company rejected his offer of help, he says. "Top management . . . doesn't care about their customers—you. They care
only about their money."

Zilterio, he claimed, is actually a pseudonym for a group of
eight hackers—three in Moscow and five elsewhere in Russia.
Mr. Zilterio, the correspondent and appointed spokesperson,
wrote in good, even colloquial English, suggesting he was either
well educated, or lying about his location.

On a web site devoted to the group's effort, there was an
extortionist's manifesto, of sorts:

The situation with online security is very bad and very dangerous now. Almost 75 percent of all big e-commerce sites
can be breaken [sic] in less than 2 hours. Customers should
not trust these sites, but they do. These online shops and
banks don't pay enough to their software developers and
technical directors maybe. We don't know why, but this is
what we have now.

Our mission is to help companies to protect their customers' data. There are many skilled hackers in our team.
We can break almost any modern computer system, including online banks and big online shops. When we get access
to such systems we notify their owners about it. Some companies are ready to cooperate and they get our help. We

send them instructions about how to improve their systems and later we track the process of this improvement. These companies care about their customers.

But some Internet sites don't want to cooperate. In this case we notify all their customers about existing security loopholes. We do it to protect people against further loss of personal information. This is our mission.

***

The world of electronic criminals is full of posers and fakes and expert liars. Armed with a near-perfect cloak of anonymity, bad guys can and do claim all kinds of wild things. But Zilterio was different. The group had claimed about a dozen high-profile break-ins during the year 2000—and most of them checked out. Russian hacker extortion plots had recently been in vogue. Only months earlier, two Russians who had extorted U.S. firms were lured to Seattle by the FBI with the promise of a high-paying computer security job and were later arrested.[2] Zilterio said he knew the two Russians, "fools" he called them. Nevertheless, early on in chat-room conversations, Zilterio himself had asked for help finding a legitimate job in the United States. He seemed to slip effortlessly between Zilterio, the genius hacker, and Zilterio, the out-of-work dot-commer.

This time, the target was a midsized Midwestern bank—Home National Bank, based in Kansas. Zilterio said he had stolen hundreds of megabytes worth of data, several years' worth of bank statements. And he was ready to provide proof of his wild claims.

He sent only a slice of the data, information on a few hundred customers. That's typical, too—he sent along enough to prove his point, not enough to tip his hand—after all, the data was valuable because he had it, exclusively. But he indicated that he had more of the same, about 1,000 times the number of bank statements he had shared.

Essentially, he said, he had the life story of every Home National Bank customer. Somehow, sitting at his computer just outside Moscow, Zilterio and friends had reached across the Internet, halfway around the world, and stolen their financial life stories.

When the bank was approached about the incident, it followed the usual pattern of silent denials. Company executives declined to discuss what happened. With great discomfort, the contents of Zilterio's e-mail bomb were sent through cyberspace again—this time to executives at Home National Bank. Comment or not, either way, MSNBC.com will write a story about Zilterio, the firm was told. Still, bank officials wouldn't talk, and the story was published, describing exposure of the bank's customers.

A week after that story ran, the bank admitted to a *Daily Oklahoman* reporter that a hacker had indeed managed to break into their systems through a hole in the firms' online banking web site. And in this story, Home National indicated it would fess up to customers. The company had decided to send letters to its customers—one year after the break-in, six months after the initial extortion attempt, and one week after a journalist had told them.

"We sent out letters to our customers not because any accounts have been compromised," Michael Walker, senior vice president, told the *Daily Oklahoman*. "But so that customers could pay more attention to their accounts."[3]

***

Word of web site hacks and Internet vulnerabilities has become so common that they are now merely background noise to most Internet users. Zilterio's adventures got attention, but only because he demanded it. So many other data leaks are kept quiet by guilty companies that the state of California passed a law requiring companies to tell consumers when their personal information has been exposed to criminals.[4] Since the pace of commerce picked up on the World Wide Web in 1996, countless consumers have been victimized by an identity theft that began

with an Internet data leak. In many cases, lazy computer practices, lax security, and poorly designed software were to blame;
in other cases, profit-minded companies have underpaid and
overworked their technology departments, leading to an
inevitable accident. Other times, hackers break directly into
consumers' computers and steal their data, or hijack their systems, assuming a consumer's virtual identity in order to commit
untraceable crimes. Whatever the method, it has become pro
forma for corporations to keep silent when consumer data is
lost; generally, they only fess up when threatened by a journalist
or a hacker.

Such leaks are an inevitable consequence of the Internet's
integration into corporate networks and retail commerce.
Nearly every corporate computer in the world is now connected
to the Internet. Not directly, of course. There might be firewalls
upon firewalls, routers, cables, secret software, all kinds of methods for erecting barriers between the Internet and that bank
computer storing all that critical data. But virtually no company
maintains two, completely different, physically distinct, totally
separate networks. If a company is connected to the Internet, its
internal computers can be attacked.

Even those consumers who have never used the Internet are
at risk of having their identities stolen from it. As this worldwide
web of computers lets us plug into the world, it lets the world
plug into us. It is a dream come true for criminals, who now can
find their victims halfway around the world and steal their
money from the comfort of home—emboldened by the relative
immunity that results from international borders. To clever
criminals, the Internet is the greatest tool ever invented.

There isn't a web site that will allow hackers to break directly
into ATM machines. But there is an innocent-looking web site
that's sitting on a computer that's trusted by another, internal
computer that's linked to a company's payroll computer. And
that's how hackers in colleges and at Kinko's sneak their way
inside major corporations in between pizza slices.

It's called "escalation"—finding a leaky computer on the edge of a network and slowly working your way in backward. It's the virtual equivalent of sneaking around a building through an air duct and dropping down into the vault room where the diamonds are kept.

That's how 18-year-old Adrian Lamo, the Kinko's hacker, managed to break into the *New York Times*'s internal networks and obtain Robert Redford's Social Security number. He also got Social Security numbers on James Baker, James Carville, and former NSA chief Bobby Inman—along with home telephone numbers for people like Jimmy Carter and Jeanne Kirkpatrick. Lamo discovered a trick that let him turn a computer security system against itself, and he used that trick on numerous big-name companies, like Microsoft and MCI. But his venture into the *New York Times*'s computers ruffled the most feathers.[5]

Lamo just browsed his way to the data, essentially worming his way onto the *Times*'s internal computers. The jackpot for him— the contact information for all *Times* Op-Ed page contributors, a veritable Who's Who of world influence and fame. And he did it all through a web browser sitting at a Kinko's.

Without the work of so-called gray hat hackers like Lamo, hackers who break into computers for sport instead of profit, we might never have any idea how the Zilterios of the world do their genuine dirty business.

Yet authorities came down hard on the fast-talking, nomad Lamo, who spent most of his later teen years busing around the country between friend's homes, working his magic at Kinko's around the country. After an FBI agent read about the *New York Times* incident on the SecurityFocus.com web site, Lamo was indicted for computer crimes in New York. He became a celebrity of sorts when the FBI made several attempts to use journalists' notes for evidence as it developed its case against him. The agency's willingness to take on thorny First Amendment issues raised by asking reporters for notes from private conversations with a source indicates how seriously some computer crimes are treated.[6]

***

Excepting the work of characters like Lamo, just how most personal data that's available on the Internet gets there is a mystery. And so is the fact that a consumer's identity has been exposed.

Dan Clements runs CardCops.com, a web site devoted to exposing credit card companies for ignoring rampant Internet credit card theft. His premise is simple: He and his band of anonymous informants troll Internet chat rooms looking for stolen credit card numbers. And when they find them, the numbers are entered into the CardCops database. Consumers can, for free, dial up CardCops and see if their credit card is in the hands of hackers. With no advertising, and meager help, Clements's database had about 1 million credit card numbers after about a year.[7]

Clements does this because credit card companies don't do this. If a credit card number is stolen from an Internet site, the credit card associations defer to the card-issuing banks, and together the two have a policy of not informing consumers. The firms wait to see if fraud occurs. Only after their neural networks detect a pattern of fraud is the card canceled and the consumer informed. It's simple economics—reissuing credit cards can cost between $10 and $25 per consumer.[8] Why spend the money if they don't have to? A consumer's right to know is not part of that neural network.

Clements's database represents a tiny fraction of the stolen credit card numbers floating around the Internet today. There are chat rooms with painfully obvious names like #creditcards where blocks of stolen account information are bought, sold, and traded like options on the Chicago Board of Trade. They are not hard to find; in fact, they are so common that the value of a stolen card can be below $1.

Hearing about stolen credit cards is one thing; seeing these chat rooms in action is quite another. Hackers regularly post stolen data into chat rooms to provide free samples, a teaser for a haul of stolen credit cards. And other times, a massive dump of stolen data is dropped into the chat room, what "carders" call "burning." Suddenly, hundreds of innocent people's names float by, their names, addresses, phone numbers, and sometimes, even more personal data, such as driver's license numbers or mother's maiden names. Within moments, every person exposed in the room becomes a victim of identity theft.

Why burn the cards? When the card numbers are dumped, and used by hundreds of other carders, the hackers think it obscures the audit trail for investigators—who now must hunt and peck through hundreds of attempted fraudulent transactions to find the criminal. Or, sometimes cards are burned when a deal goes bad and the seller intentionally makes the buyer's stolen merchandise worthless.

Whenever someone sees such chat rooms in action for the first time, the conversation always goes something like this:

"But that's someone's phone number, name, address, credit card."

"Yup. And 60 seconds from now the card will be maxed out. It's like throwing meat to hungry dogs."

"How can they get away with this? Why doesn't someone stop them?"

"It's the Internet. You can't."

"Someone should tell these people their cards have been posted in a chat room."

"OK, let's call them."

Such charitable efforts to warn consumers that they've been exposed are quickly overwhelmed by sheer volume. Following up on stolen cards in even one chat room, for one hour, could keep a small army of consumer advocates busy for weeks.

Still, it's often instructive to call a few, trying to piece together where the cards had been stolen from. Without fail, the victims are shocked to find out that a reporter knows their name and credit card number. Sometimes, their account had already been canceled by their bank, but the victims never knew why. They certainly had no idea their name and address would be published in a chat room and sold to a criminal—and that now, they are at risk for identity theft.

Credit card firms have a long, clear history of not telling victims when their identities have been placed at risk because of Internet break-ins. It is, in fact, policy. This entire area of Internet swapping is largely ignored.

In February 2003, 8 million credit card numbers were exposed to a hacker by Omaha-based Data Processors International (DPI). DPI is essentially a data middleman for credit card processing that takes place around the country. The hacker who broke in was able to spy on all manner of transactions—Visa, MasterCard, American Express, and Discover were all impacted, along with hundreds of member banks.[9]

As usual, the credit card associations left the decision to inform consumers up to issuing banks. Soon after, two banks, Citizens and PNC Bank, told some 50,000 customers they were in that group of 8 million and that their accounts would be closed and reissued. Slowly, another 10 or so banks followed suit. But the majority of member banks let it slide, hoping the data wasn't really stolen or that it wouldn't ever be used for fraud. And victims who want to find out if they are on the list the hackers might have? They'll never know.[10]

***

Do they really need to? At this point, nearly all consumers are aware that they aren't liable for charges accrued on a stolen credit card—legally, their liability is capped at $50, but even that amount is often waived. So what's the big deal?

The credit industry's generous insulation from the problems caused by the simplest form of identity theft, a single stolen credit card, is actually part of the problem. It has made credit card theft a victimless crime by muting its impact. Of course, we all pay in higher fees, and often victim merchants lose their merchandise. But the additional problems caused by credit card fraud are just complex enough to not raise any attention.

It's the ready supply of stolen credit cards that is the foundation for so many more complex identity thefts—they play a role in nearly every web-based fraud, for example, because the criminal needs to pay for web hosting service without leaving a trace. But the theft of even a single stolen credit card can enable a whole string of identity thefts, as Don's story illustrates.[11]

***

When Don's credit card number was stolen in 2002, leaked by just another careless web site, it meant just another canceled credit card, except for one thing—Don wouldn't take it sitting down. A tech-savvy Net user who works at Microsoft-owned Ensemble Studios in Dallas, Don made a few phone calls and managed to retrace the thief's steps. He agreed to share details of his cybersluething only if his last name were withheld.

Peeking through accounts at anonymous e-mail services, information brokers, and online banks, Don got a rare glimpse of an identity thief at work. Here's how that one stolen credit card became three bank checks totaling $3,000—and perhaps much more.

It all started when Don tried to buy art work online. Don stuck his credit card into a checkout form at a small web site on July 14. Unfortunately, the card number got spit out the other side of the web site, thanks to a security hole, and quickly ended up in a hacker newsgroup. By 7 A.M. the next morning, his credit card company called to say it had logged $700 in suspicious activity overnight on his card, and it had been canceled. That's normally where stories like this end. But a few days later, Don went online to check his statement and found one more fraudulent charge from a web site that sells all manner of people-finding information, including Social Security number lookups. It's a natural first stop for someone attempting identity theft. Because the account was opened in Don's name, the web site's operator agreed to fork over the user name, password, and the Hotmail e-mail address used to sign up for the site. That began Don's voyage through the ID thief's handiwork. Don tried the same password for the alleged criminal's Hotmail account—and it worked. The 15 e-mail messages sitting in his Hotmail inbox offered a blow-by-blow look at just how criminals can turn stolen data into cold, hard cash.

There was a Western Union account opened under the name of Cecilia Salow. "She" ordered a cell phone, too, through BellSouth. Then, a credit report ordered from the Equifax credit bureau on someone called Humbeto Becerra. Seconds later, a Net-Bank.com account was opened in Becerra's name. And, perhaps most important, there was an e-mail to a Michael Bradway from someone using the name Joe Angel. The e-mail indicated an $845 check was sent to Bradway via a web site named Qchex, likely funded with Don's credit card. Qchex allowed account holders to send checks via the Internet, which could then be printed by the payee and cashed just like a bank check.

In this case, the payee was Michael Bradway. In fact, according to the Qchex records viewed by Don, three checks were sent to Michael Bradway on July 19, totaling just under $3,000. Two other checks were sent a few days before Don's card was stolen, and probably from another ID theft incident, adding another $1,800 to the criminal's take. Qchex refused to comment on the incident.

Also sitting in this e-mail inbox, according to Don, was an image of a Florida driver's license for a Michael Bradway. Armed with a convincing photo ID, Bradway would have enjoyed good odds in any attempts at cashing the checks—though it's unknown if he or she ever succeeded. While it's clear the criminal tried to steal $4,800 via Qchex, it's not clear what activity was attempted with the Western Union account, so the actual take could have been more.

Blame for the string of attempted crimes is hard to pin on any of the various victim businesses along the way, but Don said he was frustrated because he had nowhere to turn with the highly detailed information he had about the criminal's wrongdoings. Chase, the card issuer, was only concerned with reverting the fraudulent charges. An FBI agent understood the case, but said "unless you can show us it's $25,000 or more we're not touching it." And the Dallas police technology crime investigator—there's only one, he was told — had a one-year backlog of cases.

But Don said he was most frustrated by the credit card company's lack of interest in pursuing the case. "I told them, 'You guys did a great job in making sure they didn't steal from me, but why don't you step up to the plate and actually stop somebody?'" Don said. "Instead, they just said to me, 'Wait a few weeks, these things work themselves out.'"

***

Trade in stolen data on the Internet can involve much more than mere credit card fraud. Most victims who had their whole digital dossiers revealed in an Indonesian-based chat room in 2001 will never know how their identities were stolen, either. The name of the chat room was #Indocarder. There's no way of knowing where its participants really were, but publicly, they said they were in the Pacific Rim nation, and most of the chatter was in Indonesian. But there were a few English words that flew by as well.

Name. Address. Account. Social Security number.

#Indocarder had always been among the most reliable Internet chat rooms that can be used for live demonstrations of serious credit card fraud. But even though he regularly frequented this dirty place, Tom Trusty, a former Citibank fraud consultant, was shocked by what he saw.

"Go stand by your fax machine," he said, practically whispering through the phone. "I will fax you something that no one else should see. Right now."[12]

He sent pages and pages of log files he had preserved from the chat room the night before. These weren't lists of burned credit cards. There were mother's maiden names. Social Security numbers. Driver's license numbers. Dates of birth. Even places of employment. These were personal lives, on full display—hundreds of them. Full digital dossiers. Somewhere in the world, some very important company had sprung a very bad leak.

Trusty had scored an invitation to the invitation-only chat room weeks earlier. He had been working undercover for months to build trust relationships in the credit card hacker world. As a hobby, he would troll for evidence of credit card break-ins and funnel them first to impacted companies, and if he was ignored, then to the media to gain attention to the problem. But he didn't expect to see this.

The appearance of the Social Security numbers was alarming. The victims faced almost certain identity theft. Once data like that is published in a chat room, there is no taking it back. There is no delete key to hit, no web page to shut down or erase. The data is copied and stored in log files and on hard drives all over the Internet. It's out there. It's not private any more. The loss of such privacy is always a one-way street.

Trusty faxed as many pages of the stuff as he could. About 100 victims were told about the chat room. Again, the conversations were always the same.

"Why do you know my phone number?"

"It's on the Internet, in a chat room, along with your Social Security number."

"Well, can I get it off the Internet?"

"No, I'm sorry, you can't."

"Where is it?"

"In an Internet relay chat."

"What's that? What should I do now?"

There was no answer for the victims then, as there really is no answer now. But there was an important question: Who leaked the data? What was the common denominator among all these victims? In data leaks like this, there is always a common point of failure, a single place where all the information was stored, for a time. Talking to enough victims often points to the place. After 50 or so interviews, some answers began to emerge.

Every victim had ordered a cell phone recently. But the consumers had used a variety of carriers and purchasing methods; some were bought over the Internet, some in mall kiosks. The data was listed in a format that mimicked the application form on several web sites, and the datasets were consistent with what's needed to run a credit check on a new customer. This was a clue, but not an answer. As often happens in Internet mysteries, the answer never came. But within weeks, Philip Cummings was arrested in New York for allegedly using a credit terminal to steal 33,000 credit reports directly from the credit reporting agencies. The arrest showed the credit application system was one of the weakest links in the identity theft chain and provided a plausible explanation for the Indonesian chat room incident.

***

You don't necessarily have to break into any computers, or even find a criminal chat room, to steal personal data online. Plenty of it is lying around in plain view. If you've never done this, try it now—search for yourself on Google.com. But don't just search for your name. Search for your personal information, like your credit card numbers, or your unlisted phone number, or even your Social Security number. Be careful, don't enter all of it— just enough to trigger a search engine hit, say the first four or five numbers. You might get an unhappy surprise.

That's what happened to Donna in March 2002.[13] One day while idly surfing, she stumbled onto her name and personal information on a web page full of stolen data, somewhere in a dark corner of the Internet. Nearly a year earlier, she had gotten one of those alarming calls from her credit card company which indicated that her credit card account had been compromised and her card would be canceled and reissued. As is normal, she had no idea why. But there she was, sitting at her home computer, looking at her address, phone number, and old credit card number. It was published on a web site based in Russia, along with about 1,000 other such records. It would have stayed there in obscurity, perhaps forever. But the know-all search engine Google.com finds every dark corner of the Internet, and it found Donna.

It's hard to say if this is good or bad. A web page that's not in a search engine might as well not exist, but for the few friends who know about it. Without Google, Donna never would have found out about her name being published.

On the other hand, simple searches like "4128"—the first four digits of a credit card account number, which indicate the name of the bank—and MC are often good enough to find some pretty private data on Google, and it found Donna's name that day. The leading search engine has an amazing ability to find everything on the Internet. When Internet shopping carts start accidentally spewing out web site checkout data onto the Internet, as PDG checkout software did in 2001, hundreds of customer lists could be found simply by searching for a particular file name on Google. For a while, a single search yielded dozens of pages full of credit card data. Google archives everything and makes it all easy to find, including things we're not supposed to see.

Google says it does all it can to avoid this unsavory situation. And when alerted to such a problem, it quickly removed the offending link from its database, as it did after the story about Donna ran.

But it doesn't always work that way. Two years later, in August 2003, Jenny repeated Donna's discovery, finding her name, address, and credit card number on a private web page. She wrote to Google on August 6; by August 13, Jenny and 500 other victims' personal information was still on the web site and still being churned out in search results by Google.

Computer hackers and identity thieves are often too quickly labeled as geniuses. Hacking and stealing are often as easy as using a search engine.[14]

***

Perhaps the only easier way to steal a consumer's identity on the Internet is to ask them for it. "Phisher" e-mails are the simplest of scams, a way of walking up to a stranger and saying, "Would you give me your credit card number?" They look incredibly real upon arrival in an inbox—complete with company logos, official-sounding language, even clickable text like www.Citibank.com, which looks absolutely real. They also usually include some kind of threat. We've lost your account information, and if you don't reply to this e-mail, we'll have to close your account, they say. And while a consumer is on the hook, they ask for account PIN numbers and other critical personal information.

It might be easy to think, "no one falls for that." Well, that's just not true.

Television anchor Contessa Brewer did, in the summer 2003, only a few weeks after taking her new job at MSNBC.[15] She was angry at herself—like most victims, beating herself up, saying she should have known better. But she had just moved for her new job and had spent the prior week filling out forms again and again, forms that requested the same information—name, address, phone, billing information.

While Brewer lost her identity, the system actually protected the criminal's identity quite well, as a hunt for the suspect revealed. Brewer's phish supposedly came from America Online, and it directed her toward a web site named Billing-Error-Online.com. There, she divulged personal information, including her Social Security number and mother's maiden name. When she clicked submit, the web page bounced back at her, insisting that she supply a bank account number and PIN code as well; she stopped short of that and suddenly realized she'd probably made a big mistake. But it was too late. An ID thief can get pretty far with a Social and a mother's maiden name.

The offending web site was actually hosted by a legitimate small Internet provider in Miami named Cybergate. Notes posted to Internet security bulletin boards indicated Cybergate had been warned about the credit card-stealing web site at least 24-hours earlier and had done nothing—even though the site was obviously engaged in criminal activity. Cybergate's administrator on call said he couldn't just pull the site down—it had to go through a legal review first, "even if it's obvious what they are doing." That might take 24 hours, he said.[16]

He also refused to reveal who had stolen Brewer's personal information. "Who pays the bill for that site?" the employee was asked. "Sorry, we can't give out customer data," he said—that wouldn't be legal. He would only release it to a law enforcement officer armed with a court order. Dead end.

The site was actually registered to a Massachusetts man, but talking to him was fruitless. The domain had been purchased via a stolen credit card. The listed site owner was actually a victim of identity theft. His information had been stolen via another phisher e-mail, sent some two weeks earlier. The trail was dead.

And now, Brewer has placed fraud alerts on her credit files, has a new credit card, and plans to regularly check her credit reports. All she can do is sit and wait and see what bad things might happen to her.

"I just let my defenses down for a moment," she said.

Thousands of others have, too. Well-designed phish e-mails can get a response rate of up to 5 percent; and their obvious prevalence is testament to the fact that they succeed. In the two weeks before Christmas 2003, two million of the criminal e-mails were sent out, according to the Anti-Phishing Working Group.[17]

Phishing is really the most common face of one of the more disturbing trends in Internet crime, what's now being called corporate identity theft. Clever criminals know that trademarks have a powerful influence on consumers, and they know how to turn this earned trust against potential victims. The Internet also makes it nearly impossible for the average person to tell the difference between a real web site and a mirage. Programming tricks make one web site look exactly like another. At a glance, a link in an e-mail that sends a consumer to Citibank's web site looks identical to a link that sends a consumer to a hacker's web site. Early in 2003, the Federal Trade Commission (FTC) issued a warning to consumers about phisher e-mails, with a series of tips consumers can use to avoid falling for scams. But for every tip, hackers quickly generated a countermeasure. When consumers get wise to one ploy, it's quickly updated. One example: Consumers afraid to send money to a stranger when they win an online auction are advised to use an escrow service for extra safety. Criminals then created an elaborate string of fake escrow web sites and services, to ease the suspicious consumers' minds.

It's easy to set up fake web sites that pose as escrow services. In the real world, a papier-mâché bank would quickly reveal itself, like the fake town of Rock Ridge in the movie *Blazing Saddles*. Online, a six-page web site can look just like Escrow.com, the top online escrow firm. The Internet is now awash in such fakes. And of course, they are all purchased with stolen credit cards, making them impossible to trace.

Consumers have lost millions, mistaking the fake web sites to be real escrow firms. Phoenix dentist Bruce Lachot is just one example. A veteran Internet user, Lachot lost $55,000 when he sent payment to one such fake escrow site while attempting to purchase a new BMW online.[18]

The cons are now so elaborate, and so authentic, by the end of the year, an FTC attorney conceded that he had stopped giving out tips to consumers on how to avoid being scammed. "I have come around to the position only recently that it's just too much to ask of people to expect them to figure out what's real and what's not on the Internet," he said.[19] Common sense is the only defense.

***

But common sense may not be a powerful enough weapon against veteran Internet auction criminals like Kenneth, who is well schooled in the twist and turns of a good multistage con. Traditional identity theft involves account takeovers and outright financial fraud. But the Internet enables many more creative ways for criminals to turn stolen private information into cash.[20]

Since reality in the virtual world of the Internet is so blurry, impersonation goes very far. Take eBay, for example. eBay is a phenomenon. If you haven't eBay'd, you will. Some day you will want to buy an Ichiro Suzuki bobble-head doll for your 12-year-old niece, and eBay will be the only place you can find it. And then you will understand why eBay is the rarest of rare success stories from the dot-com bubble. It never was a bubble; it was always a stroke of brilliance. It is the Ford Motor Company of the twenty-first century.

But on eBay, cheaters abound. It is the single most convenient tool for criminals in the world, an internationally acclaimed haunt for scam artists. If you were a criminal in any of the world's farthest corners, and you wanted to design a tool for committing the perfect international crime, you would dream up eBay. Fortunately for them, Pierre Omidyar, eBay's inventor, has already done it. Criminals steal thousands of dollars from eBay users, one at a time, every hour of every day. Auction crime is the No. 1 fraud complaint the Federal Trade Commission receives every year—outside of general identity theft complaints.[21]

Kenneth got on the eBay bandwagon early on. Part of a ring of five thieves, he and his pals claim to have taken $2 million from hundreds of eBay users from 2001 to 2003. He also liked to brag, and he was so confident that law enforcement could never trace him or his activities that he agreed to a series of interviews.

He couldn't prove he'd gotten the money. But eBay confirmed he was a well-known impersonator and nemesis. To prove himself and his prowess, Kenneth opened up one of the fraudulent e-mail accounts he used to correspond with victims and offered a peek, an e-mail account called BestBuyPlasma. Reading the back-and-forth exchanges reveals a master crafts-man at work. Through his velvety e-mail tongue, he lures victims slowly in, tempting them with outrageously low plasma television prices. The key, though, is the stolen identity.

Kenneth, the master eBay thief, starts all his cons with phisher e-mails. Kenneth is careful with his—like an accurate spammer, he sends his lists to only one or two thousand eBay members. He can get 200 responses, he says. He claims to have access to 400 eBay accounts at any given time.

And once he does, eBay users out for a good deal are an easy mark. From the start, eBay understood the problem of people buy-ing and selling to each other without ever seeing faces or feeling handshakes. In an ingenious stroke, the company elected to let eBay users patrol themselves. Through a system called feedback, users grade each other when they strike a deal. The more positive feedback a user has, the better their reputation, the more likely strangers will be willing to deal with them. Just as small businesses spend years painstakingly building their reputations, eBay users have spent years accumulating hundreds of positive feedbacks.

And Kenneth just steals them all.

It's as if a criminal could stand on a street corner and suddenly be mistaken for the family butcher, who's sold sirloin steaks to mom every Thursday for 25 years. Of course, you'd give him your money. You know he's good for it. He's the family butcher. Ken-neth hijacks the accounts of reputable eBay members, then poses as the experienced sellers and runs away with consumers' money.

Kenneth didn't remember how he hijacked the Its_Mary account involved in the con he demonstrated (the name has been changed to protect the victim). No matter. He had stolen her eBay identity, and now, 233 eBay buyers and sellers were willing to vouch for him. Armed with that reputation, he went fishing again.

Kenneth trolled auctions for big-ticket items, like plasma televisions. And he would whisper separately, in a private e-mail to bidders, "I have a better deal." Bidders often can't resist the query and ask about the terms of the deal. As his price is deeply discounted, discussions with Kenneth progress quickly. To disarm his potential victims, he's the one who brings up fraud first.

He wants to deal privately, outside of eBay's web site, because, "I have lost a certain amount of money by listing them on this site due to the NPB (non-paying-bidders) and Indonesian buyers. I also get to save the eBay fees this way."

To be safe, Kenneth steers the victims to an online escrow service, where they are told their money will sit securely until their television arrives safe and sound. And that's where the sting is. Once the money is sent to the escrow web site via a bank transfer, it's gone, and so is Kenneth.

The key to Kenneth's scheme is the stolen eBay identity. When his potential buyers get squeamish, he invokes the army of those who will vouch for him.

"I deal with people all the time and I have not received a negative feedback from anybody," he writes. For good measure, he plays the family card, too. "This is legit! I do not scam people for a living, as I make a decent living now and must take care of my family (2-year-old daughter and gorgeous wife). Would you scam a person in my case and risk everything you have for any amount of money???"

Regular eBay users often recoil at this kind of note. After all, all business transactions are based on trust—there's always a moment when one of the parties involved has both the money and the stuff. On eBay, trust is everything. If you didn't believe in the person at the other end of the e-mail, you'd never buy anything. Remember, eBay itself vouches for no one. On eBay, it's all about the reputation, all about feedback. And Its_Mary had 233 people vouching for her.

Looking at the e-mails Kenneth gets in response, it's clear he knows well the psychology of his future victims. Many are flat-out embarrassed to challenge him, even though they are about to send thousands of dollars across the Internet to a person they've never met, never even seen.

"Forgive me for being very cautious. I don't for one minute doubt you are a very honest person," wrote one. Another: "Apologies for being skeptical."

Kenneth's e-mails came from the Czech Republic, but he denied he was located there. Instead, he claimed his money flowed through his arrows, or middlemen, in the former Soviet bloc nation. He wouldn't say how he moved money out of the United States, and into the Czech Republic. But his e-mail account included an online order for a background search on a man named William—the kind an employer would do on a job applicant. The Internet is full of offers to sell such information. This one only cost Kenneth $60, on a stolen credit card—and it netted him William's Social Security number. Kenneth needed it to set up some kind of bank account in William's name. When one of his victims gave in and sent $2,500 to the Czech Republic for a television, the money would, for a time, flow through William's identity, get picked up by an arrow, then eventually be moved into an account Kenneth could access.

The magic combination of fake escrow sites, set up with stolen credit cards, hijacked eBay accounts, and stolen identities used to move money through the banking system could net Kenneth $4,000 a day at times, he said. But most of it was spent on late nights in discos, drinking Captain Morgan's with Sprite and lime, trying to impress women, he said. Kenneth, who was only 22, hadn't yet started saving much for the future.

***

An even more elaborate and more successful multistage Internet con emerged in 2003 that shows just how fast-moving identity thieves based in Eastern Europe can ply their trade and move money out of the country. Criminals using the scam had attempted to steal nearly a half-billion dollars during 2002–2003 and gotten away with millions.

Called the reshipping scam, it preys on the most vulnerable Americans: the unemployed. "It's out of control," said an exasperated Barry Mew, an agent with U.S. Postal Inspection Service. "My phone rings off the hook. My head is spinning. My e-mail is flooded (with victims)." One major credit card company has seen losses of $1.5 million to the scam, and a payment processing company for an Internet site is out $1 million, he said. He declined to mention the companies by name.[22]

The elaborate scam is a mixture of credit card fraud, identity theft, and auction fraud. The net of victims is wide, ranging from eBay auction winners to credit card firms to major online retailers like Amazon.com. But it starts with hundreds of help-wanted advertisements placed all over the Internet, on legitimate web sites like Monster.com and CareerBuilder.com. At any given time, Mew can spot ads on 25 different web sites.

The advertisements are innocuous enough.

"Our company is engaged in correspondence managing, distributing different goods worldwide, buying and reselling these goods," says one version of the ad that appeared on Career Builder.com. The ad then goes on to explain the need for employees to ship products overseas. "Everybody knows Russia is a part of Europe, but most of foreign people are afraid to have business with [sic] country. . . . We would like to prove our respectableness, but when we communicate with people from other countries they can't avoid stereotypes. So, we are looking for the persons who can represent our company in this country. Their duty will be to accept money and different goods, because often people don't want to send money to my country."[23]

Put simply, the employees, or recruits, are used to move merchandise or money out of the United States. In one flavor of the scheme, the criminals order merchandise from mail-order companies and web sites that are reluctant to ship products overseas. The goods are delivered to the recruited consumer, who then forwards the packages to Eastern Europe. Everything is ordered with stolen credit cards. To avoid raising suspicion, the con artists make sure the shipping address—the address of the recruit—is in the same state as the billing address on the stolen card. To do so, the con artists have a wide variety of recruits and stolen credit cards to choose from. They have also managed to change billing addresses on stolen credit cards so they match the recruit's locale. Some 1,300 credit card accounts were updated with new billing addresses at one credit card company victimized by the con artists.

Popular items being stolen are high-ticket electronics devices like handheld computers, digital cameras and camcorders, computers, DVD players, and flat screen monitors. All the merchandise is sent to either Russia or the Ukraine, Mew said, but it's not clear the criminals live in either country.

Auction bidders are also targeted. Con artists place auction items for sale, impersonating the recruit. When winners ask where to send the money, they are instructed to wire funds to the recruit's bank account. That gets around the barrier criminals face trying to convince auction winners to wire money overseas. The con artist only needs to fool one employee—rather than dozens of auction winners—into sending money out of the country via wire transfer. That's accomplished by enticing terms of employment. Recruits are told they will receive wire payments of up to 15 percent of sales they handle—good enough to induce thousands of victims during trying economic times.

Most victims catch on, eventually, that something is wrong, that they are falsifying customs documents to slip the shipments by authorities. But it takes some recruits longer than others. One California recruit sent 750 packages to Russia between October 2002 and March 2003. The average value of the packages was $1,500.[24]

Recruits are also at risk of identity theft, since they usually give the con artists their bank account information and other critical data while signing up for the job. One victim said that after she realized she'd been scammed and went to the police, the con artists threatened her.

"These people have my identification: Social Security number, address, and handwriting sample," she said. "Since this investigation began, I have received e-mails that state I KNOW WHO YOU ARE. I fear for the safety of myself and my family."[25]

***

As the post-forwarding scam shows, Internet identity thieves don't actually need to steal any of your money to involve you in their crime. In fact, criminals don't even need you, if they can get your computer to do their dirty work for them. Consider it theft of your computer's identity.

It's generally very easy to hijack a home computer connected to the Internet with a high bandwidth connection like DSL or a cable modem. These computers have a fixed place on the Net, a consistent address, so hackers can just bang away at them using automated tools until they find a way in. Very few consumers keep up with computer security maintenance tasks like downloading security patches and monitoring firewalls, which can be quite a bit more mysterious than regular automobile oil changes. So there's an endless supply of vulnerable home computers on the Internet, ripe to be plucked by computer hackers, who can then turn those computers into criminals.

Once there, intruders invariably leave a secret program called a Trojan horse. This little program lets the hacker access the computer he or she wants anytime, turning the victim's PC into a soldier in a computer army ready for an attack; it can also include so-called keylogging software, which copies down every key typed on that machine. Eventually, every computer user must type a credit card number or a password, and keyloggers store that information for hackers, who retrieve it later. Anecdotal research suggests as much as 5 percent of all high-bandwidth home computers are Trojaned at any given time and at ready disposal to act on a criminal's whim.

Internet users often think they have nothing on their computers worth stealing; that's wrong. Your computer is also your identity. Just ask Julian Green. Some time late in 2001, Green had a Trojan horse placed on his computer at his home in the Torquay resort community in the United Kingdom. A few months later, British police came knocking at his door, accusing him of possessing child pornography. While there were no other pornographic materials in his house, there were 172 child porn images on his hard drive. He was arrested immediately.

About a year later, Green was acquitted by a British court, who believed his story that computer hackers were using his computer to store the images.[26] He is one of the first to use the Trojan horse defense; but it's not the only successful time the "my computer did it" legal strategy has been used. In another example, Aaron Caffrey, 19, was acquitted in 2003 by a London court on charges of hacking into a computer system that controlled the Port of Houston in September 2001. Caffrey had been charged with crippling the server that provides scheduling information for all ships entering the world's sixth-largest port.[27]

The legal community has only begun to wonder about how far the "my computer did it" defense might go. It's conceivable that a criminal might plant a Trojan horse intentionally on his or her computer prior to committing a crime, laying the groundwork for a hard-to-challenge defense. But the more chilling possibility, say those in the world of computer security, is the idea that someone might go to jail for a crime he or she did not commit, set up by a computer criminal. Long considered a possibility, now it seems real—your computer might be committing crimes in your name, and you might not find out until police come looking for you.

***

Hacking one computer at a time to store pornographic images or stolen data can be hard work, so hackers have long worked to automate the process and in 2003 very nearly came upon the perfect tool. While most computer users were bemoaning the nuisance that was the SoBig computer virus, which overwhelmed millions of systems all around the world during 2003, virus computer security expert Joe Stewart of Lurhq Corp. was investigating another, more serious element of the program. In addition to the usual annoying mail bombing, SoBig dropped extra programming code on each computer it infected. On closer inspection, the software seemed to be a rudimentary e-mail program.[28]

It was spam software, Steward decided. The virus author was assembling an army of home computers that could be used as spam machines, available to flood Internet users with millions of unwanted e-mail marketing pitches. Since spammers often find their bandwidth quickly cut off by Internet service providers, hijacked home computers are a perfect alternative. After all, an Internet provider like Earthlink hardly has time to run around shutting down individual users all the time. And yet, Earthlink's Mary Youngblood does call some users at home to say, "You know, your computer is sending out spam." Incredulous customers almost never believe her.[29]

The successful tactic—really a blend of hacking, virus writing, and spamming—spread quickly about the spam community. By the end of 2003, one study indicated that one-third of all spam was being generated by hijacked computers.[30]

At about the same time that Stewart was investigating SoBig, noted computer sleuth Richard Smith was slaving away at his Massachusetts test laboratory deciphering another Trojan horse. This one also installed a sample piece of software on each victim's machine. All it did was receive a web request from one user and forward that person on to another Internet address, a sort of pass-through place, or relay.[31]

But innocent, infected home users never knew their computers were relaying web surfers on to porn sites. The virus was a secret way to push surfers at porn, ingeniously designed to obscure the porn site's tracks. Since porn pages are often shut down quickly by Internet service providers, this tactic made finding and closing the porn site difficult. Even after Smith cracked the code, it took a week before the porn ring was shut down. None of the 1,000 victims ever knew they were unwitting porn distributors.

Such computer hijackings are not new. In 1999, when computer hackers managed to shut down big-name web sites like Yahoo!, CNN, and Amazon.com, they used much the same tactic—an army of machines all attacked those sites, eventually toppling them over by sending too much traffic their way, akin to calling someone's house so many times that all other callers get a busy signal. But back then, most of the zombie computers were at universities with low security and high bandwidth.

Home users now share those qualities, ideal for computer criminals. Meanwhile, hackers are no longer just looking for fame. They seem to want fortune now. They have discovered selling porn or sending spam can be profitable. And they continue to find new ways to steal your identity, and your hard drive, and make it look like you did it.

***

The Internet's role in identity theft is not limited to hackers using it as a source to steal data or as a way to get victims to voluntarily surrender some part of their identities. It is an ID theft-equipment suppliers' market, too. As with nearly all modern crimes, from lock-picking to cellular phone cloning, the tools of the ID theft trade are easy to buy online. A credit card decoder sells for as little as $20 on eBay; encoders, which actually write data onto plastic card magnetic stripes, like the ones used by the Millennium Plot terrorists, cost around $100.[32] Armed with such an encoder, a criminal can easily swap your credit card with his. When he writes your account number onto the black magnetic stripe on his card, his card IS your card— because, as any computer will tell you, 1s and 0s don't lie. And retail clerks never check to see if the numbers on the front of the plastic match the numbers on the receipt.

Other ID theft paraphernalia on sale online: blank birth certificate paper, notary-style seals; blank credit cards, complete with holograms; and of course, fake ID cards. No need to stroll down 42nd Street in Manhattan any more. Fake IDs are a cottage industry online.

But the Internet is not simply a source for the tools of ID theft — it is, in fact, ID Theft University for most criminals. Near-foolproof simple, handy ID theft how-tos are free for download and sprawled all over the World Wide Web like viruses.

***

Computer hackers pride themselves on clarity and simplicity. Both are a sign of true genius. Hacker how-tos are often very well-written and far more clear than any government-issued step-by-step guide on how to recover from an identity theft attack. Video Vindicator's ID theft guide, a seven-step program now available all over the Internet even reads easier than IKEA furniture assembly instructions.[33]

For a warmup, the pseudonymous author explains the landscape:

There are essentially three types of identities (other than the one you're born with), and they are: Created, Forged, and Borrowed. . . . With borrowed, which is what this file is concerned with, you take over another living person's ID in order to abuse his specific credit. From the point you transfer his identity over to you, you are him.

About the longest I've ever been able to control an assumed identity is around two to three months. . . . At around this point word starts getting back to the actual person and they quickly take steps to shut down all the work which you have so carefully done. . . . But that's ok, you should have already done your damage, and now it's far too late for them to do anything of any consequence. . . . On to the next identity. It will on average take the normal Joe around five to six months total to realize just what has happened. You see, the last thing people expect is that someone is using their name and their ID and THEIR bank account for fraudulent ends. . . . But hey, in this case ignorance is definitely not bliss!

And then, much like a recipe for a simple cake, Video Vindicator describes the necessary ingredients.

Here's a list of what you pretty much need, and where you can get it

SOCIAL SECURITY NUMBER—Checks and sometimes driver's licenses

DRIVER'S LICENSE NUMBER—Checks, driver's license, DMV

DATE OF BIRTH—Checks and sometimes driver's licenses

FULL NAME (AND MIDDLE)—Checks, driver's license, bills, phone co.

MOTHER'S MAIDEN NAME— Bank

MARITAL STATUS—Bank and phone co. (sometimes)

CURRENT ADDRESS—Checks, driver's license, bills, phone co.

PHONE NUMBER—Checks, bills (sometimes), phone co.

The file's authenticity is bolstered considerably by his description of the process to obtain a fake driver's license. It is eerily similar to the tactics used by congressional investigators in 2002–2003 when they went 8 for 8 in an undercover operation to see how easily they could obtain fake IDs from motor vehicles departments around the country, as discussed in Chapter 5.

You can always get a temporary license sent to you by the DMV by telling them that you lost the original, and you're on a trip out-of-state. They will usually have one to you in about five working days, and then you're ready to have some fun. . . . Now one note on these. . . . No two states temporary ID are the same, which makes forgery of these a BREEZE!

The rest of the file marches readers through the tricks needed to get a birth certificate ("You need no ID to get this, simply say that you are the person), a Social Security card ("This is usually easily gotten, by simply going down to the Social Security office in your town, with the birth certificate"), a permanent photo license (easy as long as you "successfully completed all . . . of the above steps").

The last two steps contain advice for getting a bank to mail the thief a replacement ATM card, and how to use that card to slowly drain an account. Next comes instructions on how to use all those documents to buy cars, even take out small bank loans with the identity.

But perhaps even more troubling: When you think of Video Vindicator's recipe, picture pulling an old tried-and-true apple pie recipe from grandma's recipe box. Because Video Vindicator's instructions were first published in 1992. And today, most of them still work as well as ever.

CONCLUSION: Well, as many people have told me, my destiny lies in hell, where, of course I will just take over some poor saps identity

and then go to heaven (if hell doesn't turn out to be a challenge).
And isn't a challenge what we all are out here looking for?

***

But perhaps most troubling of all: In 1992, Video Vindicator's instructions at least involved a lot of legwork. Now, thanks to the Internet, gathering the key documents for identity theft right from home is a breeze. In September 2003, a special-interest group named The Foundation for Taxpayers and Consumer Rights purchased Social Security numbers belonging to Attorney General John Ashcroft and CIA Director George Tenet; later the group purchased Bank of America CEO Kenneth Lewis's and Wells Fargo CEO Richard Kovacevich's personal data and hired an airplane to write some of the data in the sky over Washington, D.C., just to make a point. Each cost about $30, the group said.[34] Everything is for sale in the world's largest criminal supply market.

Data merchants peddle much more than the basic Social Security numbers and mother's maiden names on the Net. A quick Google search will reveal hundreds of companies ready to sell you anyone's cellular phone bill records from the last month, for about $100. If ever you have a need to trace a person's life, cell phone records will do the trick. But that's not all. Bank account numbers and balances, license plate numbers and driving histories, voter ID information, even floor plans for homes and businesses are all for sale through e-mail. Very little of this data is obtained from the Internet, but it's all sold there.

Welcome to the information brokerage industry. Private investigators who've tuned up for the twenty-first century now make a killing by stealing private data from banks and telephone companies and selling it to everyone from jealous ex-husbands to media companies to law firms. Anything and everything about you is for sale online, if you just know where to look.

Because digital PIs know how to get it. The data merchants are pretext callers, who know just how to lie, cheat, and impersonate to get anything they want out of telephone operators working at financial institutions and other agencies that store personal data. Often the only thing between a person's medical records and a private investigator is a $10-per-hour clerk working late on a Friday night. Pretext callers, who trick clerks into divulging data by using false pretexts, have elevated such data theft to an art form. They do exactly what famous identity thieves like Abraham Abdallah and James Jackson did—only they make a living doing it. The industry is supported largely by law firms doing asset checks, on potential litigation opponents, to make sure they have deep pockets worth suing.

And we might not know much about such asset checks, but for the brave work of Rob Douglas. A former private investigator, five years ago he was making a decent living as a middleman shuttling bank account information between pretexers and big Washington, D.C., law firms. Then Douglas's conscience got the better of him. His whistle-blowing efforts cost him his business and earned him a cascade of death threats—but they led to a series of successful Federal Trade Commission lawsuits and to the creation of a federal law prohibiting some information broker activities. He is one of several individuals waging a quiet war against the identity theft epidemic. Their inspiring struggles offer some hope in this otherwise bleak battle for the preservation of privacy.

9

THE HEROES

Once it is determined a fraud has been committed the company never contacts you again. My SSN was used in Cleveland and Detroit to buy cell phones; $1,000 in charges were run up. I asked the fraud dept. if they could notify me if the people were caught; I was told "Read the newspaper." The fraud departments aren't talking to the police and no one is talking to the victims.

—Anonymous

It reads like the stuff of late-night TV drama. Whenever Los Angeles police detective Mike Gervais' beeper went off, whether it was a family member, his boss, or an undercover informant, somehow, Assaf Waknine knew. At least that's what the Los Angeles Police Department said when it arrested Waknine in 1997 and charged him with a string of six felonies, including stalking and threatening a police officer.

Snitches often spill their beans impulsively to cops, who make sure they are always available for any late-night, alcohol-induced confessions. Maybe that's what Assaf Waknine was afraid of. Waknine was under investigation by the Los Angeles Police Department's organized crime unit.[1] Perhaps he smelled a snitch, because police said he had his own undercover operation brewing. Each time Gervais' beeper went off, so did Waknine's. He had obtained a clone, a duplicate of the pager carried by the L.A. police detective, police said. No one could page

Gervais without Waknine knowing about it. As an electronic copy of the hardware, Waknine's device was a perfect copy of Gervais' beeper. The clone just plucked police pages out of the airwaves and no one—not even the technology—noticed.[2]

Later, authorities would say, Waknine had home phone numbers and pager numbers for a wide swath of L.A. organized crime investigators, enabling him to keep tabs on the movements and informants of dozens of police officers.[3]

That's how Waknine was allegedly able to terrorize a second L.A.P.D. officer's wife. One day, when the officer was at work, a Waknine henchman paid a visit to the officer's wife. "He gives his name and walks away," authorities said, suggesting Waknine had some way of knowing when the woman would be alone.[4]

Perhaps Waknine felt almost like God, having such near-perfect electronic reconnaissance on his pursuers. Waknine, an Israeli national, was eventually deported after serving jail time for a prior, unrelated federal conviction on check forgery charges. The police stalking charges against him were dropped when he left the country, according to the Los Angeles district attorney's office. But the controversy resurfaced later, as authorities in Colorado investigated the company that had allegedly supplied Waknine with the highly sensitive police information. The source: A company calling itself "Dirty Deeds Done Dirt Cheap." It was just one of the thousands of information brokers which had sprung up that claimed to be able to find out nearly anything about anyone in this country.[5]

This is the world exposed by whistle-blower Rob Douglas, a private citizen who helped unmask this underground industry in 1998. In the war against identity theft, Douglas is just one of many quiet heroes who have taken up the cause, toiling silently to rescue victims from despair, bring criminals to justice, and force corporations to accept responsibility for their role in the crisis. The efforts of these true believers shine a beacon of hope in the otherwise dark and mysterious world of identity thieves.

In June 1998, Rob Douglas and Al Schweitzer awaited their turn to testify before the House Committee on Banking and Financial Services. The topic: information brokers. Schweitzer was an obvious choice; he had been called the "Godfather of the information brokerage industry" by federal prosecutors, who had indicted him three times for data theft-related charges.[6] A man's man, Schweitzer's tone conjures up the confidence of a late-night TV infomercial host, and his resume does the talking. He claims to have lied and cajoled his way to personal data on a Who's Who of American celebrities. His techniques are essentially ancient, but updated for the Information Age. Schweitzer merely role plays his way into the data he needs, a technique called pretexting.

"Hi, I'm Joe Smith, and I've lost my cell phone bill from last month. I know it's past due. Would you fax a copy of it to me at work? Here's the number."

His impressive list of clients is diverse, ranging from major U.S. media companies thirsty for the latest on a hot scandal to big-name law firms eyeing big-ticket lawsuits. Word of Schweitzer's exploits spread so far and wide that he began offering training seminars around the country to other private investigators who recognized the easy money to be made in pretexting. Many of the hundreds of information brokers still peddling their wares online are Schweitzer's disciples. But by the end of the millennium, he had dropped out of the business, which he now says is even too dirty for him—and he's trying to make a living doing late-night infomercials teaching lawyers how to seize assets from unclaimed lawsuit judgments.

Douglas, on the other hand, was a not-so-obvious choice for the congressional hearing. He had spent the prior decade running his small D.C.-based private investigator's firm. Bright eyed, grey, and unusually self-deprecating for a PI, the former investigator for the public defender's office was making a tough but respectable living doing the types of things private investigators never do on television. He spent hours performing simple records searches, serving subpoenas, looking for cheating spouses—sprinkled with occasional high-profile assignments investigating murders and government corruption. But recently, he had expanded into a new sector of the business: backgrounding lawsuit targets. It had become a lucrative, $3,000-a-week part of his tiny four-person firm.

It's simple, really. Law firms choose their targets carefully; nothing is worse than spending a bunch of billable hours to win a big-dollar judgment against a defendant—only to find empty pockets at the end of the case. So as an insurance policy, firms run asset checks against potential defendants, to make sure they have deep pockets. It's cheap insurance; asset checks only cost a few hundred dollars. Simple bank account locations and amounts will do. And that's what Douglas did.

He didn't get the data; he was just the middleman. Douglas knew whom to call. The tiny information brokerage business was just leaving the runway at this point, and he had the contacts. After a while, his shop was a small bank account information factory, the fax machine constantly chugging out orders from law firms, and then results from brokers. It was easy money.

But something kept gnawing at Douglas. Could this be legal?

The brokers insisted it was. They were expert librarians, they always said. Information such as bank account data could be compiled from all kinds of public documents and disclosures, available in court houses and other records stores around the country. They just knew how to find the data. For 12 months or so, that answer mostly satisfied Douglas.

He was no stranger to the seedier parts of life by the time he took his first bank account search request. In fact, that work seemed rather sanitary compared to the way his career began, working as a criminal defense investigator, where he spent 17 years researching homicide, rape, and armed robbery cases. When he put out his shingle as a full-time PI, Douglas was hoping for a slightly simpler life, knowing the *Rockford Files* weren't ahead of him—he would be spending many hours behind a desk, doing simple interviews, calling on old friends in law enforcement for favors. He was headed toward the quieter life of white-collar crime. So when a postcard arrived one day advertising asset location services, he had no idea answering it would eventually lead him into the center of a national controversy, into being an important figure in the debate over the most important bank regulation legislation in 70 years. It would also lead him into telephone and faxed death threats.

"Everything told me this can't be legal," Douglas would say later. "Ninety-five percent of me said this was bullshit. But there was such uniform lying by these folks." And more important, all Douglas's competitors were offering the service. By 1996, there were a flood of postcards landing in private investigators' offices, hawking lucrative asset search services. He would quickly lose clients if he didn't play along. So he did. Asset backgrounding became the most lucrative part of his business.

What Douglas didn't know is that money from the seemingly legitimate work of law firm research propped up the entire information brokerage industry, providing steady work for shadier characters to do their Dirty Deeds, Done Dirt Cheap.

***

Information brokers are the worst kind of identity thieves, the most skilled, the most relentless, and the most elusive, and they have the most to gain from success. Regana and James Rapp and their company Touch Tone Information Inc. are the best example of how far, and how bad, the theft of data can be.

While few Americans have heard of Touch Tone, almost everyone is familiar with the company's handiwork. So much of what we know about JonBenet Ramsey and family—and we do know so much—comes courtesy of Touch Tone Communications. Working for whatever media outlet would pay them, the Rapps dug up the best hard data on the parents, perhaps the most publicly accused suspects of our times. The Rapps managed to secure American Express bills, for example, that showed purchases made at McGuckin Hardware store just days before the murder. A Touch Tone employee then wrote to the store asking for information about two specific charges, signing the letter with the name of JonBenet father, "John Ramsey."[7] Within a week, the *Globe* tabloid had a scoop about when and where the Ramseys had purchased the potential murder weapon—a roll of duct tape.[8]

As the media frenzy, which reached O.J. Simpson murder trial levels in 1997, continued to spike, the Rapps began receiving more than 100 calls a day for scoops like this. The business was grossing between $4,000 and $5,000 a day—particularly because the Rapps could resell the data many times over. Customers who called had an incredible Ramsey menu from which to choose. Their own advertisement described it clearly:[9]

1. The phone number of a Boulder police detective and cellular phone records of a private investigator hired by the Ramsey's lawyers to work on the case.
2. Cellular toll records, both for JonBenet's parents John & Patsy.
3. Land line tolls for the Michigan and Boulder homes.
4. Tolls on the investigative firm.
5. Tolls and home location on the housekeeper, Mr. & Mrs. Mervin Pugh.
6. Credit card tolls on the following:
   a. Mr. John Ramsey, AMX & VISA
   b. Mr. John Ramsey Jr., AMX.
7. Home location of ex-wife in Georgia, we have number, address & tolls.
8. Banking investigation on Access Graphics, Mr. Ramsey's company, as well as banking information on Mr. Ramsey personal.
9. We have the name, address & number of Mr. Sawyer & Mr. Smith, who sold the pictures to the *Golbe* [sic], we also have tolls on their phone.

10. The investigative firm of H. Ellis Armstead, we achieved all their land and cellular lines, as well as cellular tolls, they were the investigative firm assisting the Boulder DA's office, as well as assisting the Ramseys.
11. Detective Bill Palmer, Boulder P.D., we achieved personal address and numbers.
12. The public relations individual "Pat Kroton" [sic] for the Ramseys, we achieved the hotel and call detail where he was staying during his assistance to the Ramseys. We also have his direct cellular phone records.
13. We also achieved the son John Jr.'s SSN and DOB.
14. During all our credit card cases, we acquired all ticket numbers, flight numbers, dates of flights, departing times and arriving times.
15. Friend of the Ramseys, working with the city of Boulder, Mr. Jay Elowskay, we have his personal info.[10]

The Rapps were hardly one-trick ponies. In fact, their resume reads like a retrospective on tabloid news during the late 1990s. Investigators and court documents spelled out the allegations: The Rapps scored unlisted phone numbers for families of children killed in the Columbine High School Massacre and sold those to media outlets. They were accused of obtaining Bill Cosby's son Ennis Cosby's credit card statements after he was murdered in Los Angeles. They allegedly received records on visits by *Ally McBeal* star Calista Flockhart, to a doctor in Beverly Hills, when tabloids were buzzing with news that she might be suffering from an eating disorder. They sold information about Princess Diana and her companion Dodi al-Fayed soon after their deadly car accident, according to investigators. And, they were even accused of obtaining the phone records of Kathleen Willey, a former White House volunteer who claimed President Bill Clinton had made an unwanted sexual advance towards her.[11]

It might be possible to dismiss these incredible privacy violations as the logical end to a media frenzy, but Touch Tone didn't just do dirty deeds for thirsty tabloid journalists. When Rapp and his wife were finally targeted by the Federal Trade Commission for deceptive trade practices as they lied their way into the valuable information, the Colorado Bureau of Investigations, the FBI, and the L.A.P.D. were already closing in on the couple. Touch Tone's former name was Dirty Deeds, Done Dirt Cheap. The JonBenet Ramsey experts, it turned out, were allegedly helping a criminal keep tabs on L.A. detectives.

An affidavit filed in the Rapp case by Colorado Bureau of Investigations agent Robert Brown indicated that the Los Angeles Police Department had asked for information about the Rapps' company in connection with the Waknine case during the early part of 1999. Records seized by L.A. cops from a private detective's home revealed Touch Tone had provided home addresses, phone numbers and pager numbers for detectives on the police department's organized crime squad, the affidavit said. L.A. police believed the buyer was Assaf Waknine, whom the detectives suspected to be an organized crime figure, according to Brown's statement.[12]

There was no proof the Rapps cared to impede investigations or hurt police officers; they were just selling data to whomever would pay for it. Ultimately, James Rapp pleaded guilty to one count of racketeering and was sentenced to 100 days in jail and four years' probation. Regana was given a two-year deferred sentence after pleading guilty to one count of racketeering. The couple settled their case with the FTC by agreeing not to lie their way into obtaining financial information in the future. The settlement also imposed a $200,000 fine against the couple, which was suspended.

The fall of the Rapps and Touch Tone was the world's first look at how far information brokers can go, and how much data they can get. But if the Rapp's convictions amounted to the discovery of a new virus, the extent of outbreak remained a mystery. It took a Congressional hearing to expose the reality that Touch Tone's "Dirty Deeds" were hardly isolated incidents but rather that it was the top dog in a burgeoning industry with perhaps thousands of competitors.

***

When his asset discovery business was going well, Rob Douglas often used an information broker named Peter Easton in upstate New York's horse country to do his dirty work. He and Easton never met, but they eventually became "as friendly as two people could become on the phone." Easton was a bit schizophrenic, one day tight-lipped and secretive, the next day rambling on about his work. A veil of deception covered the transactions: After the initial setup, the work was always done by fax. Douglas faxed a request to Easton, who would fax back the same sheets with handwritten notes—bank account numbers, balances, whatever was requested. Easton wouldn't sign the document, which came with no fax header. One day, as a test, Douglas asked Easton if he could obtain a criminal background check on someone. Easton reacted emotionally, shouting that that was "highly illegal." The apparently conservative reaction actually gave Douglas hope that Easton was legit; but instead, it merely meant he was sensitive to sting operations. Easton already sensed that authorities were closing in on him. Within a year, he was sued by the Massachusetts attorney general's office for illegally obtaining and selling bank account information and forced to pay a $500,000 fine.[13]

But for now, Douglas and Easton continued to work together, and that year was Douglas's most profitable in private business. Asset checks were like printing money, Douglas recalls, because law firms "just kill for this kind of information." He started to advertise aggressively, and with a gathering reputation for finding assets no one else could, he began to romance the larger D.C. firms. He was about to hit the big time.

Then one day, one of Douglas's clients naively approached him, asking him to testify in open court about a bank account he had found. "You don't need me, I outsource the work," he told the client. At the client's request, Douglas called Easton to ask him to sign an affidavit. That phone call brought Douglas's world crashing down.

"You'd have thought I asked him to kill his mother. He went ape shit," Douglas said. He recalls Easton shouting down the phone, "'I'll go to jail before I do that.'"

Sure, there were signs that something was amiss all along. There would be times Douglas called in, and Easton would answer the phone "Source 1," and then he'd put down the phone and use a totally different accent on a second phone, obviously faking his own identity. But it was Easton's reaction to the request to appear before a court that set Douglas straight.

"It was the last conversation I ever had with him."

At that moment, Douglas couldn't kid himself about information brokers any more. Like a roach running from the light, Easton fled at the mere mention of a court of law, a sign he and everything he did was a fraud. Everything I feared is true, Douglas thought. I have to quit.

He sent letters to all his clients, saying he couldn't offer the asset backgrounding service any more, indicating he couldn't be certain the information was gathered in an ethical or legal way. Most clients bolted and found other PI's to do their dirty work. Almost overnight, Douglas's lucrative little company was collapsing. As he reeled from the implications of all this, one Saturday afternoon, while cutting his grass in a D.C. suburb, he spotted neighbor Bill Tate out in his front yard. Douglas knew Tate was a career Capitol Hill staffer, an older gentleman in his late 50s, but the two had never exchanged much more than small talk. Douglas didn't even know whom Tate worked for on the Hill. But Douglas decided to take a risk, leaned over the fence, and started to lay on Tate the story of private investigators' symbiotic relationship with shady information brokers.

"I have no idea what you are talking about," Tate confessed halfway through, Douglas says. "And you don't remember who I work for, do you?" Tate was a chief aide to Congressman Jim Leach, author of the sweeping Financial Modernization Act, what was to become the most important banking bill in the late twentieth century. It was flying through Congress at the height the dot-com mania, in part to clear the way for the banking megamergers of the late 1990s. But there was still time to address privacy issues, and Tate quickly realized Douglas was a whistle-blower with a major problem.

Leach, himself an avid privacy advocate, seized on the issue quickly. Aides researching the topic found there wasn't any federal law on the books that made the release of personal information by banks specifically illegal. Information brokers obtaining the information using fraudulent means might run afoul of consumer protection laws, but there was no way to censure banks for releasing the data. Leach decided he wanted to amend the Financial Modernization Act, also known as the Gramm-Leach-Bliley Act, with tough new provisions aimed at information brokers, but he needed to convince the House Banking and Financial Services Committee that there was a problem. Tate asked Douglas: Would you testify before the committee about what you've done?

Douglas knew his testimony would forever blacklist him in the world of private investigators; and he certainly would never work again in the lucrative world of asset location. But by now, he was determined to do the right thing. He had already spent months contacting former clients telling them they were crossing the line, in an attempt to convince them to stop dealing with brokers. He agreed to testify, and didn't look back.

***

Sitting next to Al Schweitzer in the halls of the U.S. Senate, the Godfather of the business, felt very strange to Douglas. On the one hand, Schweitzer might be to blame for this roller-coaster ride Douglas has been on, from finally striking it rich in the private sector to the months of guilt-ridden regrets, and now to the limelight of a hearing broadcast on C-Span. On the other hand, Schweitzer tells Douglas in the hallway that he's become disgusted by the business, which now sells everything and anything: police pager numbers are sold to Mafia figures; pretty girls' home addresses are sold to stalkers. Schweitzer agreed to testify to "blow the lid off the business." Maybe we can make a difference, Douglas thinks as he fumbles with the pages of his speech.

Schweitzer doesn't disappoint.

"Throughout my career, I have been involved in the gathering of confidential information of all types—credit information, unlisted telephone numbers, telephone toll records, medical records, tax information, Social Security information, credit card information, as well as other financial information obtained from banks, savings and loans, credit unions and brokerage houses. If the information exists on paper or in a computer databases, it can be obtained."

"I have provided services to every imaginable industry. My client list includes airlines, law firms, hospitals, hotel chains, insurance companies, banks, collection agencies, media, both mainstream and tabloid, manufacturers, casinos, travel and entertainment companies, high-tech firms, department stores, over 1,500 private investigators and information brokers, as well as occasionally providing information directly and sometimes indirectly, through former members of law enforcement and intelligence agencies, to law enforcement agencies on all levels."[14]

Later in the testimony, Schweitzer claimed to have provided information to all three major networks.

"The explosion of this industry can be attributed to three primary factors: Most of the confidential information can be obtained in a matter of minutes and for the mere cost of a telephone call."

That telephone call, formally called a "pretext call" Schweitzer simply calls a gag. But it is no laughing matter:

> "I have to tell you, the ease with which I obtain information from banks, credit card companies, it is almost laughable. I hang up the phone and the person at the other end probably thinks I was the biggest idiot in the world, but I am the one laughing."

> "If I wanted your bank account information, Mr. Chairman, I would first obtain your home telephone number either from public records or, if need be, directly from the telephone company using another gag. I would then call the billing office of your local telephone company and claim to be you. At this point, I know your name, address, telephone number and more often than not your Social Security number and date of birth. I would explain to the telephone company representative that although I know I paid my bill last month, I forgot to record it in my check register. I would then ask, 'Could you please tell me how much it was and when it was due?' The service rep would then tell me the amount paid and when it was due."

> "Next, I ask when my next bill is due and how much it is. The service rep would also freely tell me that."

> "Now I change hats. I call you at home and either get you or maybe your wife on the telephone. This time, I am the service rep at your local telephone company. 'Mr. or Mrs. Subject, this is Mr. Sawyer with Bell Atlantic. I am calling about your May bill that was due in June 10 in the amount of $98. We haven't received payment and now your June bill in the amount of $122 is also due. If this can't be paid immediately, I will have to discontinue your service.'"

"The majority of individuals will immediately become indignant, claiming that they have already paid those bills. 'Let me get my checkbook. Here it is. I paid you on June 5, $98.'"

"'You did? What check number was that? What bank was that drawn on? The account number, please, so we can locate it in our billing system. It was probably credited incorrectly to another account. I am so sorry.'"

"There you have it, Mr. Chairman. I now have the bank account information complete with your account number."

"The use of gags can be summed up in four steps: Identify the piece of information you are after; identify who or what institution is the custodian of the information sought; based on real-world situations or actual operational procedures of the target institution, figure out under what circumstances and to whom the desired information would be released; be that person under those circumstances."

At the hearing, Schweitzer was the convict, the insider, there for sex appeal. But Douglas was the real meat and potatoes, a regular Joe, one of thousands of private investigators who are apt to pay characters like Schweitzer. Douglas's talk puts his entire career at risk, a fact acknowledged by Jim Leach as the hearing began: "Though his own personal business interests would presumably have benefited from continued access to the data supplied by the information brokers, Mr. Douglas chose instead to alert the Committee to his concerns about the legality of their methods. By doing so, he provided us with a commendable example of public service being performed by a private citizen."[15]

Douglas isn't shy, telling the Committee that the problem is so widespread, no one should feel secure that custodians of their private data are taking care of it.

"As part of this debate we routinely hear and read of generic 'what ifs' and concerns that 'sometime in the near future' a citizen's most privately held information will be easily obtained by anyone willing to pay for it. Mr. Chairman, I am here today to tell you that we passed that point long ago and somehow it seems no one noticed.

"All across the United States information brokers and private investigators are stealing and selling for profit our fellow citizens' personal financial information. The problem is so extensive that no citizen should have confidence that his or her financial holdings are safe."[16]

Douglas didn't anticipate how quickly the hearing would change his life. Before he returned to his office that day, he had received several threatening phone calls from industry members, and one death threat came over the fax machine. It was written in crayon.

The phone was ringing when he got back to the office, a call from one of the companies he had mentioned in his testimony. "It's this guy out of New York City who was literally on verge of tears. He said, 'I expect the Feds to break through my door any second. You just put me out of business.'"

Other calls came during the coming weeks; messing with private investigators is dangerous business. "I hope you die, I hope your family dies," said one. There were even threatening and scandalous notes written about Douglas on Internet private investigator newsletters, one suggesting that he and Jim Leach were gay lovers.

But as one world closed quickly on him, another opened just as fast. Antipretexting provisions made it into the final version of the Gramm-Leach-Bliley Act, and the hearing gained for Douglas a reputation as a knowledgeable insider. Spurred on by testimony he gave at a second congressional hearing a year later, Douglas found himself acting as a consultant to the Pentagon on ways pretexting might be used against the U.S. military. Then, he was contacted by the Federal Trade Commission, which wanted help setting up a sting of pretexting firms. Douglas trained FTC employees how to sting some 100 companies advertising asset searches.

In the end, only three complaints were filed, with all three defendants settling for a fine and an agreement to clean up their act. In his initial speech, Douglas had optimistically said enforcement of the Gramm-Leach-Bliley law will require a minimal amount of resources. "A single federal agent with a computer, Internet access, fax machine and the skill to out-pretext the pretexters as I did could shut this industry down in a matter of months," he said. But four years later, in 2003, the information brokerage industry was still thriving. Thousands of offers for everything from bank account records to cell phone bills still cluttered the Internet.

Douglas, meanwhile, turned his attention to shoring up systems that enable information brokers. Moving on from his career as a PI, he set up a firm named American Privacy Consultants, which offers training to bank customer service representatives on how to avoid giving out information to pretexters. And his outspoken style has landed him a regular gig as a talk show host on Baltimore's WBAL, where he will shout to anyone who will listen about the unholy alliance between private investigators and information brokers, a fire flamed by the fuel of overeager and underpaid customer service representatives who are the custodians of our entire digital lives. His prized possession: an exquisitely framed copy of the last page of the Gramm-Leach-Bliley Act, with Bill Clinton's signature, a gift from Jim Leach.

***

At almost the same time Douglas was first glancing over the president's handwriting, Linda Foley was reeling from her first bout of identity theft. Foley's boss had taken her personal data and gone on a wild spending spree. As she battled the shock and depression of the incident while looking for work, Foley realized that she quickly wore out the generous ears of friends, who couldn't really sympathize with her trauma. ID theft victims go through a unique set of experiences, much like victims of any other form of abuse, and often need a lot of help processing the pain. When Foley found no source for that help, she decided to create one.[17]

ID theft victims can discover their plight in any number of ways. Maybe it's a call from the credit card company with word of a flurry of unusual charges. Or a denied car loan application. Perhaps there are suddenly phone calls from a collection agency. Or the motor vehicles department sends a notice saying a license has been revoked. Next comes confusion, denial, research, and dozens of phone calls with a healthy helping of irritating hold music. And if the incident is serious enough, if it involves a potential criminal record, or a determined thief who just won't stop, despair sets in. And that's when, if victims are lucky enough, they call Linda and her husband, Jay Foley.

A former teacher with a keen eye and a sympathetic ear, Foley's own battle to beat back her digital imposter made her realize there often is no help, no good advice for victims. Even before her ordeal was over, she created the Identity Theft Resource Center. Husband Jay, a Navy vet who watched his wife thrash about in the early days of her crisis, quickly jumped into the project. Together, the pair take phone calls sometimes seven days a week from desperate victims who have nowhere else to turn and no idea what to do. Intercession from the Foleys can be a godsend—police often won't believe an identity theft victim is innocent of the crime if his or her name is listed in the police database. But a call from Linda or Jay often greases the skids. They know the system. They know how to talk cop talk; they have friends at the credit bureaus. And, unlike many corporations, they become emotionally invested in carrying victims from start to finish, until their name is completely in the clear.

The center's main tool is a telephone hotline, much like suicide hotlines, available to victims any time, day or night. A small army of volunteers staff the service. Invariably, they arrive on Linda's team because they have their own story to tell, their own ID theft nightmare. That means they bring real empathy, and often, they're still hopping mad. Among the group—the woman who single-handedly forced the state of Louisiana to pass a tough new ID theft law and a former credit bureau fraud executive who quit because in his words, "This company isn't interested in doing anything about identity theft." Now, he helps victims instead.

The hotline operates on a shoestring budget. All training is done remotely, via teleconference. During a typical training session in summer 2003, callers piled into the teleconference only a minute or two before 8:30 P.M. ET—they'd been warned not to arrive early because the telecom firm charges by the minute. First, there was Lawrence from Brooklyn, whose voice showed he was obviously from Brooklyn, then Bridget, who shared she's a persistent redhead from Louisiana, and finally Judy, from Texas. Others clicked on a moment later. It was the dead of summer. There were baseball games, pools, and barbecues calling. But Lawrence, Bridget, Judy, and the rest all sat on the phone for two hours that night, and for each of the next two weeks, attending their training sessions.

From the sound of it, this could have been suicide hotline training. "Remember, it's a marathon not a sprint . . . keep your chin up," Linda tells the group. "Don't despair. Tell them, 'Remember, you can always call us. We'll be here. This is a road we're traveling together.'"

As Linda, the former teacher, walked the recruits through their paces, she stressed the devastating emotional impact of identity theft.

"First tell them 'We are sorry this happened to you.' And it's guaranteed you will be the first person who says that to them. So it's important they hear that."

Desperate victims come from all walks of life: rich, poor, abused, old, young. Only days before the training session, Linda had worked for hours with a 13-year-old boy trying to clean up his father's spoiled credit record; his dad spoke no English, only

Korean, so he didn't stand a chance dealing with the credit bureaus.

Foley's volunteers help every caller—hundreds of people every month. Linda—whose identity thief was arrested, convicted, released, and allegedly has continued committing crimes—des-cribed the process to the group:

> There's anger, denial, shame, and embarrassment. They move from numbness denial, the 'Oh my God, I've been shot,' response, to rage. How could this happen? If they have hit a lot of walls, the rage increases. I push them to rage, because from that rage comes the anger to deal with what they have to do.

The most important point of lesson one: document, document, document. Customer representatives from credit firms sometimes gloss over details—or flat out lie—to get rid of callers. That's why some companies will sell a fraudulent, overdue account to a collection agency even after a company representative has verbally promised the matter has been cleared up. If someone promises to do something on the phone, such as to credit an account, get the notice in writing, Foley says. If they won't write it down, send them a letter describing the conversation. Send all mail certified, with a return receipt. Victims must be able to prove everything. "If you keep records, judges love you," she says. Identity theft can be a nasty introduction to an informal legal education.

On this night, the rest of the call is spent swapping techniques on how to get the attention of creditors, credit bureaus, and collection agencies that simply will not listen to reason. The Foleys have an arrangement with banks and other firms—they won't step in unless the victim has at least tried the normal route of help once on their own. Only when the system breaks down does Jay or Linda place a call to a pal inside one of the firms and ask to trade in a favor—a sort of secret Radar O'Reilly, 4077 M.A.S.H. agreement.

A M.A.S.H. unit isn't a bad image for the Identity Theft Resource Center world headquarters in San Diego, California. It's Jay and Linda's rented house, outfitted with a couple of extra desks, including one in the living room, and two extra phone lines to accommodate the occasional part-time assistants who work there. The work is truly a labor of love for the couple, who sometimes find themselves answering the telephone at any and all hours of the night, weekends and holidays included. If ID thieves are working, so are we, Linda says.

The hotline center began operations in December 1999, about the time Linda also started running support groups for victims. She is adamant that those hit by identity theft often face hidden consequences, costs not quantified by industry and government studies. Her surveys suggest victims face emotional impact similar to victims of physical abuse. They feel guilty, they feel ostracized, they are left with years of hyper-vigilance and downright paranoia. Their relationships suffer as a result; many lose their jobs or suffer other employment consequences—from the obvious military personnel who are denied security clearance because of a credit foul-up to the more subtle victims who begin underperforming while all their spare time is spent compiling paper records to fight off collection agencies. This is why Linda began the hotline; not to immediately fix all the problems ID theft victims face, but just to provide listening and understanding, delivered by other people in the victims' club. Identity theft sounds annoying when you hear about it; but it's not until people see it up close and personal that they realize how devastating it can be.

In 1999, when Jay and Linda were still newlyweds, Jay worked two jobs so Linda could start the center on her own. "Our first grant was from the bank of Linda and Jay Foley," she remembers. Beth Givens, of the Privacy Rights Clearinghouse, urged her to push on with the program and allowed the Foleys to operate under the clearinghouse's nonprofit umbrella. Then, money started to trickle in. First from a bail bondsman in San Diego, who said he just believes in fair trials. Then, a few thousand from the Foundation for the Improvement of Justice, followed by more from the California Consumer Protection Foundation. By 2003, the Foleys had collected enough grants to fund a $100,000-a-year annual budget. Both Jay and Linda are paid employees, but they earn less than Linda did when she was a teacher. The 60 nation-wide volunteers all give their time, their e-mail addresses, and the telephone bills they wrack up helping victims to the cause for free.

Foley's vision for the center includes pay for the hotline volunteers, similar to the way many suicide hotlines work now. She also wants a few more employees, particularly a full-time attorney to deal with the finance companies and a full-time counselor to work with emotionally distraught victims. Eventually, she would like to move the world headquarters out of her home.

***

David Szwak has never been a victim of identity theft, but long before there was even a name for the crime, he summoned up the same kind of empathy Foley's volunteers have—and eventually turned that empathy into a career as one of the nation's most prominent consumer protection attorneys. But for his initial persistence, many identity theft victims may never have found justice against the credit industry inside a U.S. courtroom.

Back in 1992, none of the partners at his law firm would even listen to him, let alone sign the complaint he was proposing. After all, he was barely out of law school then, a former football player at LSU, a kid not yet 30 with a crazy idea. He wanted to sue some of America's biggest companies. And for what? Irritating a secretary's parents?

It was the early 1990s, in many ways the heyday of retail credit card firms, which were riding the wave of recession to new heights. People needed money, any way they could get it, and the new math of the credit card industry dictated that the very best time to shove credit cards at people is when they have little or no ability to pay the bills. The visionary thinking didn't just apply to bank cards. Retail stores started to catch on, too, pushing credit card applications at the point of sale with the new, lower standards. Also lower: the standards for making sure applicants were who they said they were. Long before anyone had even imagined the term *identity theft*, Charles and Martha Ferguson found themselves victims of the new, recession-era, loose credit policies. A year before David Szwak had taken up his starter law job in Shreveport, Louisiana, the demure, retired older couple began their ordeal: bills and more bills for things they never purchased, collection agencies hounding them, and rude phone calls during dinner—in fact, all day and all night. Somehow, someone had amassed a $120,000 debt in their name.[18] And none of the companies involved seemed interested in doing anything about it.

But David Szwak was. He had befriended the Ferguson's daughter, who was a secretary at his law office. He listened to the story of her parents' struggles, and felt the need to get involved. And because he heard their cries for help, he created a small cottage industry, reached partner within three years, and eventually became the leading adversary of the credit industry.

"At that time, no one had ever filed a suit back against the credit and credit reporting industries on behalf of a person whose ID was stolen," Szwak said. When he heard the Fergusons' story, he knew something terribly unjust was going on, and he could see the impact it had on their lives. But there were no guarantees he could actually win in court on behalf of the Fergusons, since there was no case law to support his claims—certainly his firm wasn't too sure about the prospects for the case, either.

He pitched the case to every partner at the firm, and initially, they all turned him down. "They said, 'We don't get it.'" Many laughed, either inside or out, at the prospect of suing American's biggest creditors over a secretary's parents' paperwork headaches.

Szwak was the right man in the right place at the right time. He was a geek by training—his undergraduate degree from LSU was in computer sciences. But during school, he took a job at the local courthouse. He started out in college wanting to be an engineer like his dad, not a lawyer. But he played softball with several influential judges, who took a liking to him, and urged him to take the Law School Admittance Test, just to see how well he'd do. Eventually, a couple of the judges even offered to pay for the test.

Once in law school, he had no particular interest in consumer law, which was hardly considered profitable. In fact, he didn't take a single consumer law course. When he left school and joined the firm, he was hired to litigate insurance cases for insurance companies.

But he wanted to try this case, because he cared about the Fergusons and their daughter. His programming background told him something was very wrong with the credit data reporting computers at play here. The systems designed by the credit and credit reporting companies, which made correcting errors nearly impossible, were impossibly flawed, he was sure of it. At a time when computers were still new to the common person, only a motivated young lawyer with a computer background would be able to make the case that credit firms hadn't taken even the most basic steps to avoid enabling an imposter. And that was his legal strategy. "He who deals with the imposter is in the best position to prevent the fraud," Szwak said. That meant the creditors and credit reporting agencies were to blame and deserved to pay.

The actual crime was trivial. A car salesman with access to a credit reporting terminal at the dealership simply ran the Ferguson's credit reports and applied for credit in their name—a technique that's still widespread today. The unfortunate Fergusons were chosen because they shared a last name with the car salesman—but in the end, that didn't matter because none of the creditors checked ID at the point of sale. Before he was done, the salesman had rung up charges on numerous credit cards, obtained medical services, and even purchased a mobile home using the Ferguson's name. But the imposter wasn't sophisticated. When he set up new, fraudulent accounts, he had the mail delivered to a P.O. box that he had opened in his own name, using his own Arkansas driver's license. The salesman was caught within days, once Szwak pressed the Secret Service to take on the investigation. The crime was easy to solve. It was the fallout that seemed never ending.

A year later, the salesman's spending spree was still a nightmare of bad credit and hostile encounters with collection agencies for the Fergusons—a nightmare that the financial companies were unable to end, despite the mountain of correspondence sent to creditors.

Finally, Szwak convinced one partner "with his hand shaking," to sign off on the complaint against the creditors duped by the Ferguson's imposter. The newly sworn-in Szwak then filed the case in a Jonesboro, Arkansas, federal court, suing nearly a dozen big-name defendants, including JC Penney, Bank One, and First Tennessee Bank, along with local credit reporting agencies.

But this is no Erin Brokovich tale. There was no long drawn-out discovery, no dramatic trial. The defendants settled the case almost as quickly as it was filed, and for substantial money. There would be no opening of the books in the case, no depositions about procedures inside the financial companies. Credit firms weren't interested in that kind of exposure. Szwak had called their bluff.

He was hailed as a rainmaker by the local media, which splashed pictures of him and the Fergusons across newspaper pages and television screens. Almost immediately, another dozen victims called Szwak with similar stories. Many of these settled just as quickly. "From that point, my file count just went up and up," he said.

Szwak became the highest-grossing attorney at the firm, and he was voted in as a full partner within three years. Soon, there were hundreds of cases, and then law journal articles. By 1994, just three years out of law school, he had been featured by most national major media TV news shows. Now he is the informal leader of a loose affiliation of consumer lawyers nationwide who file identity theft cases against financial companies. At 40, he is among the best-known consumer lawyers in the nation and has litigated cases in almost every state in the country.

"Somebody came by and said, I need help," Szwak said. "I always tell younger attorneys, 'People will come to you for help but if you don't listen to them and you are too busy to talk, you never know what opportunities will pass you by. Every chance meeting is an opportunity and how you handle it makes your future.'"

**

Not every heroic story has a storybook ending, however. Szwak's legal victories against both credit firms and credit reporting agencies have helped keep the industry honest; but across America, thousands of individuals whose lives are privately ruined by identity theft are toiling silently to keep their families honest. Not unlike a family battle with drug or alcohol addiction, a family dealing with a chronic identity thief can be torn apart. Roberta, grandmother of six children victimized by their own mother, speaks for all family members who must face the awful choice of looking the other way or turning in their own flesh and blood to law enforcement authorities.[19]

Roberta had spent about a year wondering how her daughter could support such a lavish lifestyle. New clothes all the time, new cars, televisions for all six of the grandkids at Christmas. And then there were these bills that sometimes showed up at Roberta's house, which was a few miles from her daughter's in a South Carolina town. They came addressed to her daughter, but displayed multiple variations of her daughter's name. Since she had been married three times, she had many name variations to choose from. Some envelopes included hyphenated names, some didn't, but there were about a dozen variations all together. Then, collection letters started to pile up. The daughter would simply throw them in the trash when she stopped by to visit. Eventually, Roberta began to dig them out of the trash to have a peek.

The fog started to lift one day when ex-husband no. 2 stopped by for a chat. Roberta's daughter had been opening a variety of credit card accounts using her children's information, the former spouse said. He wanted to say something sooner, but didn't know if he could approach his former mother-in-law. Roberta had a sick feeling in her stomach.

Nearly a decade earlier, Roberta came home from work to find her home telephone service had been disconnected. Furious, she called the phone company with her cell phone. An operator calmly told her she hadn't paid a $250 bill, so her service had been disconnected.

"But I have a $43 bill right here that I've just received," she recalls saying, stunned. Oh no, not that phone account, the other one, the operator replied, and rattled off the address. It was her daughter's address. The daughter, unable to obtain telephone service because of her own bad credit, had signed up using Roberta's name and information. Roberta stormed down to the phone company office and paid the bill herself, then gave her daughter a tongue-lashing.

A few years later, Roberta's other daughter started getting hassling phone calls from a collection agency over an unpaid water bill. A few weeks of confusion were cleared up when Roberta remembered the telephone incident and guessed her daughter was up to her old tricks. Once again, the woman had used a family member's private information to cover up her own bad credit history.

And now, it appeared Roberta's grandchildren had been caught up in the mess. Roberta suspected the worst, but had no idea what to do. She faced the most awful of familial choices: to pick between her grandchildren and her daughter. It didn't take long. They were innocent and deserved a future, she said.

"My oldest grandchild just turned 10, she's in 5th grade. She started a year early. In six years she should be applying for college loans. She's shot before she ever gets started unless it's cleared up," Roberta said.

So she went to a local police detective and asked for help, giving him the Social Security Numbers of her six grandchildren, aged 5 to 10. He came back a few days later with bad news.

"Oh my God, this is a nasty web," Roberta recalls him saying. "There's activity on every single one of these numbers you've given me."

Along with thousands of dollars in unpaid credit card bills, the detective said there was even a repossessed $70,000 double-wide trailer home purchased in one of the children's names. In all, there was $150,000 in unpaid bills.

It was clear now: Roberta's grandchildren were paying for their own Christmas gifts, paying for those new televisions, with their financial future. Further research turned up another victim, a stepdaughter from a previous marriage, who at 20 had recently tried to buy her first car and was denied her loan application.

"They said, 'You have bad credit.'" It would have been her first loan.

***

Identity theft inside families is a quiet crime, often now tagging along with some form of domestic abuse, according to Linda Foley. It's impossible to document because so many cases go unreported. Victims who call her hotline often resist or refuse to file a police report because they want to "keep it in the family." Still, they need help with the financial paperwork. There are cases where a single family member makes a mistake during hard times, makes good on the debt, and the family moves on, Foley says. But many times, the crime keeps happening, just like domestic violence, and as people look the other way, it only gets worse. Many identity thieves have silent accomplices; those who see the nice cars, the fancy clothes, who get the debt collector phone calls, but who keep quiet. Then, there are heroes who step forward in the name of the victims.

Roberta and her daughter's ex-husband no. 2 swept into action, quietly managing to freeze all the grandchildren's credit reports at the three credit bureaus. That meant, hopefully, no additional accounts could be opened in their names. Then, they spent weeks filling out the required paperwork to get copies of the actual credit reports, so they could begin the long process of cleaning up the children's credit history. The bureaus demanded copies of the children's birth certificates, Social Security cards, and the divorce settlement papers before issuing the reports. It will likely be several years, if ever, before their records are completely clean. But in this case, Roberta's trash digging quite possibly saved her grandchildren's financial future.

Roberta, meanwhile, struggled to find a law enforcement official who would take on the case. The daughter lived outside her home town, so her local detective couldn't help. Investigators at the sheriff's office wouldn't help, saying they didn't have time to follow up on all the muddied paperwork. So while she tried to build the case on her own, she still had a question to face: Would she insist on prosecuting her daughter? And if she did, what else would she find? And where would her grandchildren end up? Who would explain to them where the nice Christmas presents really came from? Roberta, like many other heroes in the war against identity theft, didn't let such questions stop her from making a stand.

10

WHAT NOW?

Clerks and customer care reps need better training . . . that training can consist of two sentences with less than ten words. Don't give out customer's information to anyone. If you do, then you will be immediately terminated.

—James Rinaldo Jackson

A sign on a community bank in Woodinville, Washington, proudly proclaims "Business loans, up to $50,000 in eight hours or less." Online mortgage companies brag about 15-minute applications. Billions of preapproved credit card applications and convenience checks wildly chase consumers around the country, filling recycle bins with ticking identity theft time bombs. There isn't a lender in America who doesn't see speed as its key competitive advantage. And there isn't an identity thief in America who doesn't see speed the same way. Haste, the ally of higher profits, is the enemy of safety. In the broken system of American credit, haste makes not only waste—it makes victims.

In fact, at nearly every turn, things are much easier for the criminals than victims.

Loan officers, software developers, poorly paid customer relations telephone operators, and even car salesman have instant access to incredibly intimate details of our lives—and have rights to see data about consumers that even the consumers can't see. Identity thieves regularly access this data and use it. It takes only a moment to fill out a preapproved credit card application and steal an identity. It can take years to clear up the mess. Victims face Jobian trials to clean their pockmarked credit reports of errors. Poorly paid investigators, increasingly based out of the country, handle disputes of credit report errors, sometimes up to 100 per day, and nearly always rule against consumers in their initial judgments.

Police officers refuse to take reports of the crime or prosecute criminals, particularly when the crime is committed someplace far away—common in the age of the Internet. The federal government trips over itself trying to mandate fixes to the problem, all the while taking away state governments' rights to experiment with their own solutions at the pleasure of the credit industry. Documents used to authenticate people who board airplanes or open bank accounts are so easily faked we might be better off using nothing at all. And criminals, often driven by the craze of methamphetamine addiction, get bolder, smarter, and sometimes more desperate every day. The perfect storm that has enabled the identity theft epidemic is indeed still raging.

What can we do?

Today, when a purse or wallet is stolen, or even when homeowners face a burglary, lost money is the least of the victim's worries. It's the stolen documents that create the most fear. Walking through the front door, finding a ransacked home, savvy consumers now know the first place to look is the strong box or safe, where the birth certificates and retirement statements were kept. Did the thief get them? If so, the house burglary may end up costing much more than lost jewelry. No one feels as helpless as the purse-snatching victim who now faces the seemingly open-ended, never-ending fear of identity theft, who hears the intensely frustrating answer from authorities: "We can't do anything until something bad happens."

The identity theft epidemic feels a bit like cancer of the finances. Some people smoke three packs a day and never get cancer; others die from a brutal bout with the disease without ever taking a drag on a cigarette. So it is with identity theft. Some answer hackers' Internet e-mails, recklessly transmitting their Social Security number and mother's maiden name across the Internet and face only minimal fraud. Others shred every last financial document that arrives in the mail, avoid the Internet, and never use a credit card—and end up having a home mortgage taken out in their name. There is no quick advice and today no silver bullet to stop identity theft, and there isn't really even a way to identify a high-risk group. Identity theft is an equal opportunity crime. In an odd twist, probably the only way to gain some protection is to completely ruin your own credit. A victim with very poor credit is of little use to an identity thief.

Aside from taking that absurd step, what can be done to regain control of our out-of-control digital twin? This incredibly complex problem requires a multipronged solution; law enforcement agencies must continue to break down jurisdictional barriers and work together to catch ID thieves across the country and the world. Consumers will have to accept radical changes in the way they validate who they are when applying for credit.

The most difficult steps must be taken by government legislators, who must stop coddling the credit industry. It has clearly failed the millions of Americans victimized by identity theft. Major reforms are needed to reel in the out-of-control industry, which has demonstrated it is not capable of safeguarding consumer privacy or financial integrity. Only when the industry is made responsible for the problem, and made to feel the pain it causes by enabling identity theft, will fundamental changes occur. A 2003 ruling by the South Carolina Supreme Court which rejected the notion that lenders have any legal responsibility to the ID theft victim when they issue credit to an imposter,[1] only points to the need for legislative initiatives mandating such responsibility. Another troubling ruling, issued in 2001 by the U.S. Supreme Court, held that consumers who want to sue a credit bureau for damaging their credit rating with bad information must file their complaints within two years of the error's entry into the system—rather than within two years of the error's discovery[2]—even though many consumers don't find out about credit flaws for months or years. The ruling effectively bars victims who don't discover errors for two years from any legal relief at all. Only a new federal law clarifying the start of the statute of limitations clock can restore victims' rights on this issue. Legislation to do just that has been proposed in Congress but not yet reached a floor vote.

Corporations that leak consumer data to hackers must face strict liability for their negligent behavior, too. Credit card numbers and other private data need not be stored by every electronic commerce site, and if they are stored, they should be encrypted so they are useless to any thief. Such encryption technology has been available since the advent of the Internet, but by 2003, only about 10 percent of companies deployed this commonsense solution.[3] Firms that don't, and then lose their data, should be held negligent for that choice.

Finally, both corporations and the government must grant consumers a permanent right to examine all the stored data that references their identity—and give them a fair chance to correct any errors, so they regain some feeling of control about their lives.

But we must admit the reality that current economic pressures mean the credit industry will do all it can, including spend tens of millions of dollars in marketing and software development, to slow down the problem enough to prevent any limitations on the free flow of credit to Americans. Virtually every ID theft initiative supported by the credit industry addresses the problem after the fact. Giving out free credit reports, for example, just tells a consumer they've already been had; and it's of little use to someone who has no reason to suspect their credit had been damaged. Almost nothing has been done to prevent identity theft.

One exception to this rule: San Diego-based ID Analytics, ironically located just a few miles from the Identity Theft Resource Center. Software developers at the tiny firm hope to beat back ID thieves by outsmarting them with technology. After all, it's generally technology that got us into this mess in the first place.

Like all of us, criminals follow patterns, particularly when they are in a hurry. When they find a pseudonym or a fake address they like, they use it repeatedly. When they get their hands on a digital dossier, they take the same steps again and again. First place a stolen credit card is used? A gas station pump, where no one is watching and no signature is required. When a new identity is used, criminals usually order a cell phone quickly, so they have a phone number to use on subsequent credit applications. Then, they often purchase electronics, such as a new mail-order PC. Only after several successful purchases will a smart thief escalate to something sizable, like a car loan. And since very few identity thieves commit only one crime—most hone their skills again and again, often as part of a loosely organized gang of experts—they are likely to order dozens of cell phones from different firms, asking that they be delivered to the same address. Even the most clever of thieves, when applying for multiple phones, will often just slightly alter addresses, telephone numbers, or Social Security numbers, perhaps incrementing the numbers by 1 on every application.

Simple steps like that easily evade basic fraud-detection procedures at most credit issuers. But ID Analytics' neural-network software, when applied to credit grantors across the industry, seems capable of peering through billions of applications and payments and detecting patterns like these as they emerge. Such neural networks, so-called because designers think they mimic the abilities of a human brain, have often met with mixed success in real-world applications. But industry insiders are taking ID Analytics seriously because the developers behind the software already have sizable success to their name. More than half of all worldwide credit card transactions are now evaluated by software called Falcon, written by HNC Software in the early 1990s.[4] Consumers might not know its name, but millions know its work. Many know that sudden overuse of a credit card is likely to trigger a phone call from the bank's fraud department. "Are you really in London buying $2,000 bracelets right now?" the operator will ask. When the consumer says he or she has never left the country, the card is immediately disabled, saving merchants thousands of dollars in stolen goods and saving consumers the hassle of disputing fraudulent charges. Falcon is behind those phone calls.

HNC executives left the firm, since purchased by credit scoring company Fair Isaac, in 2001, to take their stab at the identity theft crisis. ID Analytics plans to take the Falcon model into the far more complex world of imposter crime—more complex because the firm's solution necessarily requires instant sharing of data from nearly every kind of credit grantor, every potential target of an identity thief. Without such a thorough sharing of data, the thieves would merely adapt and hit lenders that don't use the system.[5]

In the ID Analytics system, each transaction is instantly evaluated and given a three-digit score—not unlike a credit score—which quantifies the risk that it may be an attempted identity theft. By examining other recent transactions involving the personal information listed on the application, the software looks to see if the data has been used in other attempted frauds. A sudden surge in cell phone applications listing the same address would raise a red flag or at least raise the "ID score." Within seconds, a merchant would learn that the applicant represented a high risk.

For its first trial run, ID Analytics managed to obtain millions of account applications and records from industry titans like Dell, Citibank, and Verizon. An entire year's worth of data from

2001, some 200 million credit applications, was used to test the neural network. On the trial run, eight times the amount of identity thefts were uncovered than were found by each firm's current fraud-fighting methods.

As an example of fraud caught by its software, ID Analytics shared the story of an application received by a wireless phone provider filled out with the name "O.L." and hometown of Hackensack, New Jersey. A scan of the dataset revealed that the address on the application had been used on 17 other applications for wireless service in the prior two months. By the time no. 18 was received, none of the other wireless firms had yet caught on to the identity thief.[6]

All the applications had included unlisted phone numbers, and while those phone numbers were very different, they followed a pattern. Three different area codes were used, along with 13 different exchanges (the first three digits of a 7-digit phone number). However, the final four digits were often very similar—7987 or 8978, 9879, 9898, and the like. Using current technology, none of the applications were flagged as fraud by the individual companies that received them. But the industry is hoping that by sharing application information in real time, fraud patterns will become obvious, and such crime rings could be stopped after the third or fourth fraudulent application.

It's certainly an open question if the nation's credit-granting firms will decide to play nicely together and participate wholeheartedly in such data sharing; creditors, generally queasy about sharing customer data, are watching the project with a cautious eye. And before millions of consumer vitals are shared on a real-time basis with ID Analytics, privacy advocates will likely have something to say about it. But in 2003, it was among the credit industry's best hopes.

The system almost has to succeed, in a sense—because ID Analytics fulfills the one requirement the credit industry has laid out before it will accept any true identity theft protection measures. They must not interfere with the miracle of instant credit. Risk-based solutions are a fabulous idea for the industry, for the same reason actuarial tables work well for the insurance industry. When you're dealing with billions of dollars, shaving a few percentage points off of fraud is the most workable answer. A drastic solution, such as requiring a 24-hour waiting period before issuing a new retail store credit card or allowing consumers to place outright credit freezes, would cut the flow of credit too severely and cut too deeply into revenues. A risk-based system is hardly perfect, but it would most certainly make a dent into identity theft–based fraud—perhaps enough to take the edge off the skyrocketing fraud rates and reduce the negative public relations impact of the crime. In the meantime, it would hardly dent revenues at all. And that's all the industry needs.

The irony of ID Analytics' work is it's a far more complex system than the one state legislators around the country have been trying to force creditors to adopt for some time. Currently, many credit card furnishers don't even do the most basic fact-checking when they issue credit cards. A valid Social Security number and a name are often all that's needed. A dumpster-diving identity thief can just fill out a preapproved application, enter his or her own name, address, and phone number, and sometimes even a guessed Social Security number, and often succeed in getting a stolen credit card. No grantor offers a credit card without checking the credit score of the applicant; or rather, the score attached to the Social Security number listed on the application. Simply asking credit bureaus for address or birthday verification at the same time, and matching those with credit applications, would foil a great deal of current fraud. But the simple application verification doesn't happen, largely because it would slow down the credit process—and, ultimately, give the consumer applying for a retail credit card one more opportunity to second-guess his or her purchase, a hindrance to the almighty goal of credit: closing the sale. The necessary human intervention such a system would require would be pricey—ultimately, it is much cheaper for corporations to simply let the fraud happen and deal with it later.[7]

Even when the credit industry's meager fraud-fighting measures do temporarily stop a thief, firms don't take a basic measure that would put a halt to a sizable percentage of the crimes. ID thieves are always playing the numbers, filling out dozens of applications for each dossier they obtain, knowing that some will be denied and some will be granted. If credit grantors that denied an application informed their colleagues, and the impacted consumer that a fraud had been attempted in the consumer's name, subsequent attempts could be thwarted. But a former credit bureau fraud fighter, who quit over his firm's lax security policies, says the industry is still so secretive that it is reluctant to share the valuable fraud data.[8]

Equifax brags about its membership in a fraud data sharing club, but only offers information to the group after a consumer has gone through the laborious process of reporting the fraud—which can take months, after the fraud works its way through the billing cycle. And often, it doesn't happen at all. It certainly doesn't happen under the time frame that ID thieves work in.[9]

ID Analytics isn't the only firm working to combine multiple data sources to fight fraud. Another neural network of a sort is being developed by several companies—including Equifax—that combines public and private records to make sure all the information on a credit application is internally correct. Mismatched names, birthdays, and addresses are flagged by such multiple-source data validation systems. The system is a good first step; it should be able to defeat unsophisticated ID thieves who fill out credit applications with random information, the obviously faked applications where even names and Social Security numbers don't match. But it will likely be of little use against sophisticated thieves, who generally work from complete stolen digital dossiers and can fill out a credit application accurately.[10]

Some credit card issuers, frustrated by the lack of fraud checking made available to them by credit bureaus, have developed their own algorithms to check for fraud. One system that simply checks to see if there are multiple addresses assigned to a Social Security number—a sign that an ID thief is peppering that identity with applications—worked well but cost the issuer $5 per application. It's now used only on a fraction of applications, those deemed most suspicious.[11]

Other firms are using a more complex mixture of data that allows them to challenge potential customers with surprising out-of-wallet questions. Special software cues employees to ask one simple, if intrusive, question to customers, "What kind of student loan do you have?" or "Who holds your mortgage?"[12] The questions are generated randomly and are generally harder for an identity thief to answer, since they require relatively intimate knowledge of a person's life—and a thief armed with a stolen wallet, or even a complete digital dossier, generally wouldn't have the answer. American Express has already implemented such a system. Callers who contact the firm in an attempt to report fraud are challenged by a number of questions from customer service operators. In addition to the standard "last four digits of the Social Security number," consumers can be asked to provide the first name of an immediate family member to prove they are who they say they are.[13] Ironically, consumers calling to report fraud face tougher verification challenges than ID theives applying for credit.

ID theft expert Avivah Litan says firms that have used this system have had mixed success. Sometimes, the questions are so surprising that legitimate consumers don't know the answers, and customer service representatives end up coaching them. It's not uncommon, at a time when mortgages are regularly sold and resold, that consumers don't know the name of the firm that holds their mortgage. And in the great tradition of the irony created by identity theft, correct answers can actually be an indication of trouble.

"Law enforcement officials have found stacks of credit reports in the ownership of identity thieves (perhaps obtained through inside jobs)," Litan writes. "Using this 'source of truth' data, the thieves can answer the challenge/response questions better than their victims can. Some lenders now say that if every question is answered correctly, they suspect an identity thief is responding."[14]

Still, such out-of-wallet questions represent an effective test, if sometimes a bit misplaced. When asked, "How do you know the names of my family members?" an American Express fraud service representative won't reply. These kinds of diligent fraud-fighting efforts require even more data collection, and more invasions of privacy, by corporations. And yet these same corporations still refuse to implement even basic application fraud measures up front, at the point the credit is granted. Instead, they are willing to endure wild gyrations after the fact, all in the name of keeping wide open the free flow of credit.

***

Who are you? That's the key question underlying the identity theft epidemic. In the United States, there simply is no effective way to answer that question. It's a question that America's financial institutions can't answer, as exemplified by the Know-Your-Customer controversy of Chapter 7. But outside of some kind of fraud predictive software or invasive database-based verification, the only other technology solution to identity theft is to give individuals some new thing they can hold that offer assurance they are who they say they are. The only true fix for identity theft, says Identity Theft Resource Center's Jay Foley with his tongue firmly implanted in his cheek, is implantation of a computer chip at birth that can't possibly be edited or updated. That would be the only way to prevent the creation of a digital twin, separated from each individual the moment a birth certificate is issued.

Not everyone sees the idea as far-fetched.

Biometrics—the use of biological attributes to identify individuals—run the full spectrum from simple fingerprinting to computer chip implantation. While the mere mention of the term *biometrics* often raises ominous Big Brother images, such systems are already becoming more common around the world. European nations regularly include fingerprints in identification documents, such as driver's licenses. Aggressive identity verification companies are making headway in developing simple, subdermal electronic devices that positively identify individuals.

Applied Digital Solutions, a Palm Beach, Florida, company, is already selling electronic ATM cards that are surgically implanted in human flesh. The chips emit secret codes through radio frequencies and would free consumers from having to remember PIN codes or carry debit cards. They require no batteries, sucking the tiny amount of electricity they need from external devices used to communicate with the chip, such as an ATM machine.[15]

Both private and public organizations are embracing technology to identify and track inventory. The chips are similar to inventory-tracking Radio Frequency Identifier Devices (RFID) the U.S. Defense Department plans to install on everything from chemical suits to MREs (Meal, Ready to Eat).[16] Wal-Mart also plans to force its suppliers to add RFID tags to some deliveries, easing inventory management. By 2005, Wal-Mart has said, even individual cans of Campbell's soup must have RFID chips to be on store shelves. Wal-Mart has the power to mandate such a step—its stores sell about 12 percent of Campbell's $6.7 billion in annual sales.[17]

It would be a big leap from soup cans to humans, but not as far as one might think. Chips developed by Applied Digital Solutions are already being installed in Mexican citizens, loaded with critical medical information that can be scanned by doctors and hospitals. Similar chips developed to track cattle and lost pets are now being pushed as a solution to finding lost children and even have the backing of Mexico's National Foundation of

Investigations of Robbed and Missing Children. Kidnapping is rampant in Mexico, making the radical solution not seen so radical.[18]

Security systems, unfortunately, are always a cat-and-mouse game, and biometrics is no exception. Every biometrics system developed has been defeated, using clever countermeasures. Kidnappers could simply find the microchip in the child and cut it out of their flesh with a knife. More rudimentary fingerprint systems can easily be defeated by the creation of fake shells that slip over fingertips. These might be hard to use in the presence of an arresting police officer, but they will easily defeat any ATM machine outfitted with such technology.

More limited biometrics systems have met with measured success and raise far fewer civil liberties concerns. Many police squad cars in California are now outfitted with equipment that can instantly transmit fingerprints back to a central office, which can test them against a database of known suspects. Since many suspects facing an arrest warrant already have a mug shot and fingerprint on file, instant, roadside fingerprint testing and image comparison can go a long way toward preventing false arrests.[19]

***

It is in the arena of law enforcement where perhaps the greatest progress has been made so far in the fight against ID theft. Just five years ago, many victims found it nearly impossible to get police reports when they were hit with the crime. Victims were repeatedly told a crime hadn't been committed or it had occurred outside the local jurisdiction, so a report could not be filed. Without a police report, victims had no chance at cleaning up their financial records. But dozens of states have passed laws solving the jurisdiction problem, and in some cases, requiring local agencies to take reports. Public exposure of the problem has made law enforcement more sensitive to the issue. And the increased use of computer crime task forces around the country has produced a generation of techno-savvy cops who are capable of chasing down computer criminals through cyberspace—even if they have to ask for help from officers in other jurisdictions.

But there is still a long way to go before police solve the thorniest law enforcement problem related to identity theft—the specter of false arrests. Beat cops don't have much choice when they pull over a driver for a traffic violation and find an outstanding arrest warrant in the driver's name. The situation is dire for victims; false arrests are so common that California now has a hotline number for cops to call when a suspect claims he or she is an ID theft victim. The Virginia state government has taken to issuing ID Theft Passport cards, which victims can carry around and flash to police if they are facing a possible false arrest. Today, there is greater possibility than ever that a suspect claiming "you have the wrong person" might be telling the truth, and police officers must be trained for that possibility.[20]

Meanwhile, beat cops face the other side of the coin—they will increasingly have to deal with an even more frustrating legal reality—the "my imposter did it" defense. Already, suspects charged with computer crimes are succeeding in court with explanations indicating criminal acts committed using their computer were really done by a computer hacker who had taken control of the machine. Defense attorneys will surely expand use of this tactic; the farther apart we become from our digital twin, the easier it will be for defense attorneys to create the shadow of a doubt before judges and juries.

The most promising solutions to the false-arrest problem are better identifying documents and more accurate information sharing among state motor vehicles agencies. But the idea of a national ID card creates a complex thicket of issues and stirs emotions that will not likely allow for a compromise any time soon. Even in the days immediately following September 11, 2001, when the country's appetite for civil liberties intrusions was at an all-time high, Larry Ellison's offer of free Oracle software to run a national ID card program was met with near-universal derision.

***

What's missing most from all these proposed solutions is a return to common sense. Technologies that solve one problem almost always create a new one and bring with them unexpected fallout. The one answer to ID theft that the credit industry simply cannot stomach—and the only one that would really, work—would be more rational and deliberate means for disbursing credit.

The problem of identity theft is dramatic; the solution should be, too. The only real way to get control of the crisis is the give control back to consumers. Consumers should be given the choice to drop out of the world of instant credit, placing them in a category that makes them far less attractive identity theft targets.

Put simply, it should be easy for consumers to indicate they feel no need to get a credit card, increase their credit limits, or buy a car on credit any time soon. A credit freeze would be just that—as George Bush senior might have said, "Read my lips: No new credit." No more preapproved credit card applications, no more convenience checks, no ability to walk into Circuit City and walk out with a $3,000 television on a whim. This obvious leave-me-alone solution would be a silver bullet for many consumers, making theft of their personal data far less valuable to identity thieves. Lifting the freeze would require a simple process, with really only one requirement: time. A delay of a week, or even a day, would be enough to ward off all but the most persistent identity thieves. Since many American families really do know they are planning to buy a new car or television at least a day ahead of time—and encouraging such responsible financial planning is clearly in our national interest—a well-designed credit freeze wouldn't interfere with their ability to make large purchases. The credit industry bristles at such a suggestion, posing the hypothetical of small emergencies, such as buying a new water heater when the old one breaks. But in reality, nearly all such emergencies could be handled by existing credit cards with existing credit limits.

Of course, such a drastic leave-me-alone provision would severely limit consumers' ability to go on spontaneous spending sprees. It's easy to imagine a wide swath of consumers opting for such strong protection against identity theft in exchange for surrendering the ability to make such big-ticket impulse buys. But the credit industry would never stand for it. Since the foundations of the credit card business in the 1950s, the industry has focused entirely on convincing consumers to give in to their most basic urges, to surrender tomorrow for today, to buy on credit no matter what the cost. It's an industry designed to convince Americans we can have everything we want today, and in fact, we can have a whole lot of things we don't want. Not only has the industry contributed to, and practically caused, the personal bankruptcy crisis, the credit industry has also enabled the identity theft crisis. Backing off its convenience checks, preapproved applications and instant credit limit increases is not an option, no matter how many identity thieves they enable.

Instead, the industry is driven to spend millions to build an incredibly complex software system ultimately designed to skim a percentage of identity theft frauds off the top of the problem.

Credit freezes have been attempted in limited areas, with dubious results. A California state law which took effect in 2003 gives residents the right to lock up their credit report. The service can be costly however—as much as $100 per year, unless residents can prove they have already been victims of identity theft. And lifting the freeze temporarily to enable a new home or car purchase is costly, too—up to $25 each time. Predictably, participation in the service is limited. But still, other state legislatures have taken notice, and Texas passed a similar law during 2003 allowing ID theft victims to place a "security freeze" on their accounts.

Both state provisions, however, only realistically offer relief *after* an identity theft has taken place. And the credit bureaus have already tried that route, with even more dubious result. The fraud alert system, which has been in place for years, simply places some kind of flag next to consumers' accounts indicating their personal information may have been tainted. Credit furnishers are then told not to grant credit to that consumer without contacting him or her first. Such notices give the consumer the opportunity to just say, "No, that's not me—I'm not at your retail store, I'm at home." They also offer ID theft victims a measure of peace when they are in a middle of a string of crimes committed by an imposter who is on the loose. But the fraud alerts have largely been a failure so far. Consumers who file them find credit card companies often ignore them and issue credit anyway. The credit bureaus insist on limiting their effectiveness by granting them only for a 90- or 180-day period initially. Follow-up letters are required to add time to the fraud alert, from one year to seven years. But ultimately, the system is designed to always fall back on the normal state—normal being the consumer is liable to have someone purchase a car in his or her name, at any time. That's not reassuring to victims, who know that 699 out of 700 identity frauds don't result in a conviction. The criminal is still out there, armed with their financial data, and the credit companies can't be bothered to notice a flag asking that they make a single phone call that could save a consumer hours and hours of headaches and heartaches. Instead, they insist on speed and insist on resisting human intervention.

***

The other fundamental solution is to allow consumers themselves to do the human intervention. One of the most effective fraud-fighting tools yet invented is the Internet. More and more contientious, or understandably paranoid, consumers are reviewing their credit card and checking accounts online. Some do so daily. That means they often discover a fraudulent transaction on a credit card or checking account a day or two after it happens, sometimes as quickly as the powerful Falcon fraud detection software does—and often times, consumers discover fraud even the neural networks don't. The financial industry should recognize the value of such aggressive consumer behavior and even find a way to reward it, as credit card companies reward retailers who snatch stolen credit cards from thieves at a checkout. But the culture of secrecy surrounding both public and private databases contributes to their error rate and cuts off the one best-known solutions for fixing data problems—enabling consumers.

Perhaps the most promising development of the past five years has been the new openness the credit industry has regarding credit scores. The individual credit score number, probably the most important number in any consumer's financial life, was a carefully guarded secret until the late 1990s. It was considered a state secret, an incredibly valuable, and proprietary, three digits. The industry argued consumers wouldn't understand the number even if it were revealed to them. Car dealers and banks were forbidden from sharing the number with consumers, under threats that their contracts with the credit bureau could be terminated. That would be financial death.

But a combination of public outrage, congressional interest, the rise of the Internet, and a new direct-to-consumer business model came together to change the industry's attitude about credit score disclosure in the late 1990s. Fair Isaac, maker of the

FICO score used by many credit grantors to determine credit-worthiness, decided to sell its scores to consumers over the Internet. Consumers immediately understood that an 720 credit score meant a mortgage at 6.5 percent, but a 600 credit score meant a mortgage at 8.5 percent, a difference of thousands of dollars each year. With the consequences of credit mistakes now obvious, consumers became their own private investigators, their own best advocates. They are certainly in the best position to find and fix mistakes. Combined with the now exploding business of selling full credit reports over the Internet, the new public airing of credit scores has exposed embarrassing flaws in the credit system. But it has also created the opportunity, the necessary kind of peer review, required to fix the system.

***

Predictably, just as one secret is exposed, two more are created. The expanded use of risk scoring by a variety of industries in the U.S. economy in recent years has created an entirely new class of secret numbers—numbers that consumers can't review and often can't fix when there are errors. The auto insurance industry, for example, has created a score called the insurance risk score. Consumers aren't yet allowed to see their insurance risk score, even though it is just as susceptible to error as the credit score. The home insurance industry has done the same thing. Individuals have been denied or had their home insurance canceled because their property was assigned a high risk. Yet both industries persist in their arguments to preserve the secrecy of the numbers. Such secret data will always be error prone.

The federal government, of course, has its own identity secrets. In addition to the error-riddled National Crime Institute Center database used by every police officer in the nation, the federal government is increasing its use of databases in the name of protecting citizens at airports and border crossings, such as the controversial CAPPS II airline passenger screening project, which assigns risks to fliers and instructs airport personal to inspect them accordingly. Citizens will likely never get a chance to see their own CAPPS score, or whatever metric the government eventually develops to decide who will be searched when boarding an airplane. There will never be public review of the information used to calculate that risk, never a chance to explain that it was an identity thief who purchased that unusual chemical agent that one day 10 years ago. Instead, the victim will just endure lingering looks every time he or she boards a plane, denial of government clearances, and who knows what other unexpected difficulties.

In the end, a basic premise of American justice—that suspects have a right to face their accusers—has been circumvented by the culture of the secret database. Until the culture of secrecy is eliminated, both in the government and in corporations, until ordinary people are given back the control of their own information and have a fair chance to face their digital accusers, the system will be riddled with errors, identity thieves will easily defeat it, and the frustration and pain will continue.

***

For now, in the world of identity theft, it's each consumer for himself or herself. We're left with a lot of polite and marginally helpful advice: Be a little paranoid. Shred your bills, hide your Social Security number, don't fill out any form on the Web, reject any requests by cashiers for your phone number, don't enter any mail-in sweepstakes, limit the number of times you apply for credit. Never recycle any papers with financial data on them. If you're really paranoid, you might even install anonymizing software on your computer.

It's akin to the car theft dilemma. Sure, there are things you can do to decrease the odds your car might get stolen—chief among them, take the bus—but there are no guarantees. Even 1973 Dodge Dart left in a well-lit parking lot is stolen sometimes. And even people without computers have their identity hijacked.

Ordering credit reports on a regular basis can also be helpful, but it's just a notice that something bad has already happened.

If you are a victim, expect do-it-yourself-justice, because precious few police detectives have time to chase down your imposter—you will have to develop the case yourself.

The best help comes from the consumer advocacy groups devoted to helping victims: The Privacy Rights Clearing House and the Identity Theft Resource Center. Both are nonprofit organizations staffed by sympathetic, devoted people who know how to talk to banks, credit card companies, and police officers into caring about your problem.

But the best advice of all: Just accept that it really might happen to you. Be prepared, because your first steps after becoming a victim are crucial. Hold onto old-fashioned paper bank statements for a year to prove you really did have that money in your account. Don't be careless with ATM receipts, brokerage account paperwork, anything that you might wish you had after you've been hijacked. Put critical documents such as birth certificates into a safe deposit box that's outside the home. When you are hit by ID theft, stay strong. Never pay debts that aren't yours; just keep writing letters, keep sending them return receipt, keep explaining yourself to debt collection agencies. Avoid situations where you put yourself at the mercy of a single, time-sensitive credit decision. Instead, plan for large purchases well ahead of time. Then, before house shopping or visiting a dealership, check your credit report, so if there is a problem, time is on your side.

Appendix

Signs You Are a Victim

The real problem with identity theft is that it's a silent crime, and often there are no signals something is amiss until well after the fact. Several studies have indicated a significant portion of victims don't have any idea what's happened for a year or more. There is little advice available, unfortunately, which accomplishes anything other than discovering something bad has already happened.

The surest sign of trouble is an unexpected credit denial or word from a lender that your credit rating is poor. It's best to examine your credit report well in advance of making a significant purchase, like a home or a car, which will be financed. Mortgage companies that preapprove don't necessarily pull full credit reports, so getting a preapproval doesn't necessarily indicate you are free of identity theft blemishes.

Regular examination of your credit report is a good idea and will be economically more feasible when the newest version of the Fair Credit Reporting Act kicks in. It requires the credit bureaus to give consumers one free credit report each year. Paying for more than that—say, one report every three months—is probably wise after a bout with ID theft. But subscribing to a credit monitoring service for $79 a year or more isn't necessary and will just profit the industry that has created the problem in the first place.

The appearance of unexpected charges on a credit card bill is also another sure sign of ID theft, but among the easier problems for consumers to solve. Disputes are virtually automatic when filed with the credit card issuing bank in a timely manner. But the ID thief may engage in more serious crimes later, so it's important to pay close attention to credit files even after a simple instance of credit card fraud.

Calls from collection agencies also spell trouble. So can odd telemarketing calls where an operator asks for a single piece of personal information, like a birthday, offering a prize or other compensation. That can be an identity thief looking for one more piece of the puzzle before committing a crime.

On the Internet, an unexpected e-mail indicating a change of password or login name should set off alarm bells. And so should any mail that arrives at the home announcing unexpected new credit cards or other financial accounts. On the other hand, if your credit card expires and you don't receive a new one in a timely manner, that's also a bad sign.

Tips to Protect Yourself

There are plenty of lists of dos and don'ts to protect yourself from identity theft, but the reality is there's very little you can do to insulate yourself from the crime. Some steps can be taken to decrease the odds you'll be targeted by an identity thief, and there are mistakes to be made that can virtually guarantee you'll be victimized. Ultimately, however, your personal information can be stolen from so many sources beyond your control that there is no sure-fire way to protect your identity from imposters. The best way to defend yourself, then, is to merely accept the fact that you may very well be victimized in the coming years and prepare

accordingly. That means, at the risk of sounding like Robert Ful-
ghum, doing a lot of things you were trained to do in elemen-
tary school. Keep paper records of all your financial accounts
and all significant transactions; you will need them as evidence
of account balances and such in case an imposter drains your
account.

Carefully monitor all accounts on a monthly basis, or even
more often, if you are Internet savvy. The sooner the crime is
caught, the less damage done. Web-based credit card and bank
account lookups are the most effective tool consumers have in
monitoring for imposters.

To avoid having an encounter with an identity thief, simply
hang up immediately on telemarketers. Don't let criminals use
your politeness against you; you don't owe any intrusive caller
any niceties. Simply saying "yes" to any question asked on the
telephone can be used against you by a clever con artist. Treat
spam the same way. Just don't answer any e-mail offers or
requests for information. Thousands of people are falling for
imposter e-mails designed to "phish" out personal information
because they appear to be from legitimate companies. Don't
answer any e-mail offers and you won't have to worry about it.
Using good, unguessable passwords at electronic commerce
sites like Amazon and eBay is also important, as hackers use
automated programs to brute force their way into accounts at
sites like these.

If you simply must fill out a web form to get something you
want, consider creating a fake online persona, complete with
dummy e-mail address that you won't mind filling up with spam.
Reserve your real name, address, and credit card numbers for
sites your really know and trust. Using only a single credit card
for online transactions, one you know you'll monitor regularly,
is good practice.

Properly discarding regular mail helps, too. ID thieves who
sneak their way into recycling centers can hit the jackpot when

you throw preapproved credit card applications and convenience checks into the recycling bin. Burn them or shred them instead. Better still, opt-out of receiving the offers by calling 1-888-5OPTOUT. Meanwhile, watch your outgoing mail, too. The post office will pick up mail you leave in the curbside mailbox but strongly recommends against it. That little flag you raise to summon the postal carrier also alerts ID thieves that you have likely placed a time-sensitive bill payment, complete with a singed check, in your mailbox.

Finally, hassle store clerks and other corporate agents who insist on collecting personal data, such as home phone numbers, from you. Resist divulging your Social Security number to any company, and demand an explanation when asked for it. The more uncomfortable you make data collection for corporations, the less likely they will do it.

If You Are a Victim

The first thing any victim must do is think like a lawyer. Anything might turn into evidence—phone bills, credit card applications, even notes from telephone calls. From day one, you must think about building the case you will need to present to creditors and credit bureaus, so don't discard anything. Invest in some three-ring binders, a hole puncher, and a notebook. Take detailed notes of every ID theft–related phone call, including name, time, and date. An excellent summary of how to organize your files is available at Privacyrights.org

Victims of purse snatchings or other documents thefts should anticipate an ID theft may occur and act accordingly. Street criminals are more and more aware that the paperwork inside a wallet can be more valuable than the cash.

Report any hint of ID theft immediately to the fraud units of the three credit reporting companies—Experian, Equifax, and

TransUnion. Add a fraud alert to your file, and a victim's statement. It will read something like this: "Consumer's identity has been used to apply for credit fraudulently. Contact consumer at [telephone number] to verify all applications." The alerts only remain in effect for 90 to 180 days, so ask in writing that each bureau extend the alert to 7 years. But be aware that these measures will not entirely stop new fraudulent accounts from being opened by the imposter.

Ask the credit bureaus for names and phone numbers of credit grantors with whom fraudulent accounts have been opened. Contact all creditors immediately. File an identity theft affidavit with them—the form is available on the Federal Trade Commission's (FTC) web site—and then ask them to give you and your investigating law enforcement agency copies of any documentation, such as the application forms.

Generally, banks forgive debts accumulated by imposters, but only when the victim presents appropriate paperwork. The sooner the better; outstanding or unresolved ID theft–related debt can limit your ability to obtain a loan or credit card in the future. Most victims find with the right telephone calls, they can successfully insulate themselves from real financial loss. But delays can be costly. Federal and state laws vary on consumer liability for stolen accounts. For example, reporting a stolen ATM card within two days limits liability to $50; after that, consumers are responsible for up to $500. At any sign of identity theft, call your bank, your credit card companies, and other financial institutions and ask if there has been suspicious activity on your accounts.

You must check these accounts repeatedly for fraud, religiously spying your monthly bills. Identity thieves can wait months before acting on the information they have. And even if the original thief is arrested, there's no telling if your information was sold to someone else.

As soon as you've stopped any possible financial bleeding—hopefully within hours—go to your local police and insist on filing a report. Sometimes police will say, "Sorry, there's nothing we can do" and discourage you from filing. Do it anyway. The report will be vital if you have to dispute unauthorized charges to your accounts later on.

It's terribly unlikely that your individual report will lead to the arrest of a criminal. But while you may not feel particularly inspired to civic duty at the time, the report might eventually help catch a thief, or even a ring of thieves. If there is a trend of similar crimes, your report will help police piece the case together.

For that reason, you should also file your case with the Federal Trade Commission, which, under the Identity Theft and Assumption Deterrence Act of 1998, is the federal agency responsible for collecting ID theft data. The FTC puts all the complaints—161,000 during 2002—into its Consumer Sentinel database, which is used by law enforcement agencies around the country.

There are a number of other steps to take that might head off other problems in the future. Generally, these include paperwork details such as investigating possible driver's license misuse and obtaining a new license, with a new number, if necessary.

One step that's often suggested is changing your Social Security number. But Jay Foley, director of consumer and victim services for the Identity Theft Resource Center, said that's generally not a good idea. "Because of what you lose. For example, if you have a college degree, say good-bye," Foley said. "Say good-bye to everything you have that references your Social Security number. Your employment history. Your professional licenses, your military service."

And it's likely that this step won't provide the relief the victim expects anyway. Criminal records or motor vehicles records may link the old and new Social Security numbers together. Inevitably, when you apply for a job, or a mortgage, you will be tempted to give out the old number to prove you are who you say you are. At that point, the two numbers will likely become linked anyway, and all the credit report black marks will be back. Nevertheless, the Social Security Administration will provide a new number if a victim proves their number is being misused. More information is available at the agency's web site.

The better plan is to simply take all that carefully tracked paperwork and embark on a dogged letter-writing campaign, sternly challenging every instance of fraudulent behavior committed in your name. And most important, don't give in. Don't let collection agencies harass you. Don't pay any bill that is a result of fraud. Don't cover any bad checks, and don't become paranoid about your credit rating—it can be restored, with the right paperwork and determination.

NOTES

Chapter 1

1. Most of the details in the James Rinaldo Jackson saga come from a six-month-long correspondence relationship between Jackson and the author. Attempts to verify the identity theft incidents involving Levin, Stemple, and Tisch were unsuccessful. For each of them, Jackson claims to have stolen credit card account information and wracked up tens of thousands of dollars in charges. A spokesman for Robert Stemple didn't comment. Levine didn't respond to a request for comment. Lawrence Tisch died in 2003.

2. Letter from James Rinaldo Jackson to Terry Semel, June 1, 1993. When asked about the letter, Semel, through a Yahoo representative, said he had no comment.

3. *Federal Reporter,* 3d series, U.S. Court of Appeals, Sixth Circuit 1994, *U.S. v Jackson,* p. 329.

4. Ibid, p. 330.

5. Federal presentence report, provided by James R. Jackson, 1996, p. 16.

6. Greg Farrell, "Cyber Impostors Steal Diamonds, Rolexes," *USA Today,* 8 May 2000, p. 1B.

7. Ibid.

8. Maureen Dougherty (FBI agent), interview by author, August 8, 2003.

9. Farrell, "Cyber Imposters."

10. Robert Dunn (Jackson's attorney), interview with author, August 21, 2003.

11. *U.S. v James Rinaldo Jackson,* plea allocution, 26 September 2000, p. 22.

12. Ibid, p. 21.

13. U.S. Attorney Jason Weinstein, "Argument," letter to Judge Deborah Batts in support of stiff Jackson sentence, January 21, 2001.

14. Jackson plea allocution, p. 23.

15. James Doyle (New York City detective), interview with author, August 1, 2003.

16. Martin Biegelman (former postal inspector), interview with author, August 10, 2003.

17. Murray Weiss, "How NYPD Cracked the Ultimate Cyberfraud," *The New York Post*, 20 March 2001.

18. Ibid.

19. Biegelman interview.

20. Weiss, "The Ultimate Cyberfraud."

21. Interview with Michael Fabozzi, August 15, 2003.

22. Robert Gearty, "Cyberpunte: Didn't hack celebs for Riches." *New York Daily News*, 4 October 2002.

23. Mark Truby, "Ford Credit discovers ID theft," *Detroit News*, 16 May 2002.

24. Ibid.

25. U.S. Attorney James Comey, speaking at press conference announcing arrest of Philip Cummings, November 26, 2002.

26. Truby, "Ford Credit."

27. Deposition of FBI agent Kevin Barows, *U.S. v Philip Cummings*, Complaint, Southern District of New York, November 22, 2002.

28. Ibid.

29. Ibid.

30. Statement of Teledata Communications Incorporation, November 26, 2002.

31. Barows, U.S. v. Philip Cummings, p. 3.

32. Donald Girard (Experian spokesman), interview with author, November 26, 2002.

33. David Szwak, "Theft of Identity: Roadkill on the Information Superhighway," *Trial Bar News*, Winter 1996, p. 16.

34. Avivah Litan, "Underreporting of Identity Theft Rewards the Thieves," *Gartner*, research note, July 7, 2003, p. 1.

35. Sen. Diane Feinstein, "Statement of Senator Dianne Feinstein on the Identity Theft Penalty Enhancement Act," statement before the Senate Judiciary Subcommittee on Technology, Terrorism, and Government Information, July 9, 2002.

36. Ibid.

Chapter 2

1. Darren Rovell, "The Other Tiger that Lurks in the Woods," *ESPN.com*, November 1, 2002, http://espn.go.com/sportsbusiness/s/2002/1031/1454033.html.

2. Associated Press, "Tiger's Identity," 19 December 2000.

3. David Szwak (consumer attorney), interview with author, October 3, 2003.

4. James Pittman (ID theft victim), interview with author, September 23, 2003.

5. Linda and Jay Foley, "Identity Theft: The Aftermath 2003," *IDtheftCenter.org*, Summer 2003, http://www.idtheftcenter.org/idaftermath.pdf.

6. Foley, p. 13.

7. The entire Malcolm Byrd episode is based on interviews by the author.

8. Sid Schwartz, "Traffickers Targeted Janesville, Police," *Janesville Gazette*, 28 November 2003.

9. *The Office of the Attorney General, State of California*, "Identity Theft," http://caag.state.ca.us/idtheft/general.htm.

10. *The Office of the Attorney General, Commonwealth of Virginia*, "Identity Theft: Frequently Asked Questions," http://www.oag.state.va.us/Protecting/Consumer%20Fraud/identity_theftfaq.htm.

11. Beth Givens (privacy expert), interview with author, March 7, 2003.

12. Leslie Clark, "Twelve-Year Ruse Ends; Police Say They Foil Impersonator," *Miami Herald*, 10 August 2001.

13. Robert O'Harrow, "Identity Crisis," *Washington Post Magazine*, 10 August 2003.

14. Steve Warmbir, "Man Who Blew Up Lover's Husband Gets Life in Prison," *Chicago Sun-Times*, 18 September 2003.

15. Affidavit of Ferdinand Lorenzana, U.S. District Court, Northern District of Illinois, complaint against Sienky Lallemand, February 19, 2000.

16. Affidavit of Jeanne L. Sobol, U.S. District Court, Northern District of Illinois, complaint against Sienky Lallemand, February 15, 2000.

17. John McCormick, "Wife Guilty in Bomb Plot That Killed Husband," *Chicago Tribune*, 11 March 2003.

18. Linda Foley (Identity Theft Resource Center founder), interview with author, November 14, 2003.

19. The entire Rachel Soper episode is based on interviews conducted by the author, September 7, 2003.

20. The entire Linda Foley episode is based on interviews conducted by the author, December 1, 2003.

21. Christine Pratt (spokeswoman for TowerGroup), interview with author, March 23, 2003.

22. Letter from James Rinaldo Jackson.

23. Betty Lin-Fisher, "Huge Purchase by Imposter Pushes Identity Theft Victim into Spotlight," *Knight Ridder Tribune Business News*, 12 June 2001.

24. The entire Hernandez clan episode is based on interviews with Vancouver, Washington police, October, 2003.

25. Kevin Tibbles, "Profile: Identity Theft," *NBC News Today*, July 25, 2002.

26. Adam Clymer, "Thieves Steal Homeowners' Identities and Their Equity," *New York Times*, 28 May 2002.

27. Mari J. Frank, "Identity Theft and the Elderly," Testimony before the Committee on Senate Special Aging, July 18, 2002.

28. Ted Sherman, "Big Fraud Ring Stole IDs, Even From Terminally Ill," *Newark Star-Ledger*, 20 June 2003. Sarah Henry would plead guilty to third degree conspiracy to commit identity theft.

29. Frank testimony, "Identity Theft and the Elderly."

30. Michael W. Naylor, "Identity Theft," testimony before the Senate Banking, Housing, and Urban Affairs committee, June 19, 2003.

31. Douglas Coombs, "Identity Theft and the Elderly," testimony before the Committee on Senate Special Aging, July 18, 2002.

32. Sen. Diane Feinstein, "Protecting the Social Security Number," hearing before the U.S. Senate Finance Committee, 11 July 2002.

33. Michael Forsythe (ID theft victim), interview with author, October 6, 2003.

Chapter 3

1. Howard Beales, address before the Consumer Data Industry Association, February 1, 2002.

2. "Consumer Credit," *Federal Reserve Statistical Release*, 8 January 2004.

3. Robert Manning (credit card expert), interview with author, January 9, 2004.

4. Liz Pulliam Weston, "More Games the Credit-Card Companies Play," *MSN Money*, http://moneycentral.msn.com/content/Banking/Yourcreditrating/P51865.asp.

5. Manning, Interview.

6. *Administrative Office of the U.S. Courts*, "Personal Bankruptcy Filings Continue to Rise in Fiscal Year 2003," news release, November 14, 2003.

7. Ronald J. Mann, "Credit Cards and Debit Cards in the United States and Japan," *Vanderbilt Law Review*, 2002, vol. 55, pp. 1055–1108.

8. Federal Trade Commission, "Identity Theft Survey Report," September 2003.

9. Interview with credit industry lobbyist, November 17, 2003.

10. Federal Trade Commission, "Identity Theft Survey Report."

11. Based on interviews with Mark Ishman, May 2002. The lawsuit was filed in U.S. District Court in Raleigh, N.C, number 5:03-CV-372-BO(3).

12. Based on various interviews with credit card association representatives.

13. Interview with MasterCard spokeswoman, May 22, 2003.

14. Bill Crane (merchant ID theft victim), interviewed by author, October 7, 2003.

15. Gary Howell (merchant ID theft victim), interview with author, September 13, 2003.

16. *Credit Card News*, "A New Merchant-Fraud Fighter: Neural Networks," September 1, 1993.

17. *Cards International*, "Fair, Isaac and HNC to Merge," May 20, 2002.

18. *Cards International*, "Visa Rolls out Falcon across Europe," February 12, 2003.

19. ID Analytics, "National Report on Identity Fraud," September 2003.

20. Martin Abrams (former credit bureau executive), interview with author, September 21, 2003.

21. Avivah Litan (Gartner fraud analyst), interview with author, September 21, 2003.

22. ID Analytics, "National Report."

23. Abrams, interview.

24. Robert Manning, "*Credit Card Nation: The Consequences of America's Addiction to Credit,*" New York: Basic Books (2000), pp. 84–88.

25. Biegelman.

26. David Lazarus, "A Deluge of Credit," *San Francisco Chronicle*, 7 March 2003.

27. Alan Greenspan, testimony during his confirmation hearings before the Senate Banking Committee, January 26, 2000.

28. Lazarus, "A Deluge of Credit."

29. This assertion is detailed in Chapter 5.

30. Dennis M. Lormel, chief, Financial Crimes Section FBI, statement before the House Committee on Financial Services, October 3, 2001.

31. Peter Ford, "Al Qaeda's Veil Begins to Lift," *Christian Science Monitor*, 20 December 2001.

32. Keith Johnson and Carlta Vitzthum, "Spanish Cell May Have Funded al-Qaeda," *Wall Street Journal*, 3 December, 2001.

33. Chris Hedges, "A Nation Challenged: Intelligence; A Powerful Combatant in France's War on Terror," *New York Times*, November 24, 2001.

34. Kenneth R. Bazinet, "City Leads Way in Fraud Fight," *New York Daily News*, 10 December 2001.

35. Sreeram Chaulia, review of "Inside Al Qaeda, Global Network of Terror," by Rohan Gunaratna, *Asia Times Online*, October 12, 2002, http://www.atimes.com/atimes/Middle_East/DJ12Ak03.html.

36. Jon Boyle, "Al Qaeda Turns to Crime Due to Cash Crunch," *Reuters News Service*, 22 September 2003.

37. Ibid.

38. Stryker McGuire, "'Like a Virus'; A Terror Expert Says the Kenya Attacks Prove that Al Qaeda is Alive and Well and Plotting Further Attacks," *Newsweek Web Exclusive*, 3 December 2002.

39. Richard A. Rohde, testimony before the Senate Subcommittee on Technology, Terrorism and Government Information, February 24, 1998.

40. The account of the role of credit card fraud was drawn from many sources, including a court transcript of Hanouari July 3, 2001, appearance in U.S. District Court, Southern District of New York, before Hon. John F. Keenan. An excellent reference on the entire episode is a 17-part series authored by Hal Bernton,

Mike Carter, David Heath, and James Neff for the *Seattle Times* called "The Terrorist Within," June 22–July 7, 2002. Ressam was convicted of nine criminal counts, including conspiracy to commit an act of international terrorism. He is currently serving a 27-year prison term. A potential 57 to 130 year term was reduced because he agreed to testify against Haouary: and to cooperate in other terrorism investigations. Meskini pled guilty to several counts of conspiracy to defraud, and also testified against Haouari. He is still awaiting sentencing. Haouari was convicted of conspiracy to supply material support to a terrorist act and four counts of fraud, and received a 24-year prison sentence.

41. *United States of America v Ali Saleh Kahlah Al-Marri,* returned by federal grand jury in U.S. District Court, Central District of Illinois, May 22, 2003.

42. Edward Mierzwinski, statement before the House Committee on the Judiciary: Subcommittee on Immigration, Border Security and Claims and the Subcommittee on Crime, Terrorism and Homeland Security, June 25, 2002.

43. Kathryn Kranhold, "'Identity Theft' Bill Leaves Credit Bureaus in the Cold," *Wall Street Journal,* 4 June 1997, California edition.

44. *Credit Card Management,* "California Takes Aim at Identity Theft," June 1, 1998.

45. Chris Hoofnagle (Electronic Privacy Information Center attorney), interview with author, December 22, 2003. The white paper was subsequently removed from Experian's web site.

46. Shannon P. Duffy, "Ballard Team Wins Major Identity Theft Case," *The Legal Intelligencer,* 12 August 2003.

47. Based on the author's research.

48. Sallie Twentyman, testimony before the Senate Subcommittee on Technology, Terrorism, and Government Information, March 20, 2002.

49. Based on author's interview with David Szwak, November 11, 2003.

50. Joe Rubin, interview with author, November 25, 2003.

51. Norm Magnuson, interview with author, November 25, 2003.

52. *CardFAX*, "AMEX Takes Steps against Convenience Check Fraud," June 29, 2000, Vol. 2000, No. 125, p. 2.

53. Author's interview with anonymous source, October 8, 2003.

54. Candace Heckman, "Credit Card Checks Debated," *Seattle Post-Intelligencer*, 12 February 2003.

55. Based on interviews conducted by author with anonymous sources, June 2002.

56. Henry Gilgoff, "'Loan Checks' Are in the Mail," *Newsday*, 7 December 1997.

57. Rebecca Christie, "Fed Panel Seeks Ruling on Credit Card Convenience Checks," *Dow Jones Newswires*, 24 October, 2003.

58. Gail Hillebrand (Consumer's Union), interview with author, November 25, 2003.

Chapter 4

1. John A. Ford, written testimony before the House Committee on Financial Services Subcommittee on Financial Institutions and Consumer Credit, June 4, 2003.

2. Ibid.

3. *Consumer Federation of America/National Credit Reporting Association*, "Credit Score Accuracy and Implications for Consumers," December 17, 2002.

4. *Consumer Reports*, "Credit Reports: Getting it Half Right," July 1991, p. 453.

5. *Consumer Reports*, "Credit Reports: How Do Potential Lenders See You?" July 2000, pp. 52–53.

6. *PIRG*, "Mistakes Do Happen: Credit Report Errors Mean Consumers Lose," March 1998.

7. Robert B. Avery, Paul S. Calem, Glenn B. Canner, and Raphael W. Bostic, "An Overview of Consumer Data and Credit Reporting," *Federal Reserve Bulletin*, February 1, 2003.

8. Travis B. Plunkett, testimony before the House Subcommittee on Financial Institutions and Consumer Credit, June 12, 2003.

9. *General Accounting Office*, "Limited Information Exists on Extent of Credit Report Errors and Their Implications for Consumers," GAO report to Senate Committee on Banking, Housing, and Urban Affairs, July 31, 2003.

10. Ibid.

11. Matthew Kauffman and Kenneth R. Gosselin, "Credit Laws Ignite a New Battle," *Hartford Courant*, 12 May 2003.

12. *Electronic Privacy Information Center*, "The Fair Credit Reporting Act (FCRA) and the Privacy of Your Credit Report" http://www. epic.org/privacy/fcra/.

12. IllinoisProBono.org, "Fair Credit Reporting," http://www. illinoisprobono.org/index.cfm?fuseaction=home.dsp_content&contentID=302.

13. Caroline E. Mayer, "Measure Would Hold Credit Reports Up to the Light," *Washington Post*, November 7, 2003.

14. Deposition of Eileen Little, TransUnion Consumer Relations manager, in *Roberta L. Evantash v G.E. Capital Mortgage Services and TransUnion*, 2001.

15. Chris Hoofnagle, testimony before House Committee on Financial Services, July 9, 2003.

16. Experian, written statement to the author, March 8, 2004.

17. David Lazarus, "Credit Agencies Sending Our Files Abroad," *San Francisco Chronicle*, 7 November 2003.

18. Len Bennett (consumer attorney), interview with author, August 27, 2003.

19. The description of how the credit bureau database works is based on interviews with various attorneys who have deposed credit bureau employees.

20. Erin Shoudt, Comment. "Identity Theft: Victims 'Cry Out' for Reform," 52 *Am. U. L. Rev.* 339, 34 6–7

21. Brent Hunsberger, "Victory against Credit Agency A 'Wake-Up Call,'" *Portland Oregonian*, 1 August 2002.

22. Leonard A. Bennett, testimony before the House Subcommittee on Financial Institutions and Consumer Credit, June 4, 2003.

23. Ibid.

24. *Financial Services Roundtable*, "New Center to Assist Victims of Identity Theft and Reduce Fraud," press release, October 28, 2003.

25. *Experian*, "Experian Consumer Direct Announces Second Quarter Traffic Results," press release, August 26, 2003.

26. Ibid.

27. *Experian*, "Experian Consumer Direct Announces Acquisition of MetaReward," press release, December 16, 2003.

28. *Homestore*, "Homestore Announces Completion of ConsumerInfo.com Sale," press release, April 3, 2002.

29. Based on the author's research.

30. Chris Jay Hoofnagle and Tiffany Stedman, *Complaint and Request for Injunction, Investigation and for Other Relief*, Electronic Privacy Information Center, September 16, 2003.

31. Burney Simpson, "An Unlikely Hit: Credit Scores," *Credit Card Management*, March 26, 2002, Vol. 15, No. 1, p. 16.

32. Equifax, written statement to the author, March 10, 2004.

33. *Experian*, online products catalog, http://www.experian.com/products/notification_services.html.

34. Jack Z. Smith, "What's the Score?" *Fort-Worth Star-Telegram*, 16 November 2003.

35. Michelle Levander, "Employers Turning To Credit ReportsDatabases Answer the Questions They Can't Ask," *Kansas City Star*, 22 August 1993.

36. Federal Trade Commission, "Nation's Big Three Consumer Reporting Agencies Agree to Pay $2.5 Million to Settle

FTC Charges of Violating Fair Credit Reporting Act," press release, January 13, 2003.

37. Federal Trade Commission, "Equifax to Pay $250,000 to Settle Charges," FTC press release, July 30, 2003.

38. Chris Hoofnagle, "TU v. FTC: An Important Case For Privacy," June 2002, http://www.epic.org/epic/staff/hoofnagle/tuvftc.html.

39. Federal Trade Commission, "FTC Charges against Trans-Union Upheld," press release, August 26, 1998.

40. Scott Ritter, "US Top Court Rebuffs TransUnion Appeal Over Data Sales," *Dow Jones News Service*, 10 June 2002.

41. W.A. Lee, "Ruling May Reduce Threat of Privacy Penalties," *American Banker*, October 8, 2002, Vol. 167, No. 193.

42. Experian, Fall 2003 Lift Services Catalog, http://www.listlink.experian.com/User_Doc/Fall03%20Catalog.pdf.

43. Based on a FOIA filed by the author.

44. Rob Wells, "Equifax Agrees with 18 States to Improve Credit Reporting," *Associated Press*, 30 June 1992.

45. *Hoover's*, "Equifax Inc." company profile, December 3, 2003.

46. Electronic Privacy Information Center, "The Fair Credit Reporting Act (FCRA) and the Privacy of Your Credit Report." http://www.epicorg/privacy/fcra.

47. Hoover's, "Equifax Inc."

48. Ibid.

49. Trans Union, "History of Trans Union," http://www.transunion.com/content/page.jsp?id=/transunion/general/data/about/History.xml.

50. Susan Chandler and John Keilman, "18-Year-Old Pritzker Rattles $15 Billion Family Empire," *Chicago Tribune*, 15 December 2002.

51. Hoover's, "The Marmon Group, Inc.," company profile, December 6, 2003.

52. Chandler and Keilman, "18-Year-Old Pritzker."

53. Mark Skertic, "Matthew Pritzker Files Suit on Trusts," *Chicago Tribune*, 30 April 2003.

54. Chandler and Keilman, "18-Year-Old Pritzker."

55. John O'Dell, "The Rebel's Way," *Los Angeles Times*, 15 September 1996.

56. Lisa Fickenscher, "Experian and British Credit Firm Merged in Push for Global Scope Series," *American Banker*, November 15, 1996, Vol. 161, No. 220, p. 1.

57. Lisa Fickenscher, "Experian, Not Just a Credit Bureau, Emerges as Data Base Powerhouse," *American Banker*, April 6, 1999, p. 1.

58. Kauffman and Gosselin, "Credit Laws Ignite a New Battle."

59. Brent Hunsberger, "Victory against Credit Agency A 'Wake-Up Call,'" *Portland Oregonian*, 1 August 2002.

60. Ibid.

61. Brent Hunsberger, "Award Against Credit Firm Reduced," *Portland Oregonian*, 1 February 2003.

62. Hunsberger, "Wake-up Call."

63. Kauffman and Gosselin, "Credit Laws."

Chapter 5

1. U.S. Senator Charles E. Grassley, "Homeland Security and Terrorism Threats from Document Fraud, Identity Theft and Social Security Number Misuse," hearing before the U.S. Senate Finance Committee, September 9, 2003.

2. Youssef Hmimssa, "Homeland Security and Terrorism Threats from Document Fraud, Identity Theft and Social Security Number Misuse," hearing before the U.S. Senate Finance Committee, September 9, 2003.

3. Ibid.

4. Patrick O'Carroll, Office of Inspector General, Social Security Administration, "Homeland Security and Terrorism Threats from Document Fraud, Identity Theft and Social Security Number Misuse," hearing before the U.S. Senate Finance Committee, September 9, 2003.

5. U.S. Attorney Richard Convertino, "Homeland Security and Terrorism Threats from Document Fraud, Identity Theft and Social Security Number Misuse," hearing before the U.S. Senate Finance Committee, September 9, 2003.

6. Hmimssa's background is taken from the "Summary of Senate Finance Committee Interview of Youssef Hmimssa," entered into the *Congressional Record* in lieu of an opening statement by Hmimssa.

7. Norman A. Willox Jr. and Thomas M. Regan, "Identity Fraud-Providing a Solution," *Journal of Economic Crime Management,* Summer 2002, Vol. 1, No. 1, http://www.jecm.org/archives/ 02_vol1_issue1_art1.html.

8. Farhad Manjoo, "Another Thing to Fear: ID Theft," *Wired News,* 1 October 2001, http://www.wired.com/news/conflict/ 0,2100,47201,00.html.

9. Dan Eggen, George Lardner Jr., and Susan Schmidt, "Some Hijac- kers' Identities Uncertain," *Washington Post,* 20 September, 2001.

10. James Hesse, Immigration and Naturalization Service, testimony before the House Judiciary Committee Subcommittee on Immigration and Claims, July 22, 1999.

11. O'Carroll, "Homeland Security."

12. Linda Lewis, American Association of Motor Vehicle Administrators, Homeland Security and Terrorism Threats From Document Fraud, Identity Theft And Social Security Number Misuse," hearing before the U.S. Senate Finance Committee, September 9, 2003.

13. David Myers, "Solving Security's Not Mission Impossible," *News.com,* September 25, 2002, http://news.com.com/2010-1071-959259.html?tag=fd_nc_1.

14. Vince Paragano (liquor license attorney), interview with the author, September 9, 2003.

15. Interview with anonymous source, September 2003.

16. Associated Press, "Blank Birth Certificates Stolen from Health Department Offices," May 3, 2001.

17. Alisa Ulferts, "Governor Targets Identity Thieves," *St. Petersburg Times*, 2 June 2001.

18. Associated Press, "Man Charged with Stealing Blank Birth Certificates," July 27, 2002.

19. Brian C. McCormally, "Stolen Official Documents," Office of the Comptroller of the Currency, Alert 2002-5, May 7, 2002.

20. Ryan Frank, "Police Say Lake Oswego Woman Used Records to Steal Identities," *Portland Oregonian*, 30 January 2002. Rolfe was eventually convicted on forgery, identity theft, and drug charges, and was sentenced to nearly two years in prison.

21. Holly Danks, "Hillsboro Man Gets 4-Year Sentence for Identity Theft, Forgery Charges," *Portland Oregonian*, 6 May 2002. Oates Pleaded guilty to 13 counts of identity theft and received a 4-month sentence.

22. Harry Franklin, "Examiner Charged in License Fraud Probe," *Ledger-Enquirer.com*, September 3, 2003, http://www.ledgeren quirer.com/mld/ledgerenquirer/news/6677368.htm.

23. Interview with anonymous source, September 8, 2003.

24. Bruce Alpert, "Group Says License Loophole Providing Tool to Terrorists," *New Orleans Times-Picayune*, 27 August 2003.

25. Alejandro Bodipo-Memba, "Officials Push for Acceptance of Mexican IDs," *Detroit Free Press*, 3 April 2003.

26. Ginger Thompson, "A Surge in Money Sent Home by Mexicans," *New York Times*, 28 October 2003.

27. Bank of America, "Bank of America Reaffirms Commitment to Hispanic Community," company press release, April 23, 2002.

28. Steven McCraw, statement before the House Judiciary Subcommittee on Immigration, Border Security, and Claims, June 26, 2003.

29. Robert J. Cramer, in a memo to Sen. Charles E. Grassley. The rest of the narrative about the GAO test is summarized from this draft memo, first obtained by NBC News, dated July 2003.

30. Robert J. Cramer, "Counterfeit Identification and Identification Fraud Raise Security Concerns," testimony before the Senate Committee on Finance, September 9, 2003. The summary of other GAO investigations is drawn from this report.

31. Frankie Edozien, David Seifman, and William J. Gorta, "Deranged Rival Blows Away Pol," *New York Post*, 24 July 2003.

32. Paul J. McNulty, testimony before the House Subcommittee on Immigration, Border Security and Claims and the Subcommittee on Crime, Terrorism and Homeland Security, June 25, 2002.

33. Tony Perry, "21 Indicted in Alleged Identity-Theft Scheme," *Los Angeles Times*, 19 November 2003. Both Ramirez and her husband pleaded not guilty and are awaiting trial.

Chapter 6

1. The Sheri Knudson incident is based on interviews with Knudson, Charles Rutherford, Detective Bill Sorter, and examination of the police report.

2. Avivah Litan, "Underreporting of Identity Theft Rewards the Theives," *Gartner*, research note, July 7, 2003, p. 1.

3. Linda and Jay Foley, "Identity Theft: The Aftermath 2003," *IDtheftCenter.org*, Summer 2003, http://www.idtheftcenter.org/idaftermath.pdf.

4. Linda Foley, interview with the author, February 8, 2003.

5. U.S. General Accounting Office, "Identity Theft: Greater Awareness and Use of Existing Data Are Needed," June 2002.

6. Ibid.

7. Minnesota Statutes 2003, 609.527 Identity Theft.

8. E-mail from Social Security Administration official to Charles Rutherford.

9. Star Systems, "Identity Theft in the United States: An Update," December 2002, p. 24.

10. Mike Foglia (Oregon banking official), interview with the author, June 26, 2002.

11. U.S. General Accounting Office, "Identity Theft: Greater Awareness and Use of Existing Data Are Needed."

12. Bob Berardi (Los Angeles identity theft task force), interview with the author, March 2003.

13. U.S. General Accounting Office, "Identity Theft: Greater Awareness and Use of Existing Data Are Needed."

14. The Massey incident is based on interviews with Steve Williams, prosecutor Sean Boar, and parole officer Mark Walker.

15. Nancy Pasternack, "Fraud Cases Linked to Drug Users," *The Olympian*, 31 March 2003, http://www.theolympian.com/home/news/20030331/southsound/33415.shtml.

16. Evan Hendricks, testimony before the Senate Banking Committee, July 10, 2003.

17. Mike Gray (California law enforcement identity theft trainer), interviews with the author, October 2003.

18. F.B.I., "Facts and Figures 2003," http://www.fbi.gov/libref/factsfigure/lawenforce.htm.

19. Federal Trade Commission, "FTC Releases Top 10 Consumer Complaint Categories in 2002," press release, January 22, 2003.

20. Based on interviews with Federal Trade Commission staffers.

21. Based on interviews with Federal Trade Commission staffers.

22. The author was also a speaker at this training seminar.

23. U.S. General Accounting Office, "Identity Theft: Greater Awareness and Use of Existing Data Are Needed."

24. Electronic Privacy Information Center, "Joint Letter and Online Petition: Require Accuracy for Nation's Largest Criminal Justice Database," http://www.epic.org/privacy/ncic/.

25. F.B.I., "An NCIC Milestone," press release, March 23, 2002.

26. Beth Givens (privacy expert), interview with the author, March 7, 2003.

27. Ted Bridis, "U.S. Lifts FBI Criminal Database Checks," *Associated Press*, March 25, 2003.

28. Marc Rotenberg, testimony before the Senate Subcommittee on Competition, Foreign Commerce, and Infrastructure Committee on Commerce, Science and Transportation, June 11, 2003.

29. Berardi, interview.

30. Ibid.

31. Andy Vuong, "ID-Theft Law Recognized as Deficient," *Denver Post*, 17 January 2003.

32. Sean Hoar (U.S. attorney), interview with the author, October 2003.

33. Hendricks, testimony.

34. U.S.Postal Inspection Service,"Annual Report of Investigations," http://www.usps.com/postalinspectors/ar02/ar02text.htm.

35. U.S. Postal Inspection Service, "Chronology of U.S. Postal Inspection Service," http://www.usps.com/websites/depart/inspect/ischrono.htm.

36. Biegelman, Interview cited Chapter 1 note 16.

37. U.S. Postal Inspection Service, "Annual Report of Investigations."

38. Based on interviews with Postal Inspection Service staffers.

Chapter 7

1. James Risen, "Sept. 11 Hijackers Said to Fake Data on Bank Accounts," *New York Times*, 10 July 2002.

2. Scott Barancik, "Know Your Customer Is Out; Agencies' Next Step Unclear," *American Banker*, March 23, 1999, p. 2.

3. Robert Douglas, speaking at the American Bankers's Association Regulatory Compliance Conference, June 2002.

4. *Federal Register*, July 23, 2002, Vol. 67, No. 141, pp. 48289–48299.

5. Ken Golliher, "Treasury Issues Reprieve," *Texas Banking*, November 1, 2002, Vol. 91, No. 11.

6. *Federal Register*, "Customer Identification Programs for Banks, Savings Associations, Credit Unions and Certain Non-Federally Regulated Banks," 9, May 2003, 25090, Vol. 68, No. 90.

7. John Byrne (American Banker's Association), interview with the author.

8. Bob Cusack, "Lawmaker Renews Threat to Change Patriot Act Rule," *The Hill*, November 6, 2003, http://www.hillnews.com/executive/110603_patriot.aspx.

9. Rob Blackwell, "Treasury Opts to Leave ID Rule in Patriot Act As Is," *American Banker*, September 19, 2003, Vol. 168, No. 181, p. 5.

10. Letter from John Byrne to the Treasury Department, July 31, 2003.

11. Blackwell, "Treasury Opts to Leave ID Rule."

12. Rob Douglas (privacy expert and banking consultant), interview with the author.

13. Robert O'Harrow Jr., "Concerns for ID Theft Often Are Unheeded," *Washington Post*, 23 July, 2001.

14. Ibid.

15. Review of Federal Trade Commission announcements.

16. Federal Trade Commission. "FTC issues Financial Information Safeguards Rule," May 17, 2002.

17. Federal Trade Commission, "FTC Financial Information Safeguards Rule Takes Effect," May 23, 2003.

18. Donna Harris, "FTC Audits Dealers on privacy rule," *Automotive News*, September 29, 2003.

19. Allan Jost (HNC Software), interview with the author, August 1, 2000.

20. Based on interviews with Consumer Union analyst Gail Hillebrand, and her analysis of an early version of the bill posted on

Consumer Union's web site at http://www.consumersunion.org/pub/core_financial_services/000282.html.

21. Michele Heller, "Greenspan Again Urges Preemption Renewal," *American Banker,* May 1, 2003, Vol. 168, No. 83, p. 3.

22. John Markoff, "Intelligence: Pentagon Plans a Computer System That Would Peek At Personal Data of Americans," *New York Times,* 9 November 2002.

23. Markoff, remarks at Univeristy of Washington, April 14, 2003.

24. While much has been written about Carnivore, the software still remains shrouded in mystery. A good primer on Carnivore/ DCS1000 can be found at the Electronic Privacy Information Center, located at http://www.epic.org/privacy/carnivore/.

25. Robert Rudolph, "Lawmen Explain, in General, How They Cracked Scarfo Code," *Newark Star-Ledger* 11 October 2001.

26. The Magic Lantern episode is based on extensive interviews by the author, conducted under conditions of anonymity.

27. Ryan Singel, "JetBlue Shared Passenger Data," *Wired News,* September 18, 2003, http://www.wired.com/news/privacy/0,1848, 60489,00.html.

28. *Electronic Privacy Information Center,* "Northwest Airlines Gave NASA Personal Info on Millions of Passengers; Disclosure Violated Privacy Policy," January 18, 2004.

29. *Common Cause,* "Going for Broke: Big Money, Big Banks & Bankruptcy," September 1, 1998, http://www.commoncause.org/publications/goingforbroke.htm.

30. Sarah Bouchard, "Credit Card Industry Steps Up Lobbying," *Roll Call,* July 23, 2003.

31. Ibid.

32. Sharon Theimer, "Equifax PAC Holds Fund-Raiser for Senator Behind Pro-Industry Changes to: Credit Reporting Bill," *Associated Press,* 27 October 2003.

Chapter 8

1. The Zilterio episode is the result of a series of interviews conducted during several months by the author with an anonymous source who identified himself as Mr. Zilterio.

2. U.S. Department of Justice, "Russian Computer Hacker Sentenced to Three Years in Prison," press release, October 4, 2002. Aleksey V. Ivanov and Vasiliy Gorshkov were arrested after being lured to the United States by the FBI in November 2000. An indictment accused them of hacking into U.S. banks and e-commerce sites, and then demanding money for not publicizing the break-ins. Ivanov pleaded guilty to conspiracy, computer intrusion, computer fraud, credit card fraud, wire fraud, and extortion. He was sentenced to four years in federal prison in July 2003. Gorshkov was convicted at trial of conspiracy, various computer crimes, and fraud, and sentenced to a three-year federal prison term. U.S. District Judge Alvin W. Thompson found that losses stemming from their various crimes totaled $25 million.

3. Rick Robinson, "Home National Bank Notifies Customers of Security Breach Last Year," *Daily Oklahoman*, 28 June 2002.

4. Rachel Konrad, "Law Gives Hacking Victims Right to Know," *Associated Press*, 23 June 2003.

5. Based on the author's interviews with Adrian Lamo, February 2002.

6. These included a subpoena, since withdrawn on a technicality, of the author's correspondence with Lamo. It also included 13 "preservation of evidence" notices sent to reporters around the world, including the author. Those were also withdrawn. Lamo eventually pleaded guilty on January 8, 2004, to one violation of federal law, the Computer Fraud and Abuse Act, in connection with the New York Times incident.

7. Dan Clements (CardCops.com operator), interviews with the author.

8. Ibid.

9. Based on interviews with Visa, MasterCard, American Express, and Discover, February 18, 2003.

10. Clements, interviews.

11. Based on interviews with an anonymous source, April–May 2002.

12. Tom Trusty (fraud consultant), interview with the author, June 2001.

13. Based on interviews with an anonymous source, March 2002.

14. Jenny Redo, interview with the author, August 2003.

15. Contessa Brewer (MSNBC anchor), interview with the author, September 2003.

16. Based on interviews with an official at Cybergate, September 2003.

17. Anti-Phishing Working Group, "Reports of Email Fraud and Phishing Attacks Jump Over 400% during the Holidays," press release, Tumbleweed Communications Corp. and the Anti-Phishing Working Group, December 23, 2003.

18. Bruce Lachot, interview with the author, January 2003.

19. Eric A. Wenger (Federal Trade Commission attorney), December 11, 2003.

20. The entire Kenneth episode is based on extensive interviews with an anonymous source who called himself Kenneth, July–September 2003.

21. Federal Trade Commission, "FTC Releases Top 10 Consumer Complaint Categories in 2002," press release, January 22, 2003.

22. Barry Mew (U.S. postal inspector), November–December 2003.

23. Advertisement on CareerBuilder.com, December 12, 2003.

24. Mew.

25. Interview with anonymous victim, December 15, 2003.

26. John Schwartz, "Virus Can Secretly Put Porn in PC," *International Herald Tribune*, 12 August 2003.

27. Elinor Mills Abreu, "Hackers Get Novel Defense—The Computer Did It," *Reuters News*, 27 October 2003.

28. Joe Stewart (virus expert), interview with the author, 2003.

29. Mary Youngblood (Earthlink spam fighter), interview with the author, August 1, 2003.

30. Munir Kotadia, "Report: A Third of Spam Spread by RAT-Infested PCs," *CNETNews.com*, December 4, 2003, http://asia.cnet.com/newstech/security/0,39001150, 39160133,00.htm.

31. Richard Smith (cybercrime expert), interview with the author, July 2003.

32. Based on the author's research.

33. Various hacker how-tos, which claim to be authored by a person using the pseudonym Video Vindicator, can be found on the Internet. There is no way to verify the author's identity. The one cited here is called "ID Hopping, Part 1," and was viewed at http://www.blackmarket-press.net/info/identity/ID_hopping1.htm, but the file can be downloaded from various locations. It claims to have been authored on January 1, 1992.

34. Foundation for Taxpayers and Consumer Rights, "Social Security in the Blue Sky," press release, November 12, 2003.

Chapter 9

1. Beth Shuster, "Suspect in Stalking of Detective Surrenders," *Los Angeles Times*, 16 April 1997.

2. Howard Pankratz and Marilyn Robinson, "Accusations against Rapps Widen: Pair Allegedly Sold Phone Numbers of L.A. Cops to Mobster," *Denver Post*, 29 June 1999.

3. Douglas Frantz, "Detective Methods Face Trial: Rapp Case Tests Fact-Gathering Limits," *New York Times*, appearing in *The Denver Post*, 12 July 1999. Additional research for the report was provided by *Denver Post* legal affairs reporter Howard Pankratz.

4. Pankratz and Robinson, "Accusations."

5. Much of the information broker episode is the result of interviews by the author with Rob Douglas and Al Schweitzer.

6. Al Schweitzer, testimony before the House Committee on Banking and Financial Services, July 28, 1998.

7. Frantz, "Detective Methods."

8. Douglas

9. Howard Pankratz, "Sleuth Trading in Ramsey Info Jailed," *Denver Post*, 21 January 2000, p. B-2.

10. *Denver Post*, "Letter Details Information Rapp Dug Up," 26 June 1999.

11. Frantz, "Detective Method."

12. Ibid.

13. Office of the Massachusetts Attorney General, "Supreme Judicial Court Affirms $500,000 Judgment against New York Information Broker Who Sold Consumers' Private Financial Information," press release, February 21, 2002.

14. Schweitzer, testimony.

15. Sen. Jim Leach, statement at hearing of the House Committee on Banking and Financial Services, July 28, 1998.

16. Douglas

17. The entire description of the Identity Theft Resource Center is based on interviews with Linda and Jay Foley and on the author's direct observations.

18. The entire David Szwak narrative is based on interviews with Szwak.

19. The entire Roberta episode is based on interviews conducted with an anonymous source.

Chapter 10

1. *Huggins v Citibank, N.A., et al.*, S.C. 585 SE. 2d 275, 2003.

2. *TRW v Andrews*, 534 U.S. 19 (2001).

3. Avivah Litan, interview with the author, January 13, 2003.

4. Cards International, "Visa Rolls Out Falcon across Europe," February 12, 2003.

5. Based on interviews by the author with ID Analytics executives.

6. ID Analytics, "National Report on Identity Fraud," September 2003, p. 14

7. See Chapters 3 and 4.

8. Based on interviews with anonymous sources.

9. Litan, interview.

10. Avivah Litan, "Identity Theft Solutions Start to Proliferate," Gartner research note, July 7, 2003.

11. Litan, "Identity Theft Solutions Start to Proliferate."

12. Litan, "Identity Theft Solutions Start to Proliferate."

13. Based on the author's research.

14. Litan, "Identity Theft Solutions Start to Proliferate."

15. Declan McCullagh, "Chip Implant Gets Cash under Your Skin," *CNetNews.com*, November 25, 2003, http://news.com.com/2100-1041-5111637.html.

16. Beth Bacheldor, "Defense Department Schedules RFID Pilots," *Information: Week*, December 22, 2003. p. 24.

17. Larry Dignan, "Wal-Mart's RFID Deadline: A Chunky Mess," *eWeek*, 15 December 2003, http://www.eweek.com/print_ article/0,3048,a=114625,00.asp.

18. Julia Scheeres, "Tracking Junior with a Microchip" *Wired News*, October 10, 2003, http://www.wired.com/news/privacy/0,1848,60771,00.html.

19. Identix, "Identix Receives Tenprint Live Scan Orders from California Law Enforcement Agencies," press release, November 19, 2003.

20. See Chapter 6.

INDEX